BETWEEN TOTEM AND TABOO

Between Totem and Taboo picks its way judiciously through a minefield of prejudice, myth and stereotypes. It is the first book to explore the literary representation of interracial relations between France and her former territories in West Africa through the special nexus of the white woman and the black man. Inscribed within the broader framework of the representation of Blacks in French literature, it mirrors the evolution of that representation while emphasising liberal positions which are by definition more subject to development than the unchanging intolerant stance.

BETWEEN TOTEM AND TABOO

BLACK MAN, WHITE WOMAN
IN FRANCOGRAPHIC LITERATURE

Roger Little

UNIVERSITY
of
EXETER
PRESS

First published in 2001 by
University of Exeter Press
Reed Hall, Streatham Drive
Exeter EX4 4QR
UK

www.ex.ac.uk/uep/

British Library Cataloguing in Publication Data
A catalogue record for this book is available
from the British Library.

ISBN 0 85989 649 8

Printed in Great Britain by Short Run Press, Exeter.

For Pat and Dominic,

never forgetting Becky.

CONTENTS

ACKNOWLEDGEMENTS

It gives me pleasure to express my thanks to Houssaine Afoullouss, Olympe Bhêly-Quenum, Gilbert Carr, Colette Charot, Chantal Claverie, Jean-François Durand, Nora Hickey, Bridget Jones, Lilyan Kesteloot, Henri Lopes, Moray McGowan, Aedín Ní Loingsigh, Clíona Ó Gallchoir, Derek O'Regan, János Riesz, Serge Rivière, Jill Samuel, Nicholas Saul, Véronique Tadjo, Steve Uran and David Williams for help on points of detail. I am particularly grateful to Léon-François Hoffmann, Pat Little and David Murphy for the valuable comments they made after their expert reading of the typescript. Thanks are also due to personnel at the Bibliothèque de l'Arsenal, the Bibliothèque nationale de France and the libraries of Trinity College Dublin, the École Normale Supérieure de la rue d'Ulm, Paris, and of the Université Cheikh Anta Diop, the Institut Fondamental d'Afrique Noire and the Fondation Léopold Sédar Senghor at Dakar. Scattered Osiris-like across these pages, or recycled in other ways, will be found some material previously presented in a different or fuller form in journals (the *Australian Journal of French Studies*, the *Modern Language Review*, *Research in African Literatures* and *Présence Africaine*) or other publications (by the Association for the Study of Caribbean and African Literature in French and L'Harmattan), full details of which are given in the Select Bibliography below. I am grateful to the Modern Humanities Research Association and the other relevant editors and publishers for permission to redeploy such material. I wish also to thank the Lois Greenfield Studio, New York, for permission to use the photograph by Lois Greenfield of Ashley Roland and Flipper Hope reproduced on the cover. The assistance from everyone at the University of Exeter Press, especially Simon Baker, has been much appreciated, including financial support towards the right to reproduce this photograph. But my greatest and most long-standing debt, for intellectual, moral and practical support, is to my wife, *sine qua non*.

R. L.
Dún Laoghaire and Saint-Geniès de Malgoires
Summer 2000

'... comme si tout mariage n'était pas "mixte"!'
[... as if every marriage weren't 'mixed'!]
Albert Jacquard, in Augustin Barbara, *Les Couples mixtes*

'My father says that gentlemen have horrors upon this subject, and would draw conclusions very unfavourable to a female writer who appeared to recommend such unions.'
Maria Edgeworth, letter to Anna Barbauld, 1810

'Pourquoi le bon Dieu a-t-il fait d'un côté des Blancs et de l'autre des Noirs, si ce n'est pas pour qu'ils se réunissent de temps en temps comme dans un jeu de dominos?'
[Why has God made Blacks on one side and Whites on the other if it isn't for them to link up from time to time as in a game of dominos?]
Marius-Ary Leblond, *Le Zézère: amours de blancs et de noirs*

'Dieu n'a-t-il pas créé les hommes de couleurs différentes afin de nous obliger à nous étudier?'
[Did God not make mankind in different colours so as to make us study one another?]
Bernard Dadié, *Un Nègre à Paris*

'Le phantasme accouplant le Nègre avec la Blanche est l'un des plus explosifs qui soit.'
[The fantasy coupling a black man with a white woman is one of the most explosive that exists.]
Dany Laferrière, *Comment faire l'amour avec un nègre sans se fatiguer*

'... le rapport à l'Autre est devenu le critère essentiel de la moralité.'
[... the relationship with the Other has become the essential moral criterion.]
Dominique Schnapper, *La Relation à l'autre*

'Comprendre les autres est un idéal contradictoire: il nous demande de changer sans changer, d'être un autre tout en restant nous-même.'
[Understanding others is a contradictory ideal: it requires us to change without changing, to be someone else while remaining ourselves.]
Octavio Paz, *Passion et lecture*

SOME KEY DATES

C8th   North African trade in sub-Saharan slaves revives after some evidence of it in ancient world (but most slaves then in Europe had been white)

1441   Portuguese bring first African slaves to Europe

1492   Columbus 'discovers' America

C16th   Portuguese and Spanish develop transatlantic slave-trade

1571   Slavery banned in France

C17th   British, Dutch and finally the French (in 1673) join the trade which will reach its peak in the C18th; for more than two centuries, wives were forbidden to accompany French traders, soldiers and functionaries working in West Africa and the West Indies, giving rise to temporary local liaisons called *mariages à la mode du pays* (role of *signares* in Senegal; miscegenation an inevitable consequence)

1685   *Code noir*: marriage authorised between white planter and black slave; perceived increasingly, however, to be a source of social unrest; colonial slaves automatically freed if they set foot in France

1716   (October) Regent proclaims edict regulating status of slaves in France; marriage permitted, with their masters' consent, between or with black slaves brought or sent to France; not ratified by Parlement de Paris or Admiralty Court, so principle of being free on French soil remains in practice

1724   (March) Mixed-race marriages in Louisiana banned by royal edict; unofficially this stricture is extended to other French colonies

1738   (15 December) Royal *Déclaration concernant les nègres esclaves des colonies* imposes registration and limit of three years' residence on slaves imported to France, their masters being (theoretically, but in practice rarely) fined for non-compliance; but, like 1716 edict, not ratified for Paris region

1762   (5 April) Ordinance issued by Admiralty Court requiring registration of Blacks; marked shift from mid-century towards distinction by race (colour) rather than by class (slave)

1777   *Déclaration pour la police des noirs* brings in more stringent regulations; census of Blacks in France undertaken

1778   (5 April) Royal *arrêt de conseil* prohibits Black/White marriages in France

1788   Founding, on English model, of Société des Amis des Noirs (Brissot de Warville, Condorcet, *abbé* Grégoire, Bernardin de Saint-Pierre etc.)

1791   Insurrection in Saint Domingue (Haiti)
1792   (28 March) Equality of rights decreed between Whites, Mulattos and free Blacks
1793   (29 August) Slavery abolished in Saint Domingue
1794   (4 February; 16 pluviôse an II) *Convention* abolishes slavery and the slave-trade
1798   (October) Toussaint Louverture takes power in Saint Domingue; spirit of generosity engendered by revolutionary ideals swamped by right-wing mercantile interests
1802   (20 May; 30 floréal an X) Napoleon restores *status quo ante* 1794, moreover refusing Blacks entry to France; (7 June) Toussaint trapped into being captured, but Dessalines continues his work
1804   (1 January) Independent state of Haiti established
1807   Britain abolishes slave-trade; over the next decades, the Royal Navy patrols West African coast and West Indies in an attempt to prevent its continuance
1815   (29 March) Napoleon signs decree abolishing French slave-trade; despite French and British vigilance, it is continued clandestinely by freebooters attracted by profit
1825   Charles X recognises Haiti officially
1833   Britain abolishes slavery
1848   (27 April) Slavery officially abolished in French colonies
1857   Faidherbe creates first infantry battalion of *Tirailleurs sénégalais*; they will distinguish themselves in the service of France both in the establishment of Senegal as a colony and in the two world wars, when for many Europeans they are the first Blacks ever encountered
1885   Berlin conference ratifies division of territorial spoils in 'the scramble for Africa'
1889   *Exposition coloniale*, Paris (Esplanade des Invalides)
1914–18 First World War: over 150,000 *Tirailleurs sénégalais* fight in Europe; even more Blacks from United States
1920s   Harlem Renaissance; 'Black' French writing emerges when René Maran wins Prix Goncourt with *Batouala* (1921)
1931   *Exposition coloniale internationale*, Paris (Vincennes)
1930s   Development by Senghor, Damas and Césaire of theory of Negritude, equivalent of Black consciousness
1939–45 Second World War: *Tirailleurs sénégalais* again used
1946   Martinique and Guadeloupe granted status as 'départements d'outre-mer'
1954   (7 May) Trauma of French defeat in Indochina at Diên Biên Phu; (1 November) insurrection marks start of Algerian war of independence (concluded in 1962)
*c.*1960 Independence granted to former French colonies in Africa

INTRODUCTION
BETWEEN TOTEM AND TABOO

'"White ladies and Black guys—a Hell of a subject,"
confirmed the Admiral, "You're sure to displease everybody."'
Henry Champly[1]

WARNING: you are now entering a high-risk zone. This book picks its way as judiciously as it can through a minefield of prejudice, myth and stereotypes. Most of its key terms require qualifying quotation marks: 'black' (shades of brown), 'white' (pink and blotchy, when not red with anger, green or grey with sickness or blue with cold), 'race' (supposed subdivisions of the one and only human race), 'mixed marriages' (differently interpreted in different circumstances, but as if all marriages were not mixed by gender, culture, social status, religion, age, health, politics or economics) and so forth. Constant reminders would be tedious, however, and the inverted commas will generally be taken as read after the first few occurrences.

Through a Francographic corpus—that is, one of writing in French, primarily in this case from France and its former colonies in Africa and the West Indies—covering the last two hundred and sixty years since the first French novel with a black hero, the anonymous *Histoire de Louis Anniaba*, it explores the representation of intimate relationships between 'black' men and 'white' women against the almost unshifting but shifty European agenda which determined—and still largely determines—concepts of 'racial' superiority and inferiority. As such, it is inscribed within the broader framework of the representation of Blacks in French literature, mirroring its evolution but emphasising liberal positions which are by definition more subject to self-questioning and development than the

1

unchanging intolerant stance. It is intended, in short, as a modest but original contribution to *l'histoire des mentalités*.

With France struggling, with variable success, to come to terms, between the Second World War and the debarring legislation of recent years, with an exponentially growing influx of visibly different peoples, it seems particularly timely to reflect on how earlier observers saw and represented a crucial nexus of potential assimilation. The failure of a black and white couple, in literature as in life, betokens insufficient strength and independence of mind in one or both of the partners to combat the forces of conservatism which dog them. Success requires those qualities in addition to all the factors which create continuing compatibility within a relationship. It also offers a broader model: as Albert Memmi has written, 'le mariage mixte est souhaitable afin que soit enfin possible la fraternité entre les peuples' [mixed marriage is desirable for brotherhood between peoples to be made possible].[2]

For all white observers, the Black's colour is supremely 'the visual signifier of his Otherness'.[3] Postcolonial studies have made us aware that the converse is equally true. 'The Other can possess whatever negative qualities we perceive within ourselves. But given any historical tradition of perceiving the Other, whether as Jew, black, homosexual, or woman, there are variations in emphasis and structure in the code of Otherness.'[4] Multiracial coexistence and the multiculturalism it generates are now a fact of urban civilisation in the West.

My reader's attention may well have been alerted to the consequent *Blanche/Noir* relations by their being explored in three captivating recent films: Spike Lee's *Jungle Fever* (1991), Mike Leigh's *Secrets and Lies* (1996) and James Toback's *Black and White* (1999). Yet when the word 'civilisation' is mentioned, how many white people, hand on heart, will seek a third way between the dubious relativism of Leo Frobenius, the German anthropologist who gave such comfort to the founders of Negritude, recognising the greatness of various African civilisations, and the patrician stance of the Eurocentric Kenneth Clark, taking no account of the fact that the wealth and leisure required for the production of his preferred art was generated, more than by any single other factor, by profits from the infamous trade in African slaves?[5]

Slavery, with its huge economic rewards, was justified on the basis of permutations of legal, biblical, moral, sociological and biological grounds, none of which seems now to be other than a grotesque and spurious exercise in self-justification. The blunt statement by Locke, in his *Essay Concerning Human Understanding* (1690), that 'the Child can demonstrate to you, that a *Negro is not a man*', reinforced by Hume's assertion that 'there never was a civilised nation of any other complexion than white', reflected and reinforced European prejudice.[6] Blacks became convenient chattels in the inhuman commerce of humans. The implied universalisation of European criteria, blatant or insidious, continues to this day. As to the white woman, already set on a pedestal by the courtly love tradition, she was, by the process that sociologists know as acculturation, internalised as an ideal by Blacks. While black women responded by depigmentation of the skin, black men strove to reach that ideal by intimate contact.

It never ceases to astonish me that centuries of systematic exploitation, injustice and humiliation should not have given rise to widespread acts of vengeful violence, on a scale unimagined by even the most bloodthirsty black activists and realised historically only in miniature, however traumatically, in local uprisings such as Haiti's struggle for liberation. At worst, in 'white' writing, and with different authorial motivations, suitable retribution is visited upon the emblematically individual exploiter, as in Heinrich von Kleist's *Die Verlobung in St. Domingo* (The Insurrection in Saint Domingue, written 1802–03), Eugène Sue's *Atar-Gull* (1831) or Joseph Conrad's *Heart of Darkness* (1902). Where black writers are concerned, potential resentment is more often defused by gentle irony or the factual recollection of a few unsettling truths—the equivalent, face to face, of a disarming smile. Even where, as in Aimé

Césaire's seismic metaphors, violence is postulated, it is contained within the writing, not recommended as a course of action.

By concentrating on the *couple domino*—the increasingly standardised term in French for the mixed-race partnership—and specifically on the *Blanche/Noir* rather than the *Blanc/Noire* couple (the use of French here allowing a neater encapsulation than English does of the particular pairing concerned), the present study may highlight what, in the earlier periods especially, was the rarer form of relationship.[7] In so doing it can encompass not only a greater variety of representations but also a greater proportion of those that exist. But I cannot claim completeness: no catalogue or website that I know lists cases of the *couple domino* in literature, and I have had to rely on my own inevitably partial investigations. Even so, I am persuaded that most of the texts involved are unfamiliar even to specialists in the study of French literature. In exploring an alternative canon, I like to think that I am opening avenues for further reflection.

What is particularly important from our point of view is that the *Blanche/Noir* couple traditionally encapsulates the more radically scandalous transgression of perceived power relationships, with emancipation involved for both parties, thereby reversing received notions of dominance by White and male over Black and female, a precedence which is further problematised in the white female's relationship with the black male. Each party flies in the face of the mores of his or her community by taking the genetically desirable practice of exogamy 'too far'. As Ronald Hyam has observed in relation to the phenomenon within the British Empire:

> One thing is certain. Sex is at the very heart of racism. Racism is not caused simply by sexual apprehensions, and there are many other factors involved, [...] but the peculiarly emotional hostility towards black men which it has so often engendered requires a sexual explanation. From New Orleans to New Guinea, from Barbados to Bulawayo, from Kimberley to Kuala Lumpur, the quintessential taboo to be explained is the white man's formal objection to intimacy between black men and white women. Granting political equality was perceived as giving freedom for

black men to go to bed with white women, and in the American south or in southern Africa, that stuck in the gullet.[8]

The *Blanche/Noir* nexus thus acts as a microcosm of racial, social and sexual politics, illuminating the general by the particular case, invariably perceived as the most extreme and the most provocative.

The high proportion of women writers concerning themselves with the *Blanche/Noir* couple reflects their pre-occupation with undermining the discourse of a double colonisation, that of the female by the male as well that of the Black by the White. A racist chauvinist will see women as the Trojan horse threatening the purity of the white race.[9] Penetration (*double entendre* intended) of the 'dark continent', as Freud tellingly characterised woman, using the established term for Africa when colonisation was in full swing, cried out for that twofold reversal.[10] Female and black empowerment go hand in hand in the *Blanche/Noir* couple.

As for Blacks, centuries of persuasion that they are inferior not just technologically but in every other way—except perhaps in their genital apparatus: 'the blacks' identity is as surrogate genitals', Sander Gilman suggests, or as Pius Ngandu Nkashama colourfully puts it, the Black has a 'gros phallus braqué sur le cercle magique de l'innocence blanche' [huge phallus aimed at the magic circle of white innocence][11]—has led them sometimes to believe it to be true, sometimes to overcompensate, and just sometimes, in the best cases, to dismiss it for the nonsense it is, benefit from their multicultural experience and stand proud as the individuals they are. From an analytical point of view, Gilman is as astute as ever: 'The analogy of the black with sexuality can be one of the touchstones to any examination of the problem of consciousness among the moderns.'[12] 'Pourquoi les "sauvages" seraient-ils tous entièrement bons ou mauvais, alors que nous, nous avons droit à l'indivi-dualité et à l'ambiguïté?' [Why should 'savages' be entirely good or bad, whereas we are entitled to individuality and ambiguity?], is Dominique Schnapper's entirely pertinent question.[13]

5

This book traces in broadly chronological order key texts and instances. It refers to Othello, Shakespeare's acceptable pole of black otherness,[14] and to that first literary paradigm of the 'noble savage', Aphra Behn's Oroonoko, a model entrenched by Rousseau and abolitionist writers in the eighteenth century. Passing reference is made to Freud's *Totem and Taboo*, which starts from anthropological data but wisely signals a recognition of cultural relativity, while Fanon's *Peau noire, masques blancs*, which deals psychoanalytically *inter alia* with the *Blanche/Noir* relationship and with a specific literary example of it, figures more insistently. Pervading the book's text-based investigations are the 'alternative' discourses of postcolonial criticism.

In placing this study under the implicit invocation of two psychiatrists, Freud and Fanon, I do not wish to suggest any more than a general indebtedness in my reflections to the concept of 'totemic exogamy' in the former or to the interpretation of relations between 'l'homme de couleur et la Blanche' [the coloured man and the white woman] in the latter.[15] Freud starts from general anthropological considerations already well analysed by J.G. Frazer in *Totemism and Exogamy*,[16] while Fanon's familiar thesis is based on what he calls the 'complexus psycho-existentiel' [psycho-existential complex], in effect a double bind, suffered by Black and White alike through their interactive but unequal social history.

The pervasive theme of love in literature takes on a particular coloration in the *couple domino*. There are substantial continuities across the centuries, doubtless in part reflecting unchanging half-conscious fears and conscious animosities, but also in part determined by the very nature of narrative. Antagonism was exacerbated, however, by periods of slavery and colonialism. The 1740 *Histoire de Louis Anniaba* warrants special attention: flawed, but not deserving the dismissive treatment it has generally received, it inaugurates, in an exotic fantasy remarkably free of racist bias, representations both of the near-contemporary

Black (as distinct from images of the black Magus found from the Renaissance to Anatole France and Michel Tournier) and of the *Blanche/Noir* couple in French literature. It furthermore heralded the decade in which both *Othello* and *Oroonoko* were first translated into French.[17]

Fifty years later, at the pivotal moment of the French Revolution and within the crucial nexus of contrasting discourses of power and its abolition which generated it and which it generated, the gamut of cases of biracial couplings is established—from the black stud to the easy woman, from the suitor hampered by his belief in the myth of his inferiority to the romantic idealist, from hardened racists to the 'colour-blind' *phalanstère*—for subsequent deployment and exploration. One even finds, in Bernardin de Saint-Pierre's *Empsaël et Zoraïde, ou les Blancs esclaves des Noirs à Maroc*, probably completed in 1793, the singular case of an ironic reversal of standard expectations of racial-cum-power politics which will be matched by nothing so fully as by Bertène Juminer's wickedly witty *La Revanche de Bozambo* of 1968.[18]

It is important to recall, since I am dealing with French-language literatures, that the Revolution propounded, alongside liberty and fraternity, the principle of equality, indivisible and universal. However imperfectly applied, a theoretical structure was thus put in place which, when subsequently interpreted through the colonial policy of assimilation, encouraged indigenous men to aspire to French citizenship. How better to express the desire to integrate than through intimate relations with a white woman? It was a paradoxical consequence of the theory that such practice should have been so widely deplored by both communities: at one and the same time, an *assimilé* estranged himself from his own people and remained alienated among Europeans. The ostensibly paradoxical 'Nègre blanc' [white Black] has, ever since the meaning of the term was extended beyond 'albino' in the course of the eighteenth century, been the butt of everyone's opprobrium.

As to the Revolution within the Revolution, the insurrection of Saint Domingue's black slaves and that country's emergence as the independent Haiti in 1804, the first black nation-state in the modern world, its shock-waves reverberate through literature to this day, providing a focus for arguments on every side. Some of these will be investigated through the *Blanche/Noir* couple in chapter 2, focused on literature of the 1820s.

Colonialist writers, reflecting historical circumstances (few European women explored Africa or joined their husbands there) and prevailing attitudes (contempt mixed with ignorance and fear), scarcely touched on *Blanche/Noir* relations. The 1920s, however, saw some spirited representations of the *couple domino* by largely forgotten and unjustly neglected French women writers—Lucie Cousturier, Louise Faure-Favier, Claire Goll—in the context of serious belletristic or journalistic questioning, by André Gide and Albert Londres for example, of the tenets and practices of colonialism. Indeed, the decade represents a crucial nexus, which merits extended attention here, since such liberal attitudes are to be found in parallel not only with continuing exploitation of the stereotypical white masculinist paradigms, but also with the first appearance, in a rapidly increasing body of fiction, of a black point of view. While a balanced view gradually emerges, it has to struggle against the persistent inertia of stereotypes so long and so deeply entrenched.

As far as French is concerned, and apart from occasional autobiographical accounts, Blacks have been 'writing back to the centre', to echo Salman Rushdie's celebrated phrase, and in any concerted way therefore representing their own perspectives and fantasies, only since the 1920s. It is natural, in the compass of history, that this should be so: for a West African, for example, to write in French presupposes mastery of a foreign language and culture through years of education and effort.[19] The processes of acculturation, whatever lip-service may be paid to concepts of equality and assimilation (in practice highly selective), cannot avoid prompting an awareness of difference and deprivation. That this should, according to circumstance, provoke the bewilderment of conflicting loyalties, a fundamental identity crisis, an aggressive assertion of independence, antagonistic confrontation, and a condemnation of the hypocrisies inherent in the mercantile and missionary discourses of colonisation and neocolonialism, is scarcely surprising. If Negritude could, not unfairly in some of its manifestations, be considered by Sartre as a 'racisme anti-raciste' [anti-racist racism],[20] its historical necessity has to be acknowledged too: if it had not existed, it would have had to have been invented. It allowed Blacks to relativise the universal white assumptions about their material deprivation, mechanical incompetence and cultural indigence, and to lay claim to a moral and spiritual high ground standing like a Mont Saint-Michel against the low tide of exploitation, deportation and persecution. It was almost inevitable that it should also have produced a generation of 'mimic men', to use V.S. Naipaul's telling phrase which Homi K. Bhabha picks up to such good effect.

Subsequent generations of black writers, no longer confined to representing high-flying intellectuals in varieties of auto-fiction, have had the advantage of that key *prise de conscience* while not necessarily acknowledging their gratitude towards it, preferring rather in some instances, as Sembene does, to condemn its racist premise. Rarely does Fanon's revenge model figure. In Claire Goll's 1928 novel, *Le Nègre Jupiter enlève Europa*, it is anticipated but, since Fanon was not yet born, vengeance is presented rather in the form of jealousy, with explicit reference to Othello. As to the 1985 soft-porn romp, *Comment faire l'amour avec un nègre sans se fatiguer*, by the Haitian-Canadian Dany Laferrière, its relation to Fanon may be overt, but its self-deflating ironies put its tongue firmly in its cheek with regard to its avowed psychoanalytical model. Only in some recent writings is ordinary, biodegradable love presented dispassionately as part of life's rich pattern, with free and equal partnership between the parties. This may take the form of promiscuity and, in the last twenty years, either be exploited for its own sake in forms of what René Depestre has called 'géolibertinage' or be used, as by Olympe Bhêly-Quenum or Daniel Biyaoula—parallel in this to such South African

9

writers in English as Doris Lessing, Nadine Gordimer and Lewis Nkosi—as a metaphor for a wider and deeper psycho-sociological or political investigation. Véronique Tadjo brings our chronological survey full circle, since the skin-colour of the *Blanche/Noir* couple in her 1999 novel, *Champs de bataille et d'amour*, is mentioned no more than it was in the *Histoire de Louis Anniaba* of 1740.

This study therefore sets out to act as a touchstone for reflection over several interactive disciplines, concludes that the mixed-race relationship is likely to remain a site of special scientific as well as social and therefore literary interest for generations to come, and calls for a society in which multicultural awareness replaces racial prejudice, recognising the latter as primarily skin-deep. In the process, some re-evaluation of earlier works, hitherto neglected or marginalised, will take place, shifting the emphasis away from the established canon.

I have been struck by the fact that virtually every writer exploring a *Blanche/Noir* relationship believes that he or she is doing so for the first time, that there is no tradition or pre-existing set of literary patterns. I hope that even those rare souls who, with the benefit of cosmopolitan exposure and a liberal mind, are entirely free of racial prejudice, will recognise the value of exploring earlier and different attitudes in the interest of increasing their number.

We shall find ignorance and prejudice represented in full measure and astonishingly resilient in persisting beyond the availability of facts to explode their myths and fantasies. On the other hand, a liberal stance is no guarantee either of a happy outcome or of good literature. Most of the texts, especially those by Whites, are drawn from 'minor' writers or are the minor works of 'major' writers, but we have to beware of the self-fulfilling classification of works deemed peripheral for reasons other than literary.[21] By exploring 'popular' representations, this study can observe the stereotypes in sharper focus, whether they be the myth of the noble savage or the fact of the tortured slave, the fantasies of exoticism and eroticism, bestial Blacks endowed with generous genitalia or superior sexual appetites and prowess, the counter-image of black men effectively emasculated by the white man's general social domination of Blacks and specific sexual control of black women, or Fanonian notions of individual coitus wreaking revenge for centuries of European oppression and exploitation.

Transgression is fraught with excitement as well as danger. Yet for transgression to be sensed as possible, and even in some instances desirable, a taboo or a barrier has to be perceived to exist. It is therefore one of the paradoxes of the present study that it cannot help but throw into relief the very racism that it deplores. Its exploration of a black–white axis leads to a polarisation which needs to be set in the broader rainbow context of multiracial complexity. One reason for the lack of illustrations in the present volume is that relevant images of black man and white woman alone together tend graphically to reinforce the stereotype, leaving the imagination no purchase for a visual counter-discourse. Explicitly or implicitly, the heightened sexuality or animality of the Black is presented as raping the innocent White.[22] Even where the image of a mixed-race couple, with or without their child, is seemingly neutral, the accompanying commentary appears to be shot through either with repugnant white supremacism or with what some would consider scarcely less offensive self-congratulatory liberalism.[23] Words can perhaps navigate between such a Scylla and such a Charybdis, but the idea that their author should be tied naked to the mast for the purpose, with all the Freudian implications, leaves me distinctly uncomfortable.

Not being a black male or a white female may be considered insuperable handicaps in a critic embarking on an analysis of the literary representation of intimate relationships between black men and white women. Certain schools of black nationalists and of feminists would undoubtedly think so, but by definition their requirements are mutually exclusive. What is more, since the chosen corpus is writing in French, not to be French might be seen as definitively disabling. I like to think that such apparent disqualifications should, on the contrary, lend greater detachment and objectivity to my investigations. Whether

11

or not there is any truth in the assertion that 'interracial sexuality between white women and black men symbolizes the ultimate threat and insult to white masculinity',[24] it is clearly a subject eminently worthy of exploration.

An exhaustive psycho-sociological review of the possible permutations of relationships between Blacks and Whites has been published.[25] By contrast, there have been few studies of *Blanche/Noir* relationships in 'Black' Francographic writing,[26] and characteristically not one of them also considers writing by metropolitan French authors. Indeed the representation of Blacks in French literature before the advent of Negritude in the 1930s is a somewhat neglected field, viewed no doubt with legitimate embarrassment by white critics but also largely ignored—with varying degrees of contempt for its 'doudouist' propensities—by black scholars.[27] I like to think that one of the merits of the present book is that it is not limited to pre- or post-Negritude writing as is usually the case but seeks rather to cover both. As a result, it reveals continuities and discontinuities within the representation and self-representation of Blacks, albeit from a special angle.

Outside imaginative literature, European travel writers and factual reporters, from intrepid explorers to slave traders and from merchant adventurers to colonial officials, have, even if selectively, fared rather better: it is recognised that their observations shaped awareness and attitudes, and it is a healthy sign that a substantial doctoral thesis has recently been devoted by a Senegalese scholar to exploring the relationship between their accounts and the creative literature of his homeland.[28]

The period of colonialist writing has also been extensively studied, though by an understandable paradox it is not prominent in this study, being as light on *Blanche/Noir* intimacies as it is heavy on *Blanc/Noire* ones, whether as passing affairs—'une nécessité physique qui illumine la solitude d'un broussard' [a physical necessity which lightens a bush-ranger's loneliness], as one African critic has charitably described it[29]—or as marriages à la mode du pays. A full relationship is still unthinkable in many minds:

> Un mariage entre Blanches et Noirs s'avère pratiquement impossible en Afrique coloniale. Si la société africaine tradition-nelle s'y oppose, la société blanche le combat par tous les moyens, afin de maintenir sa position de prestige et de supériorité.

> [A marriage between white women and black men is practically impossible in colonial Africa. If traditional African society is opposed to it, white society fights it with every means at its disposal, so as to maintain its position of prestige and superiority.][30]

'Really, Tom, I cannot contemplate how a white woman could have anything to do with a native' encapsulates the European woman's attitude at the time.[31] In the late 1960s, Eldridge Cleaver postulated a polar opposition so absolute as to show its manifest absurdity: 'The psychic bride of the Supermasculine Menial is the Ultrafeminine. She is his "dream girl."'[32] In the anonymity of a large cosmopolitan city, and with increasing interaction between Blacks and Whites, the unthinkable is becoming increasingly common-place, but the familiar question 'Would you let your daughter marry a black man?' still, all too often, prompts a viscerally negative response.

White women novelists of the last forty years have continued to contest such a prejudice: while Guy des Cars and Georges Conchon serve to reinforce the stereotype (the former by paying ludicrous lip-service to its reversal), Christine Garnier and Claire Etcherelli, like the English novelists Catherine Cookson (in Colour Blind) and Marina Warner (in Indigo), have questioned its validity with open-mindedness and acumen. Geneviève Billy adds her largely positive personal account. Even where the female writer concludes that Blanche/Noir marriages generally end un-happily, as in four out of the five cases presented by Michèle Assamoua in Le Défi of 1987, it is not a presupposition. Con-servative 'popular wisdom' continues, however, to parade the old prejudice: 'Ces mariages mixtes ne marchent jamais!' [Those mixed marriages never work!].[33]

One might imagine, given the interracial admixture of the West Indies, that the majority of instances of *Blanche/ Noir* relationships would be drawn from that part of the world. The detailed racial permutations presented in tabular form by Moreau de Saint-Méry towards the end of the eighteenth century make it clear, however, that the starting-point is rather the white male. 'Triste société, où les qualités sont définies par la couleur de la peau!' [It's a sad society in which value is defined by skin-colour!].[34] This is a reflection of the social reality of the time: the rare white woman who ventured to the islands may attract a black slave's attention and even feel impelled to reciprocate it, but decorum was paramount and the rare intimacy severely punished.[35] The very fact that all Blacks of African origin in the New World had at some time in their family history been uprooted, transported and subjected to slavery distinguishes them from Africans who had managed to stay put. For while internal African slavery is by no means unknown, even to this day, the degree of trauma in those carried off across the Atlantic was inevitably greater. Present-day Caribbean society is so mixed that the racial absolutes represented by 'Black' and 'White' scarcely obtain. Indeed, the promotion of *créolisation*, like that of *métissage*, implicitly reflects the rejection of such absolutes, but it will be a long time before someone biracial feels able to write: 'Métis, ce n'est pas une couleur. Ça n'existe que dans la tête de certaines personnes' [Mestizo is not a colour. It only exists in some people's minds].[36]

What then are the variables within the literary corpus concerned? The principal ones would appear to be the date of composition, the culture of the author, and the location of the action. Subsumed under the date of composition are considerations of historical events, socio-political and legal circumstances, and prevailing fashions of literary style, while the questions of the author's culture and the impact of where the action occurs may, in particular cases, be less than straightforward. The western liberal is rapidly forced to recognise that racism is not the exclusive prerogative of white societies. But what is certain is that the three main variables interact to produce complex patterns of which the individual shape is determined, as in all literary composition, by the author's ideological stance, narrative competence and projective imagination. A given reader will inevitably sympathise more with some attitudes than with others, but it should be remembered that the economy of a text is a delicate balance of forces, the interplay of which is integral to its composition and effect. At its simplest, for good to triumph over evil, evil must be represented, and it has the disturbing literary characteristic of being inherently more dramatic.

Different works may emphasise the viewpoint of the black man or that of the white woman, and this viewpoint may correspond or not with the race and gender of the author. In any case, no author can be familiar from the inside with *both* points of view and it is therefore unlikely that stereotypical fantasies can be avoided altogether. It will be part of our evaluative judgement to determine not just the degree of subtlety with which racist stereotypes are characterised (degree zero in some instances) but also how they contribute to the narrative progress and outcome. Quotation will further help to give the flavour of the writing, all the more necessary where texts are little known and not readily available. As to the literary product, the fact that it remains part of a regenerative process in successive readers means that it is open to reinterpretation and re-evaluation. This seems to me particularly true of the representation of Blacks by Whites in all the 'pre-Negritude' period: once the French Empire started 'writing back', the earlier work takes on a whole new coloration and with it new and sometimes startling relevance.[37]

One psycho-sociological yardstick is the attitude of characters and, insofar as it can reasonably be deduced, of the author towards the natural product of miscegenation: biracial children, whether actual or projected. The phenomenon is more widespread in the African diaspora than in Africa itself, becoming a significant social and literary issue in the nineteenth century. 'Half-castes' may be viewed as enjoying double benefit or, more often, suffering double jeopardy, reminding one of George Bernard Shaw's caustic response to the idea of a child that he might hypothetically have by Isadora Duncan, idealised as having her beauty and his brains, whereas his wry scepticism envisaged rather the converse. Mulattos, whose very name derives from the sterile product of horse and ass, belong to both black and white communites—or to neither. The social consequences of the uneasy paradox that 'hybridity is heresy' were most clearly seen in Haiti at the time of independence: once the common (white) enemy had been ousted, the latent antagonism between mulattos and Blacks erupted into confrontation.[38]

Moral disapproval has been expressed in the broad-shouldered name of sound medicine and good social order:

> au lieu d'avoir la somme des éléments de résistance du blanc et du nègre [les mulâtres] n'ont au contraire que la somme de leurs imperfections physiques et morales;

> [instead of enjoying the soundness in wind and limb of Black or White, mulattos combine their physical and moral imper-fections];

or again:

> ivrognerie et prostitution sont les tristes apanages de cette classe de gens qui détestent le blanc et méprisent le noir.

> [drunkennness and prostitution are the sad prerogatives of this category of people who detest Whites and look down on Blacks.][39]

James Walvin observes that 'Edward Long, always reliable as a spokesman for racial extremism, described miscegenation as a "venomous and dangerous ulcer that threatens to disperce [sic] its malignancy far and wide, until every family catches infection from it"'.[40] In the nineteenth century, a decade before Gobineau's now infamous *Essai sur l'inégalité des races humaines* (1853–55), Alphonse Esquiros promoted a limited type of miscegenation in the mistaken belief that

l'union d'un individu de la race éthiopique avec une femme
blanche est douloureuse, antipathique, le plus souvent impro-
ductive. La condition inverse est, au contraire, favorable au
mélange des sexes; l'union d'un Blanc avec la femme noire est
facile, sympathique et presque toujours féconde. [...] La nature veut
l'élévation des races, elle ne veut pas leur abaissement. Or, dans
le premier cas, le produit descend vers la race éthiopique; dans le
second, c'est-à-dire dans le cas de l'union de l'homme blanc avec
la femme noire, le produit est élevé vers la race caucasique. On
entrevoit déjà que le mélange des races, dans certaines limites
fixées par la nature, est un des moyens de perfectionnement de
l'espèce humaine.

[the coupling of a man from the Ethiopic race with a white
woman is painful, unwelcome, and most often unfruitful. The
opposite relationship is, on the contrary, advantageous to the
mixing of the sexes: the coupling of a white man with a black
woman is easy, agreeable and almost always fruitful. [...] Nature
seeks the elevation of the races, not their degradation. Now, in
the first case, the result descends towards the Ethiopic race; in
the second, i.e. in the case of a white man coupling with a black
woman, the result is raised towards the Caucasian race. It
emerges from this that the mingling of races, within certain
limits fixed by nature, is one means of perfecting the human
species.][41]

Esquiros compounded his tendentious and baseless
assertions by adding, with no less confidence in the accuracy
of his genetic information, that

quand le mélange de deux individus de races diverses est fécond,
la race supérieure fournit au moins les deux tiers à la nature du
produit.

[when the coming together of two individuals from different races
is fruitful, the superior race supplies at least two thirds of the
make-up of the result.][42]

Such a farrago of nonsense, supported by the science of its
day (in itself a cautionary tale regarding unquestioning
belief in today's science), seems to be the result of wishful
thinking as much as of ingrained prejudice. In short, as
Champly underlines with evangelising fervour and
apocalyptic horror: '*Beware, White race! The Coloured races*

have discovered your supreme treasure, the White Woman!'[43] It is unfortunately a fact available for an easy pun to writers with quite varied purposes that 'en notation musicale, une blanche vaut deux noires' [in musical notation, one minim/white woman is worth two crotchets/ black women].[44]

To relativise such a position, one has only to reflect on the very different viewpoint powerfully propounded by Awa Thiam in her ground-breaking feminist study of West African women:

> Prise de force par le colon—violée—ou séduite par lui grâce à quelque artifice, parce que perçue comme objet de plaisir, la Négresse se trouve ravalée à un statut dégradant. Son essence étant niée, que reste-t-il d'elle? RIEN. *Elle n'est plus rien*, ou plutôt elle est réduite à l'état d'instrument. Dans ce contexte, y a-t-il une possibilité d'amour vrai entre le colonisateur et la colonisée? Ou une possibilité de rapports humains?

> [Taken by force by the colonist—raped—or seduced by him by some other artifice, because perceived as an object of pleasure, the Negress finds herself reduced to a degrading status. As her essence is denied, what is left of her? NOTHING. *She is nothing any longer*, or rather she is reduced to the state of an instrument. In this context, is there any possibility of true love between the colonist and the colonised woman? Or any possibility of human relations?][45]

At various times and in various places, legislation was brought to bear in an attempt to regulate—i.e. to prevent— miscegenation,[46] but since slavery was abolished in particular, many influential voices have, on the contrary, seen it as a positive way forward for society:

> Le jour où mulâtres et surtout mulâtresses se diront nègres et négresses verra bientôt disparaître une distinction contraire aux lois de la fraternité et grosse de futurs malheurs

> [The day when mulattos and particularly mulatresses call themselves negroes and negresses will herald the disappearance of a distinction which is against the laws of fraternity and fraught with the seeds of disaster]

declared Schœlcher in echo of the *abbé* Grégoire, while Senghor's familiar 'métissage culturel' [cultural miscegenation] is proposed as a desirable model for human understanding.[47] As the son of a Congolese father and a French mother, the contemporary writer, politician and diplomat Henri Lopes acknowledges some existential problems for a person of mixed race such as he, but capitalises on his privileged vantage-point to explore in his novels the complex roots of his double culture.[48] Véronique Tadjo, a biracial Franco-Ivoirian, makes a contribution to *Blanche/Noir* literature which, by its total absence of reference to skin-colour, provides a keystone to my chronological arch of instances drawn from both Blacks and Whites and symbolically points the way forward to mixed-race relationships which are as unexceptional (or exceptional) as any other.

Set against that, however, is the racist discourse of Nazism, apartheid or the various persistent forms of fascist or neo-Nazi white supremacism which fantasise about innate superiority. A noted French geneticist makes the general point that

> la présence d'un couple "mixte" est le scandale majeur pour ceux qui ne peuvent imaginer de vérité que dans leur vérité.

> [the presence of a 'mixed' couple is the worst scandal imaginable for those who can envisage no truth other than their own.][49]

An American critic has further observed that 'while interracial sexuality between all whites and all nonwhites is taboo in this [white supremacist] discourse, the plethora of images and articles about interracial sexuality focuses almost exclusively on white woman and black man.'[50] That the *Blanche/Noir* couple should be singled out by fascists for special excoriation is another good reason for investigating it more dispassionately from a different perspective and through a wider corpus.

When tragedy occurs in the literary representations of the *Blanche/Noir* couple, does it arise from within the characters and their interaction, as traditionally tragedy should, in a framework of social prejudice (Jean Malonga's *Cœur d'Aryenne* written in 1948 and Mariama Bâ's *Un chant écarlate* published in 1981 are cases in point), or is it the result of a 'chance' occurrence interposed by the author (as in Ousmane Socé's 1937 *Mirages de Paris*)? Or again does it stem from the patronising but persistent assumption that such a relationship is unthinkable, whether this assumption be made by the author, the white female character, or both, leading to the narrative equivalent of *coitus interruptus* (Hugo in *Bug-Jargal*, originally written in 1818, Balzac in *Le Nègre* of 1822, Madame Cashin in *Amour et liberté* of 1847, Félicien Champsaur in *La Caravane en folie* of 1926, Ferdinand Oyono's *Chemin d'Europe* of 1960)? Once again the *Blanche/Noir* couple can be seen to encapsulate a theme more broadly observable: that of the clash—the 'ambiguous adventure' or the *écart* (to echo the titles of key novels by Cheikh Hamidou Kane and V.Y. Mudimbe)—which generates schizoid and even suicidal tendencies in the attempt to straddle two cultures.

Where an optimistic stance is promoted or a happy ending achieved, is it soundly based? Louise Faure-Favier's *Blanche et Noir* of 1928 may be as misty-eyed as the anonymous *Histoire de Louis Anniaba* from nearly two centuries earlier, but by comparison Guy des Cars's 1963 *Sang d'Afrique* is both more crass and more dishonest. Social pressures in matters of biracial relationships are such that the *dénouement* of Sembène Ousmane's 1957 *Ô pays, mon beau peuple!*, with the death of Oumar at the instigation of white colonists who see him as a multifaceted threat to their way of life, appears more realistic than the hopeful but untested projections of René Maran's *Un homme pareil aux autres* (1947) or Bhêly-Quenum's as yet unpublished *C'était à Tigony*, even if, at the personal level, the *Blanche/Noir* relationships are unusually satisfactory in all those cases. Such optimism has of course to be tempered by realism, and the depressing daily news of racist attacks, tribal conflict and confrontation inclines one to scepticism and even to cynicism, but the more we endeavour to see ourselves objectively and others subjectively, the greater the pool of understanding is likely to be and the more rewarding the world a place to coexist in.

If at different times and in different societies there has been a stated or unstated taboo erected, within the healthy practice of exogamy, against interracial marriage, it is equally apparent that there have always been transgressors more than willing to convert that taboo into a totem. Neither extreme position is healthy for the individuals concerned or for the society at large. Equally, it is clear that the thrill of transgression is always likely to be a minority sport, however significant a model. Intolerance must be condemned but patronising tolerance recognised as suspect. Barriers have to be transformed into thresholds of exchange, understanding and respect. The aim is a stance beyond both difference and indifference, beyond the fear of the former and the apathy of the latter.

CHAPTER 1
EIGHTEENTH-CENTURY ENWHITENMENT

> 'Black man, what can you have to do with love?
> Give over chasing white girls if you have any sense!
> An Ethiop black like you can have no way to reach them.'
> Nusayb the Younger[51]

IN THE YEAR 1738, when it is estimated that there were only some four thousand Blacks in France out of a population of about sixteen million people, the *abbé* Prévost was prompted by his reading of *Othello* to remark: 'une femme blanche ne peut pas tomber amoureuse d'un noir' [a white woman cannot fall in love with a black man].[52] Certainly the context was unpropitious for a liberal-minded attitude, for 1738 also heralded an era of intolerance towards mixed-race marriages in France and its colonies.

A celebrated court case, the details and implications of which are fully presented by Sue Peabody, occupied the summer months of 1738 and led to an acquittal of the plaintiff, a black servant married, it seems, to a white woman, who claimed and won his freedom.[53] Official displeasure came swiftly. Louis XV's *Déclaration concernant les nègres esclaves des colonies* of December that same year smacks of disproportionate retribution: not only did he rescind the legal principle, established since 1571, that nobody on French soil could be a slave, but he also extended to France his 1724 edict forbidding interracial marriages in Louisiana. Although the courts did not ratify the declaration, thereby leaving the status of the Black in France open to litigation (until the 1777 *Déclaration pour la police des noirs*, which both deprived Blacks in France of many rights and initiated a census of them), it is clear that, in 1738,

22

attention was drawn to Blacks in a prevailing mood of increased hostility.

In respect of marriage, article IX of the 1685 *Code noir*—issued in the same year as the intolerant Revocation of the Edict of Nantes—had regulated religious worship (restricted to the Roman Catholic church) and, in particular, marriages both between Blacks and between a white master and his black slave. In the latter case, the woman and any children were confiscated but never freed. As to Blacks in France, article X of the 1738 declaration makes explicit reference to an interim decree:

> Les Esclaves Negres qui auront esté emmenez ou envoyez en France, ne pourront s'y marier, mesme du consentement de leurs Maistres, nonobstant ce qui est porté par l'article VII. de nostre Edit du mois d'Octobre 1716. auquel Nous dérogeons quant à ce.

> [Black Slaves who have been brought or sent to France may not marry there, even with their Masters' consent, notwithstanding article 7 of our Edict of October 1716, which We hereby rescind.]

That earlier edict had declared:

> Les Esclaves Negres de l'un ou de l'autre sexe, qui auront esté amenez ou envoyez en France par leurs Maistres, ne pourront s'y marier sans le consentement de leurs Maistres; & en cas qu'ils y consentent, lesdits Esclaves seront et demeureront libres en vertu dudit consentement.

> [Black Slaves of either sex brought or sent to France by their Masters, may not marry there without their Masters' consent; and in the event of such consent, the aforesaid Slaves will be and remain free by virtue of that consent.]

As to the interim ruling in respect of Louisiana, a practice which was extended to France's other American colonies, article VI of 1724 reads as follows:

> Deffendons à nos Sujets blancs, de l'un ou l'autre sexe, de contracter mariage avec les Noirs, à peine de punition & d'amende arbitraire; [...]. Deffendons aussi à nosdits Sujets blancs, mesme aux Noirs affranchis ou nez libres, de vivre en concubinage

avec des Esclaves; Voulons que ceux qui auront eu un ou plusieurs enfans d'une pareille conjonction, ensemble les Maistres qui les auront soufferts, soient condamnez chacun en une amende de trois cens livres; Et, s'ils sont Maistres de l'Esclave de laquelle ils auront eu lesdits enfans, Voulons qu'outre l'amende ils soient privez tant de l'Esclave que des enfans, & qu'ils soient adjugez à l'Hospital des lieux, sans pouvoir jamais estre affranchis.

[We hereby forbid our White subjects, of either sex, to contract a marriage with a Black, on pain of punishment and an unlimited fine. [...] We further forbid our White subjects, as well as our freed Blacks or those born free, to consort with Slaves. We require those who have had a child or children from such cohabitation, and also the Masters who have allowed it, to be severally condemned to a fine of three hundred *livres*. And, if they are the Masters of the Slave with whom they have had the aforesaid children, We require that in addition to the fine, the Slave and her children be taken away from him, assigned to the local almshouse and never be freed.][54]

This legal framework has not been taken into account in the generally adverse criticism accorded to the first French novel with a black hero, the anonymous *Histoire de Louis Anniaba, roi d'Essenie en Afrique sur la côte de Guinée*, published in 1740. The novel's benign stance may contribute to the weakness of its literary qualities, but it displays no little courage in adopting that position.[55]

The preface to the story conventionally protests its veracity; drawn from Anniaba's memoirs, it is narrated in the first person with, we are assured, only minor adjustments. Anniaba was born at Guadalaguer, the son of the King of Essenie. At the age of eighteen, bent on travelling to Europe, he entrusts himself to a Marseilles merchant and meets on board an aristocratic young Frenchwoman, Dalo..., rescued from Essenie after her capture by Barbary pirates in the Mediterranean. Married in Essenie to a young Provençal captive who had taught her Arabic, she has him die in her arms from joy at seeing his homeland. Anniaba consoles her on their return to Antibes and the Château de Bart... where she was brought up. Eternally grateful, she falls in love with him while remaining sensitive to the moral code of her upbringing. But her protestation, 'je dois ménager ma gloire' [I must safeguard my honour], has to do not with his colour but with her recent widowhood and sense of a class difference between them. He refers to her as his Queen, then as his 'Épouse' [wife], promising to renounce his faith for the purpose of marriage:

> Ah, lui dis-je, charmante Beauté, vous y êtes maintenant à l'abri de l'esclavage, & moi j'achève d'y perdre ma liberté!

> [Ah, said I, my lovely one, you are now safe from slavery and I am about to lose my freedom!],

to which she replies:

> Il y a en tous sens une si prodigieuse distance de vous à moi, qu'il est impossible que je puisse vous approcher? [sic] Votre Trône, votre Religion, vos qualités personnelles, tout s'opose [sic] au retour que vous doit ma tendresse. Tout conspire contre notre union.

> [There is in every respect such a gulf between us that I could never come near you. Your throne, your religion, your personal qualities, everything militates against your reciprocating my tender feelings towards you. Everything conspires against our marriage.]

All such barriers, however, of which race is not one, are finally overcome: 'Prenez donc, mon cher Prince, la possession irrévocable d'un cœur qui vous doit toutes ses affections' [Dear Prince, take possession for ever of a heart which owes you its total affection]. The resentment of a rival suitor, Baron de Lasc..., sent packing by Anniaba, will trigger subsequent twists in the plot.

The couple goes to Paris, where Anniaba joins the *Mousquetaires Gris* under the name Marquis d'Outremer. Relaxing in the Bois de Boulogne, they are attacked, and Dalo... is abducted. The first volume ends with Anniaba's conversion to Christianity and his stated intention to present himself in his Company of Musketeers to King Louis XIV at a review. Volume II opens on the review of troops at which Anniaba is singled out by the King and informed that his father had died a fortnight before. He is then baptised by Cardinal de Noailles at Notre-Dame de Paris (the chronicles suggest that this function was performed by Bossuet, with the Cardinal rather administering the first communion) and leaves for Africa via Toulon, where he searches in vain for his wife. He fortuitously finds her at Tripoli living as a slave but resolute in her love ('Heureux mile [sic] fois l'Epoux à qui le Destin a donné une femme de ce caractère!' [A thousand times happy the husband to whom Fate has given a wife of such character!]) and he has her freed. Baron de Lasc... is revealed as the *ravisseur* of the Bois de Boulogne, but while the couple's reunion resolves the personal problem, the political plot thickens.

In Anniaba's absence, he is assumed to be dead, and Bacha Osman has mounted the throne of Essenie. With help from Louis XIV and the Grand Master in Malta, Anniaba sails to Meknes (or so it is said, despite that town being some one hundred and forty kilometres from the sea) to enlist further Moroccan support to reclaim his throne:

> Je n'atendois plus que des nouvelles de France pour aler [sic] planter mon étendart [sic] sur les bords du Sénégal.

> [I was waiting only for news from France to go and hoist my flag on the banks of the Senegal river.]

Although the African place names may be imaginary, confused, or unknown to modern cartographers, the fictional location of Essenie on the Senegal river is confirmed when Bacha Osman is said to make a treaty with the neighbouring 'Troulles', 'peuples qui habitent sur les Rives du Sénégal' [people living on the banks of the Senegal], upstream, in other words, from where, at Saint-Louis, the French had their oldest trading-post in the region. The rumour of Anniaba's death was compounded by another suggesting that a Frenchman was impersonating him so as to accede to the throne. Anniaba is thus greeted by general opposition, but his army wins the day, lands with considerable pomp and is finally acclaimed. Anniaba's rival

suitor, Baron de Lasc..., complete with ludicrous false mous-
tache, is dissembled among Anniaba's troops, but his ruse is
foiled, and he is left to face his crime. The Queen participates in the battle and, although slightly wounded, beheads
Bacha Osman. With his head stuck on a spike, she marches
at the head of her troop. Anniaba is recognised as rightful
king, and the Queen's niece turns up to complete the
coincidences, prompting celebrations all round. While an
effort is made to promote Christianity, it is not imposed by
force: people are left to worship as they think fit. All is peace
and felicity. The welcome accorded to the Queen by her
former slave-mistress hints at a broader acceptance of her
difference.

The historical facts are first recounted in the *Mercure de
l'Europe* of 1701 (the date of the death of James II, exiled in
Paris since 1688 and mentioned in the text as being present
at the royal review of troops). A prince Louis Hannibal from
Syria, said to be on the Gold Coast of Africa (just to
compound the geographical confusion), had been presented
to Louis XIV, who gave him his Christian forename and
had him baptised by none less than Bossuet, Bishop of
Meaux from 1681 to his death in 1704. The convert made his
first communion with the celebrated Cardinal de Noailles
and placed his country under the protection of the Virgin
Mary. Such an account prompted a highly sceptical response in Bosman's celebrated *Voyage de Guinée*.[56] For him,
Anniaba was a quick-witted slave turned con-man, and the
French court and church dupes of his machinations all the
more inclined to credulity because of possible political and
commercial advantage on the profitable Guinea coast.
Another near-contemporary reaction, by *père* Labat (1722),
no doubt inspired by Bosman, embroidered on the latter's
scepticism.[57]

The novel has likewise been dismissed in modern times
with scathing comments, for example by Roger Mercier:

le romancier semble ignorer que son héros avait la peau noire, et
dans un épisode l'usurpateur qui s'est emparé de son trône l'accuse
d'être un seigneur français qui s'est substitué au prince mort. Quant
à l'action, elle est constituée par les amours du prince pour une

grande dame européenne, qu'il finit par épouser, histoire purement imaginaire. Il est difficile de trouver un récit qui fasse fi aussi scandaleusement de toutes les réalités historiques et géographiques.

[the novelist seems unaware that his hero has a black skin, and in one episode the usurper who has seized his throne accuses him of being a French lord who has taken the place of the dead prince. As for the action, it is made up of the prince's love for a high-born European lady, whom he finally marries, a totally imaginary story. It is hard to find a tale which so scandalously flouts historical and geographical truth.][58]

Carefully documented realism is not part of the author's preoccupation, however, and to judge his work by such criteria is misplaced. However inaccurate the geography— the history being far less questionable—what if Essenie (Issinie, Issyny or Assini) is placed on the Senegal river rather than on the Gold Coast, nearly two thousand kilometres away as the crow flies?[59] It is an inaccuracy surely more forgivable than recent observations by reputable journalists about 'a village called Mali' or 'the Pacific coast of Africa'.[60] Behind the imprecision lies a significant fact of which the author must have been aware from travellers' tales: by the Senegal river, which is where the French set up their first trading-post in West Africa, live the Hal-pulaar'en or Fulbe (Peuls, in French), who pride themselves on their descent from Nilotic peoples, their pale skin-coloration and their lack of negroid features.[61] That Anniaba should, at different times, have been mistaken for an Italian or a swarthy Frenchman, is therefore less far-fetched than Mercier suggests. It is also less important. The *Blanche/Noir* relationship in *Histoire de Louis Anniaba*, while central to the tale, is not foregrounded as problematic in its own right, and this seems to be the result of narrative choice and perspective rather than of an incapacity to confront it. Of itself, it is not considered as something of consequence, an attitude which it would take a couple of centuries to regain.

The degree of improbability about the narrative, more intent on scary adventures and suspense than on sociological analysis, no doubt warrants its classification as exotic fantasy. Yet the very epigraph to the book, 'Aliquid novi fert Africa quod non est monstrum' [Something new out of Africa which is not monstrous], pointedly contradicts the ancient proverb first recorded by Pliny and affirms the novelist's intention to portray an African in a favourable light. In this—perhaps a major reason for the author's anonymity—it flies in the face of the contemporary legislation against Blacks. Colour is deliberately and symbolically discounted as a matter of supreme irrelevance, the French integration of Anniaba being matched by Essenie's acceptance of his Queen. Only a critic steeped in the essentialist racism generated during the intervening centuries can fail to see that. The novel's grounding in reality puts the colourbar into human perspective by focusing on a love-affair, the vicissitudes of which centrally involve an understandable preoccupation among sea-going travellers of the time: the ever-present danger of capture on the high seas by Barbary pirates or Sallee rovers.

Aphra Behn's 1688 portrayal of Oroonoko as a noble savage, benefiting from the author's acquaintance with the slave colony of Surinam yet shot through with improbabilities, is no more realist by comparison. Interestingly in the present context, Thomas Southerne felt free, in his stage version of it first performed in 1695, to change Imoinda from black to white. As to Othello, his character enjoys outstanding psychological density, and any improbability is reduced to the episodic (such as Desdemona's medical conundrum of being smothered and yet having the capacity to speak at some length before she dies). It is clear in this last case that we accept the impossibility as of less consequence than the psychological and dramatic coherence of the episode. In a similar way, there are psycho-sociological lessons to be learned from the *Histoire de Louis Anniaba*: its preparedness to countenance a *Blanche/Noir* marriage shows it to be blissfully free of the contemptuous and contemptible racism of later times, whereby Blacks represented a threat because they were seen as 'socially inferior but sexually privileged'.[62] While the anonymous author's lack of adherence to fact may be judged by a positivist critic to be a disqualification for serious consideration, it is far more significant that the first French novel presenting a Black, however flawed by inconsequences and *invraisemblances*, should be colour-blind, to the point of freely and positively imagining his marriage with a white woman.

Even Louis XIV's reported comment to Anniaba: 'il n'y a donc plus de différence de vous à moi que du noir au blanc' [there is no more difference between you and me, then, than between black and white], quoted by Yambo Ouologuem in his novel *Le Devoir de violence* and made to serve Christopher L. Miller's argument that Blacks, like Africa, are merely a void to be filled at the whim of white people's imaginations, can alternatively be seen as a recognition, both by the King and by the author, of identical status and stature against the skin-deep difference of colour.[63] Such is Robert Delavignette's reading of Louis XIV's remark as recorded by Ouologuem. While this may still be wishful thinking and far from realisation in practice, the King's view is a sensible reminder that colour-blindness, like tolerance, should not of itself be an aim (even if, as a starting-point, it is preferable to antipathy), since the superficial difference should rather be acknowledged, and respect then accorded to the cultural differences it denotes.

It must be acknowledged, however, that in France the literary representation of the *Blanche/Noir* couple was characterised by a number of false starts and ill-grounded fantasies. Even before the eighteenth century, there had been such representations, but there were largely determined by a baroque aesthetic of reversals, with no purchase on social realities.[64] The vogue for orientalism focused attention on the Levant in much seventeenth- and eighteenth-century writing. France was behind Britain both in establishing a major image of a 'noble savage'—*Oroonoko*, like *Othello*, was translated into French, we recall, only in 1745—and in following Shakespeare's lead, through the characters of Aaron and Othello, into a dramatic and psychological exploration of the *couple domino*.

In France, a false start of a different kind was made in 1774 with the publication of Dorvigny's play *Le Nègre blanc*. Focused on entertainment like the *Histoire de Louis Anniaba*, but with no social message to convey beyond ridiculing the gullibility of pretentiousness, it has a desperate suitor black up in order to gain access to his girl-friend's house, fool her protective but simple-minded mother, and reveal his identity only to his beloved.[65] However slight, it was none the less sufficiently popular to prompt Godard d'Aucourt to produce an *opéra-comique* based on it under the title *Le Nègre par amour* in 1809.[66] In the meantime, however, a Revolution had occurred, one which accepted, after some heated debate, that the Black was 'a man and a brother'.[67]

The establishment of a 'République une et indivisible' [single and indivisible Republic] which had as its motto and watchwords 'liberté, égalité, fraternité' gave rise to an un-comfortable and still unresolved paradox with regard to France's overseas subjects. As Simone Weil expressed it:

> Quand on assume, comme a fait la France en 1789, la fonction de penser pour l'univers, de définir pour lui la justice, on ne devient pas propriétaire de chair humaine.

> [When you take on the function, as France did in 1789, of thinking for the whole world, of defining justice for it, you do not become an owner of human flesh.][68]

In the last decade of the eighteenth century, articulate voices from the colonies, supported by some members of the French parliament, pressed for logic to be pursued to its con-clusion.[69]

A favourable attitude towards 'noble savages' was by then entrenched by both philosophical and creative literature. While Rousseau propounded the theory in his early *Discours* (*sur les sciences et les arts*, 1751, and *sur l'origine ... de l'inégalité*, 1755), Saint-Lambert provided in the eponymous *Ziméo* (1769) an influential literary expression of the type, ending his tale with a swingeing attack on slavery.[70] Parallel to it, however, and backed by a powerful lobby of those who had made money from the slave-trade, was a counter-discourse of continuing contempt. Although speculation, both imaginative and commercial, was more avidly focused on the New World than on Africa, it fed on and fostered ignorance. The 'blank darkness' of Africa (I purposely echo the title of Christopher L. Miller's 1985 book) might fascinate by its novelty or repel by containing monsters: it was primarily a space to be filled, as Swift observed by comparing it with epithets in a line of verse:

> So geographers in *Afric* maps
> With savage pictures fill their gaps,
> And o'er unhabitable downs
> Place elephants for want of towns.[71]

What filled the gaps depended entirely on the point of view adopted, and these polarised as the century proceeded.[72]

Towards the end of the eighteenth century, as a flurry of texts representing Blacks reflected the current philosophical debate about their status, the specific location of a narrative assumed sociological significance. The triangular traffic between Europe, Africa and the New World determined those locations. Almost by definition, sexual opportunity on board ship was exclusively between white men and black women. In Europe, increasing numbers of Blacks generally retained the lowly status allowed them by their masters. There are historical instances of *Blanche/Noir* marriages among the working classes, while members of the aristocracy took a patronising and sometimes sexual interest in their blackamoors. Before such exotic creatures, the blandishments of curiosity combined with opportunity should not be underestimated. As to Africa, a very few white women were there, and only by constraint. In the plantation settlements, by contrast, some white women accompanied their husbands and were thereby exposed to the daily sight of near-naked bodies toiling on their property as well as exposing their daughters to the care—and sometimes attention—of their black slaves. As Maryse Condé recalls:

La femme blanche créole [...] ne peut même pas, comme le maître, chercher l'apaisement dans le commerce sexuel, car on veut qu'elle symbolise la pureté et la respectabilité, face à la négresse et à la mulâtresse, objets de plaisir.

[The white Creole woman [...] cannot even, like her husband, seek comfort in philandering, for she is expected to symbolise purity and respectability, unlike the negress and the mulatress, who are objects of pleasure.][73]

In matters of interracial congress, the law continued to discriminate in its application to Black and White, the former suffering a severe, even capital, penalty, while the latter, even if the case came to law, was sometimes, if a man, admonished but more often let off scot-free, while a woman would suffer greater opprobrium. Of the situation in the West Indies in the seventeeth and early eighteenth centuries, Clarence J. Munford writes:

Freedmen often had sexual encounters with white women of the humble classes, particularly with female indentured servants and with the oppressed 'undesirables' who had been forcibly transported from France to 'service' male white colonists—i.e. orphans, beggars, vagrants, insolvent mothers, petty offenders, prostitutes, etc. While less frequently admitted, sexual intercourse also occurred between slaves and white women. Most frequent was that between male slaves and concupiscent white female slaveholders, couplings usually commanded and initiated by the women. Under her planter husband's very nose, many a *habitation* mistress, 'devoured with a guilty passion' slipped a handsome virile slave into her bed and took delight in his arms. But it was always perilous and emotionally-taxing [*sic*]. For one thing, the Black lover endured deep chagrin at being powerless to shield his partner from reprisals. For another, there was the humiliation to his male pride at having to be protected by her. Terrifying consequences sometimes ensued for the adultress as well as for the slave, for in an age without modern contraceptives it was not easy for a white mother to disguise the birth of a Black child. Liaisons of this sort scandalized planter society, and once exposed inevitably elicited knee-jerk white racist male chauvinism.[74]

Fiction reflects these emerging patterns. In a French setting, restrictions of authorship and readership led to a flurry of Blacks frolicking in an upper-class setting. The 'accouplements bicolores' [two-coloured couplings] in Crébillon's *Le Sopha* of 1742 and Voltaire's 1768 tale *La Princesse de Babylone*, taking advantage of the vogue for fake orientalism, gave way to other instances of similar *libertinage* set in France. Occasional and passing *Blanche/Noir* affairs tended to mirror the rape of the old woman captured by a Sallee rover in *Candide* (1759, chapter XI), a scene as (porno)graphic in its own way as those of *Blanche/Noir* sex in such 'adult' films of the 1970s as *Behind the Green Door* and *Emmanuelle 2*. Towards the turn of the century, Rétif de la Bretonne (Ursule and Antonini in *La Paysanne pervertie*, 1784), Sade (*La Nouvelle Justine*, 1797, chapter XX), Andréa de Nerciat, Grasset de Saint-Sauveur and others indulged this propensity, while dramatists exploited its varied theatrical potential.[75]

Nerciat's libertine novel *Le Diable au corps*, written in 1789, published in 1803, and partly composed as a *récit dialogué*, is not untypical of that exploitative streak. Its plot does not depend on interracial couplings: they are merely one of the many permutations and variations on sexual relationships, via all possible orifices, between men and women, women and women, men and men, men and boys, and even women and a donkey. 'L'infatigable Zamor' [the indefatigable Zamor] is no more than a token black stud, a colourful variation on a licentious theme, and he has his female counterpart in 'l'incomparable Zinga'. In a scene of group sex with a vengeance, his prowess makes the beneficiaries swoon: 'Zamor sait si bien goûter et faire goûter le suprême bonheur!' [Zamor knows so well how to enjoy supreme happiness and help others enjoy it]; his 'richesses viriles dont la Nature l'a si largement pourvu' [virile attributes with which Nature has so generously endowed him] are remarked on with favour, as is 'ce boute-joie nerveux qui n'a pas moins la dureté que la couleur du fer' [that dynamic bringer of joy which has both the stiffness and the colour of iron].[76] Penetrating the Marquise—'Rien de plus beau que le grouppe [sic] de ces deux corps admirables, chacun le chef-d'œuvre de son sexe et de sa couleur' [What could be finer than the combination of these two admirable bodies, each one a masterpiece of its sex and colour?]—he has Le Tréfoncier enter him from behind. But he remains 'le vulgaire Zamor, mi-parti du singe et de l'homme' [plain Zamor, half-monkey, half-man], scarcely the best advertisement for racial equality, since Hitler's view of Blacks was identical.

Yet there are many episodes in which attention is drawn beyond the immediate circumstances of the sexual romp. One such is the following, involving Zamor, but where the psychological observation has sufficient finesse to warrant our interest. Countess Sourcillac recounts to her friend the Marquise (pp. 144–45) an amusing instance of her husband's self-engrossed obtuseness:

LA COMTESSE

L'autre jour, tandis qu'il [le comte] lisait la gazette près de ma croisée, Zamor, sous prétexte de me passer ma chemise, m'enfilait, nue, dans mon alcôve…

LA MARQUISE

Zamor! ce superbe nègre qu'il a payé si cher pour vous l'offrir?… il vous a?

LA COMTESSE

froidement.

Ou je l'ai; comme il vous plaira: fort à votre service, si vous pouvez en être tentée… Parlez?

LA MARQUISE

Un nègre, ma chère! y pensez-vous? Et s'il arrivait qu'on devînt grosse?

LA COMTESSE

On ferait un petit mulâtre, cela est clair… Sourcillac donc était assistant; il me prit une idée bien folle! Tu sais que souvent il m'appelle Minette?

LA MARQUISE

Eh bien?

35

LA COMTESSE

Au fort du travail du vigoureux Zamor, je prends la liberté d'interrompre la lecture du Courrier, et dis: "*A propos mon ami?*" Zamor, effrayé, de vouloir s'ôter et de battre en retraite: mais je l'enlace, le presse, et lui fais sentir que j'entends qu'il reste là.

LA MARQUISE

Vous aviez donc perdu l'esprit?

LA COMTESSE

Un moment.—"Que veut ma Minette? (me répond-on bien gracieusement).—Justement, mon bon ami, je voulais te prier de ne plus m'appeller [*sic*] Minette, parce que cette nuit j'ai rêvé que j'avais couru les toits, et qu'un gros matou, couleur d'ébène, m'avait violée: je me suis éveillée mourant de peur, et me disant qu'infailliblement j'allais mettre au monde une demi-douzaine de chats d'Espagne.—Rien de plus original! s'est écrié le bon Sourcillac (riant comme un fou, et laissant aller par la fenêtre la gazette qui lui échappait des mains,) je veux conter ce drôle de rêve à tous mes amis. —Et lui de rire... rire!...—Cette duperie, moncœur, avait quelque chose de si piquant pour moi, que jamais passade de cette espece [*sic*] ne me fit autant de plaisir: il semblait que Zamor lui-même y entendait finesse; il se surpassa...

[THE COUNTESS

The other day, when he [the count] was reading his magazine near my window, Zamor, under the pretext of handing me my shift, took me, naked, in my bed-chamber...

THE MARCHIONESS

Zamor! that superb Negro he spent so much on giving you?... He *has* you?

THE COUNTESS

coldly.

Or *I* have *him*, as you will; and he's at your service, if you are tempted by him... What say you?

THE MARCHIONESS

A Negro, my dear! what are you thinking of? What if he made you pregnant?

THE COUNTESS

We'd have a little mulatto, that's clear... Anyway, Sourcillac was close by; I had a wild idea! You know that he often calls me Pussy?

36

THE MARCHIONESS

So?

THE COUNTESS

When Zamor was in full, vigorous swing, I took the liberty of interrupting my husband's reading, and said: 'By the way, my dear...' Zamor, terrified, wanted to withdraw and beat a retreat, but I clung on to him tightly and made him aware that I intended him to stay where he was.

THE MARCHIONESS

Were you out of your mind?

THE COUNTESS

One moment. 'What do you want, my Pussy?' came the courteous reply. 'Precisely, my dear. I wanted to ask you not to call me Pussy any more, because last night I dreamt that I was out on the tiles, and that a big tomcat the colour of ebony had had his way with me. I woke up dying of fright, wondering how I could prevent myself having a litter of half a dozen alley-cat tabbies.' 'What could be more original?', cried dear old Sourcillac, laughing like a madman, and letting his magazine fall out of the window, 'I want to recount this curious dream to all my friends.' He went on laughing, laughing!... I enjoyed the piquancy of this ploy so much, my dear, that no sex ever gave me greater pleasure. It even seemed that Zamor appreciated it: he surpassed himself...]

It remains the case that Zamor is reduced to a sexual cypher in a licentious fantasy typical of Nerciat. It is worth noting, however, that this reflects the Royal judgement in council of 5 April 1778 that marriages between Blacks and Whites were prohibited in France.

Bernardin de Saint-Pierre's play *Empsaël et Zoraïde ou les Blancs esclaves des Noirs à Maroc*, probably completed by 1793, is of a very different temper and turns the scene to Africa, where no such prohibition obtained.[77] Bernardin's sympathetic treatment of Blacks in both his celebrated novel, *Paul et Virginie* (1788), and, more explicitly and outspokenly, in his *Voyage à l'isle de France* prepares us for the abolitionist play, in which the eponymous *Blanche/*

Noir couple takes centre-stage.[78] At its heart lies the irony, encapsulated in the sub-title, which depends for its effect on the European assumption of automatic white superiority and the cognate supposition, enshrined during the course of the eighteenth century, that masters will always be white and slaves always black. But that it should, like *Histoire de Louis Anniaba*, present a happily married couple, whatever the initial duress, marks it out for special attention in our review of the literature. Enduring love, and not just transient affairs, across what W.E.B. Du Bois, in *The Souls of Black Folk*, was to call 'the color-line', is shown to be not only possible but socially desirable.[79]

The location of the drama is an historically accurate Kingdom of Morocco, geographically defined as Cap d'Aguer, the modern Agadir, where the despotic Moulay Ismaïl, who ruled from 1672 to 1727, holds sway and where his black prime minister, Empsaël, reaps the benefits of piratical attacks on ships leaving the Mediterranean. He has married a French captive, Zoraïde, who, in the midst of much anti-slavery debate by representatives of various beliefs—Catholic, Protestant, Quaker, Jew—persuades him to soften his sentence on one of his latest prizes, Don Ozorio, a slave-owner from Saint Domingue who had once been his own master. The circumstances of Empsaël's capture, enslavement, escape and rise to fortune are recounted at length. The element of chance reuniting him with his brother, Don Ozorio's faithful servant, stretches credibility. It is no doubt flattering to France, and an indication of Bernardin's residual Eurocentricity, that one of her daughters should be seen 'civilising' a 'savage', but the central point that people from all races and backgrounds can and should live in harmony is forcibly made.

It is made differently, but with even more Eurocentric focus, in Adrien de Texier's *Les Colons de toutes couleurs, histoire d'un établissement nouveau à la côte de Guinée*, of 1798. Differently because we are presented with settlers joining forces of their own free will; more Eurocentrically because the colony assumes entirely French values: the French language, the Catholic religion, and exclusively

French social and psychological stances. In both works, characters are spokesmen for different positions rather than rounded, but Texier deploys a markedly narrower range.

Returning to Saint Domingue in 1791, the narrator, Philippe B..., takes pity on his slaves, treated harshly by the overseer he had left in charge. His fellow-planters disapprove of his progressive ideas, and when the arrival of a black captain seeking settlers for a colony established in West Africa by a Frenchman, Adrien G..., coincides with the start of the insurrection, he takes the opportunity to escape with several hundred slaves. A kind of colour-blind *phalanstère* has been set up by Adrien, who has himself married Zara by way of example, while his sister is married to Prince Iglof of the Bambouki tribe. This *Blanche/Noir* pairing merely participates, therefore, in the general proposition of interracial harmony which, because it is so fanciful in the circumstances, remains frustratingly untested.

When, in the programmatic novel by Grasset de Saint-Sauveur, *Hortense ou la jolie courtisane* (1796), the scene shifts to the New World, the high-born heroine turned courtesan is abducted by two Blacks. One, Zéphire, kills the other and, not without reservations, is befriended by Hortense, who grows to love him and, as Hoffmann nicely puts it, without benefit of philanthropic treatises, realises the injustice and absurdity of colour prejudice.[80] She is made to declare, and the author to acknowledge, an element of cultural relativity:

> Je raisonnois, je comparois et je disois: si cet esclave étoit aussi loin de la nature que notre orgueil le suppose, s'il n'avoit pas comme nous le cœur fait pour aimer [...], s'il étoit enfin ce qu'on nous les dépeint et ce que nous les forçons à devenir, que ferois-je au milieu de ces déserts qui me séparent à présent du reste de l'Univers?

> [I reasoned, I compared and I said: if this slave were as far away from Nature as our pride has us suppose, if he did not, like us, have a heart made for loving [...], if he were as they are portrayed to us and as we force them to become, what would I do in the middle of this wasteland which now separates me from the rest of the universe?]

39

This sense of relativity is reinforced by Zéphire's inability to speak French until, after the birth of their child, Hortense undertakes to instruct him. While a process of cultural colonialism can thereby follow, Grasset is at pains to portray a paradise in which his protagonists can flout European conventions, for example by going innocently naked and rediscovering a natural religion which, however suspect in itself, escapes the hypocrisies of a corrupt society. The metaphorical snake turns out to be Donsel, a French officer who, having found Hortense in the jungle, imitates so many literary Blacks of the age, and rapes her. The degree of improbability increases as further adventures befall the hapless couple but, as Hoffmann has pointed out, the author misses an opportunity to set the seal on his apparent belief in racial equality when, after the birth of Donsel's white daughter, Hortense is forcibly married to a native Indian but has no child by him:

> L'expression symbolique de sa régéneration dans le Nouveau Monde aurait été complète si Hortense avait porté dans ses flancs les trois races destinées à en assurer le peuplement.
>
> [The symbolic expression of her regeneration in the New World would have been complete if Hortense had carried in her womb the three races destined to furnish its population.][81]

Where, in eighteenth-century French literature, the Black is not simply a sex-machine, he is more often than not a peg to hang a theory on. The myth of the noble savage predominates in presentations of Blacks who aspire to the hand (or bed) of a white woman. In the very word 'aspire', however, we see the compulsive myth at work: it reinforces the superiority assumed by Whites by suggesting, not without ample evidence, that Blacks accepted it as a fact of life, that they longed, in short, for enwhitenment. For as long as Whites wrote Blacks' stories, such a double assumption would remain entrenched. Where a *Blanche/Noir* couple is central to a narrative or drama of this period, the generously inclined—often abolitionist—author tries to show, more or less programmatically and more or less adequately, that equality is not just an idle boast, and that racial harmony is both a possible and a desirable aim for a truly civilised society. But white writers engaged in what could only be a monologue for two, or a dialogue for one, however ostensibly polyphonous. If the posture remains suspect, however laudable the ambition, we may blame the human incapacity to imagine ourselves other than we are. Cultural colonialism will remain a feature of attitudes to our day, and it often has less noble motivations than those we have seen in *Histoire de Louis Anniaba, Empsaël et Zoraïde* and *Les Colons de toutes couleurs*. Turning to the nineteenth century may show progress in certain respects, but also how barbed and illusory this can be. The 1820s, which we shall investigate in the following chapter, mark a shift in sensibility which, countered by the thrust of colonialism later in the century, will not find a response until the 1920s.

CHAPTER 2
FROM TABOO TO TOTEM

'My mother bore me in the southern wild,
And I am black but O! my soul is white.'
William Blake[82]

ALTHOUGH the Convention formally abolished slavery and the slave-trade with regard to French overseas possessions on 16 Pluviôse, an II (4 February 1794), the *status quo ante* was reintroduced with a vengeance by Napoleon on 20 May 1802. The question of Blacks and their status effectively went off the French agenda for twenty years, to be raised only when Britain's abolition of the slave-trade in 1807 and its consequent monitoring of the seas, in which material advantage could be presented as high-mindedness, was perceived, for example by Chateaubriand in correspondence with Wilberforce, as an economic threat to France.[83] It was a bleak period for Blacks until, paradoxically, and in the very different circumstances of his brief return to France and power ('les Cent-Jours'), Napoleon signed the decree abolishing the slave-trade in 1815.

The Revolution marked a major shift in sensibility, but in many respects attitudes towards Blacks remained unchanged, with the agenda still being written by Whites. The Haitian Revolution within a Revolution certainly sharpened the focus for both conservatives and liberals, but it traumatised everyone in providing ammunition for both condemnation and continuing equivocation. As Ronald Hyam has rightly remarked: 'The shock waves generated by the unprecedented explosion against white rule there reverberated around the world.'[84] That impact was predominantly negative, with *abbé* Grégoire's voice virtually the only one at the time to recognise the justice of the Blacks' cause. None seems to have been raised in 1825 against the iniquitous imposition on Haiti of economically crippling compensation for French losses in return for recognition of its sovereignty.

Even Ourika, the eponymous black heroine of Madame de Duras's novella, is plausibly made to react adversely to news of the insurrection in Saint Domingue.

> On commençait à parler de la liberté des nègres: il était impossible que cette question ne me touchât pas vivement; c'était une illusion que j'aimais encore à me faire, qu'ailleurs, du moins, j'avais des semblables: comme ils étaient malheureux, je les croyais bons, et je m'intéressais à leur sort. Hélas! je fus promptement détrompée! Les massacres de Saint-Domingue me causèrent une douleur nouvelle et déchirante: jusqu'ici je m'étais affligée d'appartenir à une race proscrite; maintenant j'avais honte d'appartenir à une race de barbares et d'assassins.

> [The negroes' right to liberty next began to be debated; and I, of course, felt deeply interested in the question. One of my remaining illusions was, that at least I had countrymen in another land, and knowing them to be unhappy, I believed them virtuous, and pitied their fate. Alas! here again I was undeceived. The massacre of St. Domingo added fresh grief to my soul; and to my despair at belonging to a proscribed race was added shame at their being likewise a race of barbarians [and murderers].][85]

While it is undoubtedly the case that someone in Ourika's position would, through her upbringing, education and environment, have espoused the sensibilities and views of a European of her generation, and therefore be a prototype of the *assimilée*, her dismayed response is that of anyone who sees indiscriminate violence as no way to redress even the most inhuman of grievances. Even that rare phenomenon for its time, a liberal European, found it hard to defend such lawlessness, whatever the intense provocation: moral arguments for colonisation joined the powerful economic ones. Fear of recurrence did nothing but entrench the combined forces of evangelising self-righteousness, a sense of adventure, and the overriding greed for gain.

During the course of the nineteenth century, following the formal French abolition of the slave-trade, slavery itself was abolished in the French colonies in 1848. Privateers flouted the first law for a couple of decades, while West Indian planters replaced Blacks by coolies imported from India after the second, thereby creating yet another layer of complexity in the racial cocktail of the Caribbean. The Africans who had reaped considerable profits from selling their enemies, captives and unwanted tribesfellows to Europeans had to revert to the centuries-old traffic with North Africa which the Atlantic trade had largely interrupted.

The insurrection in Saint Domingue and its subsequent liberation as Haiti were major sources for imaginative literature. In the area of *Blanche/Noir* relationships, the circumstances of a major social-cum-racial reversal offered a series of dramatic possibilities, if only because, in a settler society, white women were present and were now seen for the first time, whether for lust or love, as available.[86]

Sociologically speaking, the dark imaginings of Europeans invested the idea of sexual relations between Blacks and Whites with more fantasy than fact. Plantation owners, whether in France or in the colonies, would dismiss the issue as either too trivial (the master's self-gratification) or too unthinkable (the Negro's 'assaults' on his wife or daughter). A sympathetic commentator of 1823, Garnier-Hombert, indulged in a measure of wishful thinking:

> Lorsqu'au milieu des désastres de Saint-Domingue, les blancs ont vu leurs femmes exposées à tous les outrages des Nègres, ils ont pu juger de ce qu'ils avaient fait éprouver à ces derniers en commettant les mêmes excès contre les négresses.

> [When, in the midst of the disasters in Saint Domingue, the Whites saw their wives exposed to all the outrages of the Blacks, they could reflect on what they had made them suffer by committing the same excesses against Negresses.][87]

One might legitimately wonder how many such *habitants* were sensible of the equivalence between the two acts.

The relevant literary corpus of the period covers what are generally classified as minor writings. While such a departure from the established canon may appear inappropriate to some, it has the singular merit of showing more clearly than 'high literature' certain stereotypical attitudes of the time towards delicate areas of human relations where angels fear to tread. That such stereotypes are still current in the popular literature and representations of our own time means that an exposure of early examples throws light on many still-unquestioned assumptions. The postcolonial discourses of literary criticism, benefiting from the findings of anthropology and fuller and more rapid communications between peoples as well as from the upsurge of interest in 'Black' studies and women's studies, impose a readjustment of viewpoint. Through a better understanding of the mechanism whereby 'Others' are postulated, they prompt a more tolerant reflection on the Other. So it is of particular interest to focus on those instances which themselves manifest tolerance, even if that is only a staging-post still redolent with paternalism. The absolutely intolerant remains depressingly unchanged as well as unedifying over the centuries.

It is noteworthy that women writers seem particularly sensitive to the issues involved and are consequently to the fore. But some continued to exploit the stereotype that Aphra Behn had inaugurated with the image of the noble savage in *Oroonoko*. Olympe de Gouges and Madame de Staël, a century later, with no experience of the colonies, were reduced to exotic-cum-erotic flights of fancy in *L'Esclavage des Noirs* (1792) and 'Mirza' (1795) respectively.[88] Maria Edgeworth's short story 'The Grateful Negro' (1802) is in the same tradition.

The earliest sustained representation by a woman of a *Blanche/Noir* relationship occurs, to the best of my knowledge, in a German short story first published in 1817: 'William der Neger' by Caroline Auguste Fischer.[89] It is interesting, however, that Maria Edgeworth had aborted her attempt to introduce a *Blanche/Noir* couple even fleetingly into her novel *Belinda* (1801: chapter XIX). Clíona Ó Gallchoir has written:

> The detail that caused the most discomfort, however, was a relatively minor episode in which a black servant [Juba], arrived from the British Caribbean, meets and marries a white woman [Lucy]. Subsequent editions of this novel contained awkward revisions to remove the offence. Edgeworth wrote in 1810: 'My father says that gentlemen have horrors upon this subject, and would draw conclusions very unfavourable to a female writer who appeared to recommend such unions; as I do not understand the subject, I trust to his better judgement.'[90]

The innocence of the episode is emphasised by its setting between one in which Mrs Freke, a 'fiery obeah-woman' is throwing her witchy weight about and another where Lady Delacour's maid arrives to demand Belinda's instant presence at her mistress's convenient illness. In respecting her father's views, Edgeworth does not, it would appear, subscribe to them.

Fischer's story proves abortive in another sense, but is worth dwelling on since it throws into relief the originality and generosity of Duras and Doin. William, captured in his native Africa and taken into slavery, is bought by the abolitionistically inclined Sir Robert. William's imagination is fired both by the prospect of playing a leading role in the newly liberated Haiti and by Molly, a local shopkeeper's daughter. We rapidly reach a point where he exclaims: '„Ach warum bin ich schwarz! Molly, du himmlische Weiße!„' [Alas, why am I black! Molly, you divine white girl!], rapidly followed by a direct echo of the motto of the Society for the Abolition of the Slave Trade: '„Ja, ich bin schwarz! Aber bin ich kein Mann?„' [Yes, I am black! But am I not a man?]. Molly is fully persuaded that he is, but the authorial commentary is illuminating:

> Wenn ein veredelter Schwarzer eine schöne weiße Frau liebt, so mag seine Liebe wohl schwerlich mit der eines Europäers zu vergleichen seyn. Bey William war sie eine heilige Gluth, die Molly in ein zitterndes, fortwährendes Staunen versetzte. Wie fern war seine Rede von jenem süßlichen, tändelnden Geschwätz

gemeiner Verliebten! Welch eine Reihe herrlicher Bilder führte er vor Molly's Seele! Welch ein Herz, welch einen Geist entfaltete er in den Gesprächen, die es ihr von nun an unmöglich machten, ihr Schicksal von dem des hohen begeisterten Jünglings zu trennen!

[When a noble black loves a beautiful white woman, his love can hardly be compared to the love of a European man. For William it was a holy, consuming fire which put Molly into a trembling, continuous ecstasy. How far removed was his speech from that trifling and mawkish twaddle of the usual lover. What magnificent images he revealed to Molly's soul; and the heart and mind he unfolded before her in conversation made it impossible for her to separate her fate from that of this noble and spirited young man.]

However noble and high-minded William may be, Fischer explicitly precludes the possibility of his equality with a white man. Indeed she goes on to observe that Sir Robert's common sense told him that this could have a tragic outcome. It transpires, however, that his caution, born at first of his caring philanthropy, emerges in due course as being at variance with it and is not entirely disinterested. When Sir Robert and Molly eventually meet, primarily for the former to approve of the match with William, a *coup de foudre* is presented in precisely that metaphor: 'Beide wurden wie von einem Blitze getroffen' [Both were struck as if by lightning]. In passing, the author hints at William's animal passion, ready to be roused if Molly should refuse him: 'er aber auch entschlossen war, die Gewalt der Stärke und der Liebe zu gebrauchen' [he had already decided to use the force of his love and his superior strength]. The impeccably civilised Sir Robert is portrayed, on the other hand, as mastering his passions and proceeding with the betrothal of his ward and his neighbours' daughter.

At this point, however, a significant motif is introduced: that of the mirror, which also plays a notable part in the 1823 tale of Ourika: 'je n'osais plus me regarder dans une glace', 'j'avais ôté de ma chambre tous les miroirs' [I no longer dared to look in a glass; I would have no looking-glasses in my room]. Seeing himself reflected alongside Sir Robert and Molly, William is struck not just by a similar self-disgust but also by a sense of incongruity: so imbued is he with European attitudes that he cannot imagine Molly ever being happy with him.

Such doubt is prompted not, as both Fischer and Duras recognise, from any intrinsic lack of worth but on the basis of European society's preoccupation with, and prejudice born of, a difference of skin-colour. In this atmosphere of patronising superiority, William falls into a decline. In the process of tending him, Sir Robert and Molly become aware of something William had sensed: feelings towards each other which they had barely begun to admit to themselves. The patient recovers, has various adventures, and returns to Haiti where he distinguishes himself. A letter is received from William renouncing his claim to Molly in favour of his benefactor.

A few months later the news of William's death arrives; Sir Robert and Molly are married, in due course having two children. However benevolent they may be towards Blacks, they are apparently unable to inculcate colour-blind reactions in their children: their daughter screams and hides when a small black face peers round the door, its owner then dashing vivaciously round the room and finally announcing that his father, 'William der Retter' [William the Saviour], is nearby. The extraordinary closing paragraph of the narrative follows Sir Robert's embrace of his former ward:

> Keiner von beiden konnte ein Wort vorbringen; aber als Molly erschien, rief William, sich losreißend: „Zurück, Molly! Ich habe ein schwarzes Weib genommen! Die Nachricht meines Todes war vergeblich! So mußt' ich dich zwingen. Aber vergessen sollst du mich nicht! Ich lasse euch meinen Sohn! Er heißt William! Ein Freygeborner! Lebt wohl! Ich darf nicht verweilen!—Zurück! Haltet mich nicht! Wenn das Werk ganz vollendet ist, sehn wir uns wieder!„

> [Neither could say a word; but when Molly appeared, William shouted, pulling himself away with vehemence: 'Go back, Molly! I have taken a black wife. The news of my death was a ruse; only that way could I force you! But you shall not forget me. I am leaving my [sc. freeborn] son with you. He is named

William. Farewell! I may not stay. Go back! Don't stop me!
When the task is complete, we shall see each other again!']

Neither the vehemence nor the stock ruse is astonishing, nor indeed is the determination to fight on for complete victory for the Blacks in America, though it will take more than William's lifetime to accomplish it. What seems psychologically unacceptable is that William should, with or without his wife's consent (her interests in the matter not being deemed worthy of comment by the author), abandon his son to the doubtless tender but fundamentally racist care of Sir Robert and his wife. Even the conventional renewal of the cycle with a child of the same name as his father firmly suggests no improvement in attitudes, and the tale ends in a blur of wrongheadedness and wishful thinking.

The marked progress from Fischer's attitudes to those we shall find in Sophie Doin is perhaps mediated both by historical developments such as a renewal of abolitionist demands in the 1820s and the official French emancipation of Haiti in 1825 and by writings which appeared between 1817 and 1826, not just the hugely popular *Ourika* but also early works by Hugo and Balzac.[91] Their representations of relations between black men and white women are markedly less positive than in the women writers of the period. More than one critic has noted the particular interest of women writers in the subject.[92] One of them has indeed remarked:

> Même lorsque des auteurs reconnaissent aux hommes de couleur le droit au sentiment, la liaison est présentée comme impossible.

> [Even when authors acknowledge a coloured man's right to feelings, the relationship is presented as impossible.][93]

An exception to this general rule, however, well after the anonymous *Histoire de Louis Anniaba*, Bernardin's *Empsaël et Zoraïde* and Sophie Doin, to whom we shall

49

return shortly, is the occasional mulatto author, whether the forgotten Louis Houat or the unforgettable Alexandre Dumas, whom we shall meet again in the next chapter.

Thus Balzac's 1822 play *Le Nègre* depicts the platonic love of the black hero, Georges, for his mistress, Émilie de Gerval. Driven by his passion to declare himself to her, he is haughtily rebuffed, but forgiven in terms which, however typical of the time, now appear not merely insensitive but positively uncouth: 'L'offense se perd dans la distance qui nous sépare' [The offence is lost in the distance which divides us].[94] A trap is set, in which Émilie is pursued by her husband to a rendez-vous which is innocent but is assumed to be improper. Georges's revenge is to obey his master's order to kill Émilie. Balzac was to be as frustrated as Georges with regard to his melodrama when he submitted it for consideration by the Théâtre de la Gaîté. The report from the reading committee elicits the following comment by Sylvie Chalaye:

> Intrinsèquement impossible selon les préjugés de l'époque, l'amour du Noir pour une Blanche n'a le droit d'exister que comme souffrance, comme torture intérieure.

> [Intrinsically impossible according to contemporary prejudices, the love of a Black man for a White woman has the right to exist only as suffering, as inner torment.][95]

If death is inflicted by others in Balzac's *Le Vicaire des Ardennes*, also of 1822, it is a minor variation on the same unimaginable relationship: an escaped slave carries his young mistress off and covers her with kisses before being cut down by her outraged companions.

As for Hugo's better-known first novel, *Bug-Jargal*, it has, thanks in part to its use of Pamphile Lacroix's eye-witness account of the Saint Domingue uprising but also in large measure to Hugo's precocious talent, a wealth of boisterous, melodramatic detail familiar from his later work. Bug-Jargal's (aka Pierrot's) intense love for Marie, the fiancée of the internal narrator Léopold d'Auverney, makes them improbable rivals: 'tout en moi se refusait à la révoltante supposition d'avoir un esclave pour rival' [everything in me rejected the revolting notion of having a slave for a rival]. Recalling the mindset of the time (but suggesting by the present participle that it is still widespread), Hoffmann observes:

> La plupart des Blancs étant d'ailleurs persuadés que le souhait le plus ardent de tout homme noir est de posséder des femmes blanches, les lecteurs de *Bug-Jargal* étaient peut-être indignés, mais pas surpris de ce que Pierrot convoite Marie.

> [Most Whites being persuaded that the most fervent desire of every Black is to possess white women, the readers of *Bug-Jargal* were perhaps indignant, but not surprised that Pierrot should covet Marie.][96]

Like so many of his literary forebears, Bug-Jargal had been a king in his (unspecified) homeland, and his argument runs:

> Tu es blanche, et je suis noir; mais le jour a besoin de s'unir à la nuit pour enfanter l'aurore et le couchant, qui sont plus beaux que lui!

> [You are white, and I am black; but the day needs to combine with the night to engender dawn and dusk, both of which are more beautiful than itself!]

D'Auverney's attitude is such that he cannot envisage 'l'hypothèse d'un amour impossible pour la fille de son maître' [the hypothesis of an impossible love for his master's daughter]. As Hoffmann again rightly records:

> Le raciste qui postule que tout Noir désire les Blanches postule également qu'une Blanche qui désire un Noir frôle la dépravation.

> [The racist who assumes that any Black desires white women also assumes that a white woman who desires a Black is close to being depraved.][97]

D'Auverney's marriage is duly celebrated, but on a date remembered in history as that of the outbreak of the insurrection in Saint Domingue, 22 August 1791, allowing, in chapter XVIII, the melodramatic juxtaposition of joy and devastation which includes the sight of Marie being carried off by Bug-Jargal, giving a foretaste of the prowess of Tarzan or King Kong, saved from the flames before the marriage can be consummated. Many cliff-hanging adventures occur before husband and wife, each preserved by Pierrot's interventions showing superhuman powers and super-human restraint, are reunited. Tortured by the sight of their embrace he shouts repeatedly: 'Pas devant moi!' [Not in front of me!]. Marie is innocence incarnate:

> Marie se souleva de mes bras à demi, et s'écria en le suivant des yeux:
> — Grand Dieu! mon Léopold, notre amour paraît lui faire mal. Est-ce qu'il m'aimerait?
> Le cri de l'esclave m'avait prouvé qu'il était mon rival; l'exclamation de Marie me prouvait qu'il était aussi mon ami.
> — Marie! répondis-je, et une félicité inouïe entra dans mon cœur en même temps qu'un mortel regret; Marie! est-ce que tu l'ignorais?
> — Mais je l'ignore encore, me dit-elle avec une chaste rougeur. Comment! il m'aime! Je ne m'en étais jamais aperçue.

> [Marie raised herself half out of my arms and, following him with her gaze, cried: 'Good God! Leopold, our love seems to pain him. Could he possibly love me?'
> The slave's cry proved that he was my rival; Marie's exclamation proved that he was also my friend.
> 'Marie!', I replied, as indescribable happiness flooded into my heart at the same time as deathly regret, 'Marie! were you not aware of it?'
> 'But I'm still not aware of it', she said to me, blushing chastely. 'What! Does he love me? I had never noticed.']⁹⁸

Such purity of thought and deed also betokens a total lack of consideration of the black hero as a human being and is scarcely compensated by the subsequent protestations of gratitude and friendship. Yet it is clear that the author does not entirely share his characters' narrow prejudices. Hugo shows himself aware of European presumption when he has Léonard here, for example, in a neatly modulated formula, recognise Pierrot as both 'rival' and 'ami', and later recount an exchange he had with Pierrot: 'je lui promis un grade dans l'armée coloniale' [I promised him an appointment in the colonial army], which is countered by: 'Frère, est-ce que je te propose de t'enrôler parmi les miens?' [Brother, did I offer you a place in mine?]. In terms of Pierrot's aspiration to love Marie, however, it must remain at the level of an unsatisfied aspiration: neither its propriety nor its realisation is countenanced either by the character or by the author.

So despite the totemic flirtation with a biracial relationship, the taboo is still manifestly in place in *Bug-Jargal* as it is in Fischer's tale, just as it remains out of the question in Madame de Duras's *Ourika*, where the eponymous heroine's existential impasse is caused on the one hand by her inability to return, given her upbringing in an aristocratic Parisian milieu, to her native Senegal, and on the other by the inflexibility of her adoptive society, obsessed with class and lineage, towards the idea of a transracial marriage. The only way in which marriage is envisaged for her is by the purchase of a husband. The brutally realistic Marquise de ..., who twice intervenes crucially in the narrative, declares to Ourika's benefactress:

> A qui la marierez-vous, avec l'esprit qu'elle a et l'éducation que vous lui avez donnée? Qui voudra jamais épouser une négresse? Et si, à force d'argent, vous trouvez quelqu'un qui consente à avoir des enfans nègres, ce sera un homme d'une condition inférieure, et avec qui elle se trouvera malheureuse. Elle ne peut vouloir que de ceux qui ne voudront pas d'elle.
>
> [Who can you marry her to, with the education you have given her? Who will ever marry a negro girl? And if you should find any man who, for the sake of money, would perhaps consent to have negro children, must it not be someone of inferior condition, with whom she would be unhappy? Will a man whom she would choose ever choose her?]

Small wonder that Ourika is conveniently indisposed when her dear 'brother', Charles, is married. She can only go into a decline, retire to a convent, and die young.

Ourika is a masterpiece of psychological penetration and finesse. Being set in Paris, in a society the author knew intimately, and alluding only in passing, as we have seen, to the insurrection in Haiti, it avoids the over-simplifications one finds in Sophie Doin's short story 'Blanche et noir' of 1826.[99] This is set as one panel of a diptych, the other being the story 'Noire et blanc', in which a servant, Nelzi, saves her young master's life during the Haitian insurrection of 1791, in recognition of which Charles lives with her in America, effectively as common-law man and wife, until the prospect of a handsome legacy takes them to Paris. A requirement of his inheritance, however, is that he marry his cousin. Several stratagems later, and with an alternative income secured, Charles and Nelzi jointly acknowledge their irreplaceable love in the presence of a friend who, having schemed to help them, has the last word:

> Voilà bien l'amour, et l'amour sans reproche, dit en soupirant Eugénie; blanc ou noir, oh! qu'il est joli, cet amour là!'

> [This really is love, irreproachable love, said Eugenie with a sigh; black or white, oh! how pretty it is, that kind of love!][100]

The marital permutations are completed by 'Le Négrier', in which Léon, a reluctant slaver, abandons the trade for Laure, the only daughter of a hardened dealer in the 'commerce de vivants' [trade in human beings][101] whose business she deplores and who, under pressure from her, at the eleventh hour and much against his better judgement, consents to the match.

Set entirely in Haiti, also at the time of the insurrection, 'Blanche et noir' has none of *Ourika*'s empathetic penetration or supreme elegance of style, but it does take an unconventional step forward towards a recognition of a common humanity beneath surface appearances. When read in conjunction with the other short stories briefly outlined above, it appears to institute transracial marriage as a totem, albeit sociologically circumscribed and, as we shall see, fraught with ambiguities, where previously the taboo had been paramount. By its nature, however, a totem is a long way from realism, and continues to embody characteristics both of the sacred and of the forbidden.

Domingo is a black slave taken in as an orphaned child by Madame de Hauteville, the wife of an archetypally self-seeking plantation owner, 'fier, hautain, plein de préjugés' [proud, haughty, full of prejudices]. Their baby daughter, Pauline, is given Domingo, only a few years older than herself, as a servant and playmate. Also in the household is Léopold, the son of a friend in France, who predictably falls in love with Pauline. With the smell of freedom in the air, Domingo presumes to encourage other Blacks to rebel:

> Quelquefois il s'approchait de noirs, les questionnait, plaignait leur sort plus amèrement que de coutume, cherchait à leur communiquer quelque énergie, à les tirer de l'abrutissement où la douleur les avait plongés.

> [Sometimes he approached the Blacks and put questions to them, pitying their fate more bitterly than is usually the case, and trying to instil some energy into them and to draw them out of the torpor into which suffering had plunged them.]

This is, inevitably, badly received by Hauteville's factors, but fortunately for him his master is preoccupied with Léopold and Pauline's engagement, to which the latter is not at all committed. In parallel, the unthinkable scenario is prepared by sententious observations about Domingo:

> La culture de la pensée agrandit l'âme, étend les dispositions naturelles, développe les sentimens; Domingo, élevé par le cercle de ses occupations et les connaissances qu'il avait acquises au-dessus du sort commun des esclaves, Domingo osait penser, et sentait se développer en lui toutes les sensations d'un homme libre.
> L'amour, ce sentiment impétueux, était fait pour cette âme neuve et brûlante. Il devait la déchirer, et lui faire payer chèrement l'agrandissement de son être. Esclave encore par toutes les institutions, son esprit seul commençait à soulever ses chaînes; il pouvait donc ressentir les émotions d'un homme libre, sans goûter les joies qu'elles produisent pour lui.
> Amour, fils chéri de la liberté, toi qui ne peux souffrir de chaînes que celles que tu donnes, tu changeas, pour le malheureux noir, tes délices en poison cruel! tu l'embrasas pour une maîtresse

adorée, de tes flammes dévorantes; tu désolas ses regards par
l'horrible spectacle d'une rivalité triomphante; enfin, tu brisas
toutes les facultés de son cœur, rempli par toi d'un désespoir
infructueux, d'une fureur impuissante.

[Cultivating reflection enlarges the soul, extends natural
capacities and educates feelings. Domingo, brought up in the
bounds of his occupations and the knowledge that he had
acquired above and beyond what slaves could generally expect,
Domingo dared to think, and felt all the feelings of a free man
swelling within him.

Love, that impetuous feeling, was made for this new and fiery
soul. It was to rend it and make him pay dear for the ennobling of
his being. Still a slave as far as all institutions were concerned,
he sensed his mind alone beginning to throw off its shackles; so he
could feel the emotions of a free man without tasting the joys they
prompted in him.

Love, dear child of liberty, who suffer only those shackles
which you impose, you changed your delights into bitter poison
for this wretched Negro! With your all-devouring flames, you set
his heart on fire for his adored mistress; you condemned him to
gaze on the dreadful spectacle of a successful rival; in the end, you
broke his heart, having filled it with fruitless despair and
impotent fury.]

Progress towards the arranged marriage is stalled by the
outbreak of violence, displeasing M. de Hauteville to the
point where a misplaced word or glance is heavily
punished. Domingo is guilty of such a look, but escapes
from the threatened punishment, pausing only at Pauline's
room to declare his love for her and promise her his
protection on his way to join the rebels. In the heat of the
insurrection, Hauteville is shot, and his dying words, as
Domingo comforts him, are:

ne perds pas de temps, sauve ma fille chérie; cours, Domingo,
porte-lui mes adieux. Va, tu méritais d'être blanc.

[don't lose a moment, save my darling daughter; run, Domingo,
and give her my farewell. Go on, you deserved to be white.]

The well-established distinction between physical blackness and moral purity, symbolically white, assumes
narrative force on the repentant lips of the dying plantation

owner.[102] Its force is undermined, however, precisely because it depends on the stock association, fostered in the white world for its own advantage, of skin-colour and inner worth. The western world has entrenched the stark oppositional symbolism of black and white as part of its assumed superiority. In so far as we read Hauteville's 'Va, tu méritais d'être blanc', as we are clearly intended to, as an approving badge of merit bestowed on a lesser being, we connive in the continuation of white superiority.

Aware of that reaction in her European readers, Doin turns it to dramatic effect at the end of her tale. The power of love sets Domingo above thoughts of revenge: 'l'amour l'a élevé au-dessus du préjugé de couleur, l'amour lui a enseigné la clémence' [love has raised him above colour prejudice, love has taught him clemency], so he helps Léopold to escape from the island, but not before the unhappy suitor has proposed to Pauline one last time. Her blunt answer prompts a brisk reaction:

"Non, Léopold, dit-elle d'un ton ferme; non, je n'augmenterai pas la rigueur de vos destins et l'embarras de vos voyages; non, je ne quitterai pas ces lieux où tant de cruels souvenirs me ramèneraient sans cesse. Qu'irais-je faire dans d'autres climats? L'honneur de Domingo sera mon protecteur dans ces contrées, je veux y mourir. Adieu, Léopold, l'embarcation va s'éloigner, partez, je le veux, ma résolution est inébranlable."
La certitude de ne pouvoir ni la fléchir ni lui être utile décida Léopold, il partit, l'âme déchirée, et tourna ses pensées vers sa famille.

['No, Leopold', she said firmly; 'no, I shall not increase the inflexibility of your destiny or the difficulties of your journey; no, I shall not leave these shores to which so many memories would constantly bring me back. What would I do in another country? Domingo's honour will protect me here, where I want to die. Farewell, Leopold, the boat is about to depart. Leave me, that is what I want, my mind is made up.'
The certainty of not being able to persuade her or to be of any use fixed Leopold's course; he left, his soul in tatters, and turned his thoughts towards his family.]

While such an exchange is psychologically and narratively underdeveloped, consistent in this respect with Doin's writing in general, its very briskness announces the impending closure of the tale. Domingo's cry: 'Ah! [...] que ne suis-je digne, moi, de votre époux!' [Oh! why am I not worthy of your betrothed?], elicits the following response from Pauline:

> Domingo, vous avez adouci les derniers momens de mon père, vous avez sauvé la vie de celui qu'il nomma son fils; vous vous êtes élevé au-dessus des préjugés, je saurai vous imiter; mais je veux fuir ces scènes de carnage: qu'une forêt soit notre refuge, qu'elle nous cache à tout l'univers; consentez à vivre pour moi seule, et je suis à vous.

> [Domingo, you cradled my father's final moments, you saved the life of the man he called his son. You have risen above prejudices, and I shall imitate you. But I want to escape from these scenes of carnage. Let a forest be our refuge and hide us from the world. Consent to live for me alone, and I am yours.]

Beyond prejudice: the concept is central. Pauline speaks here as a woman, liberating herself from society's conventions in a non-violent manner which parallels but improves upon the violent self-liberation of the Haitian slaves in which Domingo had found himself drawn to participate. In the opening words of the story, which subsequently proceeds in flashback, he had equated freedom with being a man: 'Terre de liberté, je te salue; je suis homme enfin, je suis libre!' [Land of liberty, I salute thee! I am a man at last, I am free!].

Doin is not of course the first to suggest that love has an ennobling and civilising effect, even in her stress on the active role of woman in the process of stooping to conquer: Marivaux is only her most celebrated French precursor in that respect. Nor, as we have seen, is she the first to focus narrative attention on colour difference where Marivaux confined his reversals to social class. Pauline, however, unlike the Zoraïde of Bernardin's play, starts as a free woman and in no way stoops to feminine wiles to influence Domingo in his actions. Emphasis is placed on his vaguely Rousseauistic 'natural philosophy'. His unbounded love for Pauline is the catalyst for what in white eyes was a social and racial presumption which would still, in the 1820s and beyond, attract only reproof and castigation. It is Pauline's willingness to break the mould inculcated in her by her social position and paternalistic assumptions that raises her to a level of colour-blind humanity and allows her love to flourish.

It is fully reciprocated, and a happy ending is thereby ensured. It comes immediately: there is no development, such as Grasset de Saint-Sauveur provides in *Hortense*, to suggest how the Negro's abilities complement the white woman's in various practical ways.[103] The closing paragraph of the tale shows an unusual awareness, rarely voiced by European writers, that racial prejudice exists among Blacks as well as among Whites and, in a final pirouette, turns Hauteville's dying words on their head, making Pauline an honorary Black just as he had made Domingo an honorary White:

> Domingo resta long-temps [*sic*] prosterné devant sa divinité. Douze ans après, lorsque la république d'Haïti fut assise glorieusement sur de solides bases, on trouva, par hasard, au fond d'une épaisse forêt, une chaumière adroitement construite. Un homme noir et une femme blanche l'habitaient; ils y vivaient de chasse et de fruits sauvages; on admira l'amour et les mœurs douces des époux, mais les nègres étaient mécontens [*sic*] qu'une femme blanche fût l'objet du culte d'un noir; il fallut pourtant respecter celle que ce noir adorait. "C'est dommage, disait-on en soupirant, elle méritait d'être noire!"

> [For a long time, Domingo lay in worship at his goddess's feet. Twelve years later, when the republic of Haiti was gloriously established on a sound basis, a cleverly constructed cottage was discovered by chance at the heart of a dense forest. A black man and a white woman dwelt there, living off hunting and wild berries. The couple's love and gentleness were admired, but the Negroes were unhappy that a white woman should be the object of a black man's worship. Yet they had to respect the person this black man adored. 'It is a pity, they said with a sigh: she deserved to be black.']

The emphasis on worship—'divinité', 'culte', 'adorait'—is fortunately counterbalanced by notations of equality and reciprocity: 'Un homme noir et une femme blanche', 'l'amour et les mœurs douces des époux'. The final neat twist of Hauteville's condescending praise is all the more striking because it reverses the viewpoint and assumptions of the reader, exclusively white at the time and still predominantly so, and so prompts further reflection on the implications of otherness.

Sophie Doin is given short shrift in biographical dictionaries. Born in 1800, she disappears, following a turbulent and abbreviated marriage, after 1845. One catty comment runs: 'Cette femme incomprise était bien faite pour devenir une muse romantique: elle n'y a pas manqué' [This misunderstood woman was well placed to become a Romantic muse, and in this she succeeded].[104] Her maiden name, Mamy, possibly African in origin, suggests that she may herself have been of mixed race, so prompting her interest in promoting interracial understanding through her writings. But it is by no means necessary to accept such a hypothesis to recognise in her work a singularly generous mind. Like so many negrophile writers, she would court the opprobrium of such as Gide, who was to insist that 'c'est avec les beaux sentiments qu'on fait de la mauvaise littérature' [Fine sentiments make bad literature].[105] This is in the manner of a provocative *boutade*, however, and should therefore be seen as an over-simplification rather than the truism Gide declares it to be. While no great claim should be made for Doin's work, she took a significant step forward in the development of greater sensitivity towards an oppressed and exploited people, disparate in their origins but yoked together in misery. After all, Gide also wrote in his diary: 'Le monde ne sera sauvé, s'il peut l'être, que par les *insoumis*' [The world will be saved, if it can be, only by *people who refuse to submit*].[106]

CHAPTER 3
TRADITIONS AND TRANSITIONS

'And we, father, can never guess from looking at a negro ...
what he may be when there is no white man to fear and hate.'
Harriet Martineau[107]

WHILE important legal and sociological developments occurred in the decades following the 1820s, treatment of the *Blanche/Noir* couple went largely into abeyance, with only sporadic occurrences. It was as if the literary *topoi* relating to the Negro temporarily lost their relevance and dramatic force once the slave-trade had been abolished and consciences were thereby salved.

With the development of the sugar-beet industry in Europe, it was no longer necessary or appropriate to have black workers toiling in the cane-fields of the New World. In consequence, the abolition of the slave-trade proved less of a hardship than the plantation-owners had feared; it was in any case less expensive to allow slaves to breed new generations of slaves. While the abolition of slavery, finally achieved in 1848, was still the enlightened action of a mere handful of determined liberals taking advantage of a political opportunity, its opponents were fighting a rearguard action. They were to some extent comforted by the sense that indentured labourers could be more profitable, having to pay for the food and shelter which slaves had had for nothing.

Yet an attitude of innate superiority had been engendered and, in the West Indies in particular, was applied with mathematical precision in respect of the increasing number of biracial children fathered by the planters and in turn by their mulatto children. As Louis de Maynard de Queilhe wrote in *Outre-mer*, published in 1835,

61

'les mulâtres méritent tout le mépris des blancs, et les blancs toute la haine des nègres' [Mulattos deserve the total contempt of Whites, and the Whites the total hatred of the Negroes]. His biracial hero, Marius, rejects the passionate advances of a mulatress, Flora, and after the suicide of his black wife turns his ardent attention to Julie, the daughter of the Marquis de Longuefort, a wealthy plantation owner, winning her affection and eliminating successive rivals as well as her dissolute brother. Twists in the plot come thick and fast; Flora survives Marius's attempt to have her killed and returns to haunt him; a negro uprising and, in a reminiscence of *Jane Eyre,* the big house in flames form the backdrop to Marius stabbing first Julie and then—but not before discovering that he is Longuefort's son—himself.

The perception of gradations of skin-colour as social status is still a highly significant and scrupulously registered part of the West Indian mentality. As the Haitian Jean Price-Mars was to write passionately in the 1920s:

Toutes les turpitudes des promiscuités coloniales, les hontes anonymes des rencontres de hasard, les brèves pariades de deux paroxysmes sont devenues des titres de considération et de gloire. Quel peut être l'avenir, quelle peut être la valeur d'une société où de telles aberrations de jugement, de telles erreurs d'orientation se sont muées en sentiments constitutionnels?

[All the turpitudes of promiscuity in the colonies, the anonymous shame of chance encounters, the brief couplings of two climaxes have become titles of consideration and fame. What can the future be, what can the value be of a society in which such aberrations of judgement, such errors of orientation have changed into constitutional feelings?][108]

The hierarchy of superiority and prejudice was now re-inforced by the ostensibly incontrovertible proof provided by science. Cranial measurements and facial angles became yet another yardstick for contempt and the 'legitimacy' of domination.

The imperial penetration of virgin territory, historically linked with virile adventurers, traders, colonists and armies, is manifestly at odds with the practical as well as the imaginable possibility of a relationship between a black man and a white woman. 'La colonisation, acte de pénétration, de fécondation, était par nature incompatible avec ces situations' [Colonisation, an act of penetration, of impregnation, was by its very nature incompatible with such situations].[109] The masculinist agenda has been shown to have a life well beyond colonisation, even in certain major and influential black writers of the present century.[110]

Individual acts of revenge by Blacks against Whites—as in Eugène Sue's melodramatic *Atar-Gull* (1831) and Édouard Corbière's *Le Négrier* (1832)—reflect the sense that there was good historical reason for such retribution. Similarly, the rape of a white woman by a Black, as in Victor Escousse's drama, *Farruck, le Maure* (1831), continued to excite audiences in more ways than one. On the other hand, Anicet Bourgeois and Philippe Dumanoir's *Le Docteur noir*, of 1846, has a rich heiress marry a poor Black.[111] The *abbé* Dugoujon, in correspondence from 1840 published five years later, seems almost surprised to acknowledge, on the basis of his experience in the West Indies, that 'l'antipathie des dames blanches pour les noirs est loin d'être une vérité' [antipathy for black men on the part of white ladies is far from being a truism].[112]

Haiti still acts as a conventional backdrop for Madame A. Cashin's *Amour et liberté* of 1847, in which the planter's daughter, Hortense, inspires the unrequited love of their slave, Maki. He, raised to the status of Colonel Saint-Paul at independence following events which have seen Hortense lose her mind, presumes to carry her off. Both Hoffmann and Ruscio quote the closing lines in understandable disbelief at the *dénouement*:

> Il ose déposer un baiser sur les lèvres d'Hortense. Oh! bonheur, ses lèvres ont tressailli sous ce baiser de feu! Il lui semble qu'il lui a été rendu. [...] Maki murmure ces mots: Ange du ciel, je meurs heureux! Il expire tué par l'excès de sa félicité.

> [He dares to place a kiss on Hortense's lips. Oh joy! her lips have trembled at his passionate embrace! It seems to him that she has returned his kiss. [...] Maki murmurs these words:

'Heavenly angel, I die happy!' He expires, killed by an excess of bliss.][113]

Such inanities join the ranks of other stereotypes of the time, in which love between Blacks and Whites

> apparaît comme le symbole de la pire des mésalliances, [...] comme une monstruosité de la nature, un sentiment inavouable et interdit qui ne peut conduire qu'à la mort et provoquer la plus effroyables des tragédies.

> [appears as the symbol of the worst possible mismatch, as a monstrosity of nature, an inadmissible and forbidden feeling which can lead to nothing but death and trigger the most appalling of tragedies.][114]

However, the representation of mulattos sometimes softens the image. So in de Comberousse and Antier's *Le Marché Saint-Pierre*, of 1839, a version of the prolific Eugène Scribe's *L'Épave*, a mulatto is saved from the rigours of the *Code noir* by his young mistress marrying him *in extremis*.[115] The brilliant mulatto Chevalier de Saint-Georges, in Mélesville and Beauvoir's play of that title (1840), has the Comtesse de Presle ask for his hand in marriage: 'il incarne enfin un héros noir qui tient la dragée haute aux Blancs' [in sum, he embodies a black hero who makes Whites dance to his tune].[116] Such instances lead Sylvie Chalaye to suggest that the white woman in the partnership takes the initiative in every case, thereby defying the social code and affirming her independence.[117] We have seen, however, that this is not invariably the case: the Black or mulatto can also make the first move, however disastrous the results, and he too, in so doing, is affirming his identity as a man and a potential lover. It is, after all, the freed slave Chevalier de Saint-Georges, treated by another character as an 'Othello poudré' [powdered Othello], who confesses his undying love for Madame de Presle and prompts her to admit her love in return.

If the mulatto can be presented as enjoying a special advantage, because of his intermediate skin-colour, in entering white society and aspiring to the hand of a white woman, this runs counter to his widely applied legal classification as a Black. It also ignores the predominant perception of him as being subject to a double jeopardy, being, so to speak, neither fish nor fowl. His potential as a embodiment of evil is therefore no less than the Black's in the stereotypical view; indeed, with his indeterminate status he can be portrayed as particularly slippery. The unrequited love of a mulatto overseer for his master's daughter in Lafont and Desnoyer's *Le Tremblement de terre de la Martinique* (1840) allows the authors full rein to exploit melodramatically the supposedly two-faced characteristics of half-castes. As overseer, Dominique already enjoys an intermediate status, and he uses his authority over the slaves to further his obsession with Julie de Beaumont. Having saved a slave from death at the hands of a man whom he kills, and who turns out to be Julie's brother, he is torn between his hatred for Whites and his passion for Julie. With his own crime undetected, he plays false with both Blacks and Whites in pursuit of his aim. Learning that Julie is betrothed to Henri, he foments a slave uprising and murders him; when the Comte de Beaumont is threatened by a similar insurrection, Dominique asks him for her daughter's hand, something he rejects as unimaginable. So the mulatto resorts to abducting her, and it takes the cataclysm of an earthquake to restore 'order', as understood at the time.[118]

As mulattos formed an increasing proportion of the Creole population, and often, thanks to their white fathers, enjoyed the benefits of education, it is not surprising that they should increasingly be represented in literature or indeed that from among their number should spring authors ready to present their inevitably different agenda.

In 1843, the mulatto Alexandre Dumas *père* set his rumbustious and complex novel *Georges* in multiracial Mauritius. In it, Laïza, a black slave from the Comoro islands, is enamoured of 'la Rose de la rivière Noire' [the rose of the Black River], Sara, the white niece of M. de Malmédie, a wealthy landowner, but she loves and finally marries (in dramatic circumstances, as he is on the way to his execution) Georges, the eponymous mixed-race hero. The following year, Louis-Timagène Houat, a mulatto from Réunion, published *Les Marrons*, but envisages no biracial hero. However, his sympathy allows him to imagine a Negro slave saving his mistress from drowning and marrying her secretly. When this is discovered, however, they are put under such pressure from the society around them that they flee to the mountains and live out their idyll in a cave.[119]

In 1844 too, Anaïs Ségalas puts herself into the mind of a Black and so joins earlier endeavours to relativise notions of beauty:

> Un nègre a sa beauté: bien sombre est ma couleur,
> Mais de mes dents de nacre on voit mieux la blancheur;
> Tes yeux rayonnent bien sous tes cils fins, longs voiles,
> Mais regarde, les miens ont un éclat pareil:
> Ton visage est le jour, tes yeux c'est le soleil;
> Mon visage est la nuit, mes yeux sont des étoiles.

> [A Negro has his beauty: my colour may be dark,
> But the whiteness of my pearly teeth stands out;
> Your eyes glint from the long veils of their lashes,
> But look, my own have no less of a sparkle:
> Your face is day, your eyes the very sun,
> While mine is night, and my eyes are the stars.][120]

Such a sympathetic projection, in which a woman's sensibility seems to play a significant part, will, if my extensive but inevitably not exhaustive trawl through the relevant literature can be considered a fair measure, disappear from the scene until the 1920s. The emphasis on masculinist derring-do, with official approval as colonisation gathers pace, seems to direct the sexual energy of the colonists, with no less a sense of encouragement by the authorities, towards passing affairs with local women, seen as fostering good relation with the natives. The occasionally present but insufficiently occupied *memsahib* of settler societies is seen as at best a diversion and at worst a threat to good order, a phenomenon long since noted by Tacitus:

better to leave the wife or fiancée at home, her frustrations coralled by propriety, her sense of duty, and her family.[121]

During the whole period between the Berlin agreement of 1885 which 'regulated' the scramble for Africa according to the interests of the major European players and the onset of questions about the practice and principle of colonisation in the 1920s, *Blanche/Noir* relationships virtually disappear from the scene. It is as unthinkable in the coloniser/colonised situation as it was in the master/slave one. Just as the Haitian revolution gave rise to a sub-genre by calling the latter relationship into question, so the very principles of colonisation had to await powerful critics before an exploration of *Blanche/Noir* relations could re-emerge in literature. Conversely, of course, accounts of *Blanc/Noire* relationships abound, even if they rarely had any permanence or profundity.

Colonialist novels are full of 'amours exotiques' [exotic passions], of sensual complicities with a 'mousso' [native girl], of marriages 'à la mode du pays' [after the local fashion], of housekeepers who do more than keep house. White women are largely absent, protected by distance from the Black's presumed sexual capacity, exaggerated all the more because of the strutting masculinity of European arrivals. As Mineke Schipper-De Leeuw writes:

Il est certain que le mythe du nègre créé pour la danse et pour le rythme du tam-tam qui invite à la licence sexuelle, existe dans le subconscient occidental. Lorsque l'homme blanc a une peur inconsciente de la prétendue puissance sexuelle extraordinaire du Noir, il en vient facilement à considérer le nègre comme un être bestial, fait pour l'accouplement et qui menacerait la société occidentale par son désir de la femme blanche.

[It is certain that the myth of the Negro designed to dance and created to enjoy the rhythm of the tom-tom which leads on to licentiousness, is present in the western subconscious. When white men have an unconscious fear of the supposed extraordinary sexual power of the Black, he has no difficulty in believing in the

Negro's bestiality, made for copulation and therefore a menace to western society through his desire for the white woman.][122]

Towards 1910, Colonel Baratier expresses the common view: 'Nous serions stupéfaits qu'une femme blanche s'éprenne d'un nègre' [We would be amazed if a white woman were to fall in love with a Negro].[123] The overview is summarised by Jean-Pierre Houssain:

les amours entre hommes blancs et femmes noires occupent dans la littérature coloniale une place envahissante.

[affairs between white men and black women occupy a huge amount of space in colonial literature.][124]

Yet the black woman, reduced to the status of an object, offers no more than passing relief, physiological escape, a routine form of hygiene, in short, for the coloniser far from his beloved.[125] If there is a (Snow) White on the horizon, as unreal and disembodied as in a fairy-tale, she is invisible and mute, immured, or supposedly so, in her patient wait for the return of her hero... who, as husband, will without question continue his dominating role. Apart from the occasional administrator's wife,[126] or some pioneering adventuress whose enquiring spirit leaves her prudishness intact, the only white women in French West Africa before the First World War—whereas by 1926 there are nearly 1500 white women in Senegal alone[127]—are those excluded from polite society in the motherland: at everyone's disposal, 'elles font la ligne' [they do the line], as was said in Senegal, or else indulge in less peripatetic promiscuity.[128] In 1916, Louis Le Barbier noted that prestige had been lost among Blacks as a result of the arrival of white women.[129] One such, Marie-faite-en-Fer, around whom a complete short story is written, impartially conceives her sexual role as a charitable one, serv(ic)ing Black and White alike, and encapsulates one type of social marginality.[130] Another, the mistress of Dr Antoine Thibault, is not above recalling the welcome she gave a young Togolese with whom she had previously exchanged no more than a glance.[131] Yet another, Vania in Mille and Demaison's *La Femme et l'homme nu*

(1924), whose case we shall investigate more fully, is a 'poule de luxe' [high-class whore] who is carried away by a transitory attachment to the negative image of herself.

Such *Blanche/Noir* couples as are presented by French writers during the time of high colonisation are all marginal in one way or another. Anatole France's *Balthasar* (1889), a syncretist reworking of biblical fragments and other Arabic traditions, reverts to the legend of the three wise men in giving his Balthasar a brief but intense affair with Balkis, the Queen of Sheba, on his way to Bethlehem. Among the inconsequential fantasies of Alfred Jarry's Ubu is one, in *Ubu colonial* (1901), where his wife travels to Africa and has a black baby. In *Le Zézère* (1903), Marius-Ary Leblond puts a question (p. 268) which suggests, in its simile, the origin of the expression 'couple domino':

> Pourquoi le bon Dieu a-t-il fait d'un côté des Blancs et de l'autre des Noirs, si ce n'est pas pour qu'ils se réunissent de temps en temps comme dans un jeu de dominos?

> [Why has the good God made Whites on one side and Blacks on the other, if it is not for them to get together from time to time, as in a game of dominos?]

Such reasonableness, however, merely acts as a foil for the pervasive attitude in this novel that intimate relations between black men and white women are unthinkable.

Considered geographically and sociologically marginal by the European criteria of the time, the mulatto poet known as the Haitian Frédéric Mistral, Oswald Durand, entered his plea for understanding in 'Le Fils du Noir' in a sonnet sequence *Rires et pleurs* (1896):

> [...] A vingt ans j'aimais Lise; elle était blanche et frêle;
> Moi, l'enfant du soleil, hélas! trop brun pour elle,
> Je n'eus pas un regard de ses yeux étonnés.

> .   .   .   .

> Pourtant ma mère était aussi blanche que Lise!
> Elle avait des yeux bleus où s'endormaient les pleurs;
> Quand elle rougissait de crainte ou de surprise,
> On croyait voir soudain une grenade en fleurs.

69

Sa chevelure était blonde aussi. Sous la brise
Elle couvrait son front pâli dans les douleurs.
Mon père était plus noir que moi. Pourtant l'Église
Dans un pieux hymen maria leurs couleurs.

Puis l'on vit, doux contraste, à sa blanche mamelle
Pendre un enfant doré comme nos bruns maïs,
Ardent comme un soleil de notre beau pays.

Orphelin, je vis Lise et je l'aimais comme elle;
Mais son front pur pâlit à mes aveux tremblants:
Le fils du noir fit peur à la fille des Blancs.

[The Black Man's Son

At twenty I loved Lise, white and delicate;
I, a child of the sun, far too dusky for her,
Earned not a glance from her astonished eyes.

.   .   .   .

And yet my mother was as fair as Lise!
She had blue eyes in which her tears were cradled;
When fear, surprise or something made her blush,
It was as if a pomegranate bloomed.

Her hair was also blond. Beneath the breeze
She veiled in shade her pale and grieving brow.
My father had a blacker skin than I,
And yet their marriage had the Church's blessing.

Soon a sweet contrast showed at mother's breast
A child as golden as our ripened corn,
With all the fervour of our country's sun.

Orphaned, I loved fair Lise like my mother;
Her brow went pale before my stuttered feelings:
The black man's son aroused the white girl's fear.][132]

The French masculinist tradition, self-perpetuating and to a large extent, however obliquely, self-congratulatory, took an unconscionable time to die. While male writers did not have the monopoly on the maintenance of stereotypes, their vision took full advantage of the privileges accorded to men in bourgeois and particularly in colonialist society. So André Salmon, in *La Négresse du Sacré-Cœur* (1920), has the colourful, artistic milieu of Montmartre enjoy Cora, the Negress at the chosen centre, who leads a free life and the free love that goes with it. Equivalent to her is Philippe Soupault's freewheeling Edgar Manning, in *Le Nègre* (1927), who, in the Lisbon episode, goes with the symbolically named white prostitute, Europe, before stabbing her to death.

Equivalent too are the highly sexed, highly stylised Negroes of Georges Ribemont-Dessaignes's *Le Serin muet* (1920) and A.-P. Antoine's *Le Démon noir* (1922).[133] In the former, the nymphomaniac white Barate falls (literally, from a height) for Ocre. In the latter, the title role is occupied by Ti-Saao, a randy Black, whom Catherine fights off with a whip before the curtain falls on the threat of gang rape. In Félicien Champsaur's *La Caravane en folie*, of 1926, Freya uses an equivalent weapon. Surrounded by black porters who rebel and all want to possess her, she is provided, in a moment of high melodrama, with a stratagem to maintain her modesty and, as it were, the whip hand:

> — Que le plus amoureux de vous se détache et vienne jusqu'à moi.
> Tous s'élancèrent. Mais elle les arrêta d'un geste bref.
> — J'ai dit: un seul!
> Alors un colosse à bouche lippue repoussa brutalement ses camarades, se fit un chemin comme un sanglier une trouée; se campant devant Freya, il la dévisagea effrontément et dit:
> — Moi, je t'aime plus que les autres...
> Il roula sur l'herbe, la tête fracassée par le coup de revolver que Freya lui déchargea dans la figure.
> — Qu'un autre se présente et il aura le même sort! cria-t-elle. Chiens que vous êtes! ... Vous avez cru que la reine vous laisserait lever les yeux vers elle? ... Aviez-vous pensé, crapauds immondes, que j'apaiserais vos ignobles désirs?"
> Les Noirs, matés, reculent, comprenant soudain la monstruosité de leur avidité sexuelle... On en entend certains demander pardon.

['Let the man most in love step forward and come up to me.'

71

They all dashed forward. But she stopped them with a curt
gesture.

'I said: one only!'

Then a thick-lipped colossus pushed his comrades aside and
strode forward, making a path for himself as a wild boar makes a
breach through undergrowth; planting himself in front of Freya,
he stared at her and said, 'I love you more than the others...'.

He rolled onto the grass, his head shattered by the bullet
which Freya had fired into his face,

'Someone else can come now: he will share the same fate!' she
cried. 'Dogs that you are!... Did you believe your queen would
allow you to look up at her? Did you think, you filthy toads, that
I would satisfy your base desires?'

Crestfallen, the Blacks step back, suddenly realising the
monstrosity of their sexual passion. Some even beg forgiveness.][134]

The colonialist novel in which, to my knowledge, the love
of a white woman for a black man is most sustained, if still
fleeting, is *La Femme et l'homme nu*, by Pierre Mille and
André Demaison (1924). In an extended prologue, we are
presented with the portrait of Vania, a symbolically copper-
haired Russian aristocrat given to extravagances of all sorts
and with a marked taste for revolutionary anarchism.
Abandoning her husband, she moves to a social whirl in
Paris, seeking

cette affection définitive dont, inconsciemment, malgré l'insolence apparente de ses écarts, elle avait faim et soif...

[that definitive affection for which, unconsciously, in spite of the
apparent insolence of her waywardness, she was thirsting...]

Tricked out in fashionable furs and feathers, she contrasts
pointedly with the naked African of the title, Tiékoro,
whose description occupies the first chapter.[135] His sole
garment, as a member of the Koniagui tribe from southern
Senegal, is, like that of the Bororos studied by Lévi-Strauss,
an *étui pénien* [penis case].[136] Demaison compensates for
such nudity by a surfeit of ethnographic detail which, by its
very indulgence in para-scientific documentation, distracts

and detracts, as is often the case in colonialist literature, from the artistic balance of the novel.

Mille and Demaison are too experienced to be considered naive in their writing or character-portrayal, but their over-simplification appears not only in the stark contrast between Vania and Tiékoro, who are mere pawns on the racial chessboard, but also in their acceptance of the inevitability of an unhappy ending for the *Blanche/Noir* relationship central to the plot.

Partly under the influence of alcohol, the means of tricking Behn's Oroonoko and Mérimée's Tamango into slavery, Tiékoro is recruited as a *Tirailleur sénégalais* [West African infantryman]. Wounded in battle and taken into hospital at Saint-Raphaël, he finds himself, under a war-time system whereby soldiers were attributed female penfriends, given a French *marraine de guerre*. This is none other than Vania, on the hunt for exoticism, who visits him and gradually allows her compassion as a mother-substitute to be transformed into erotic desire.

The contrast between the two characters is heavily underlined:

> Les actions, les pensées mêmes du Noir lui sont dictées de l'extérieur, par des usages, des traditions, des injonctions spiri-tuelles, dont il n'a même pas l'idée qu'il soit possible d'enfreindre les ordres. Pour Vania, tout ce qui n'est pas sa fantaisie n'est que préjugé négligeable, convention illégitime à laquelle il est beau de ne pas se soumettre. [...]
>
> Vania prétend retrouver en ce moment en Tiékoro un frère d'exil, de race inférieure, qui pourrait être à la fois son esclave et, pour une heure, un passe-temps... Mais elle soupçonne que ce passe-temps ne doit pas être chose commune, et peu à peu monte en elle le désir de s'en convaincre. Les confidences de sa caymériste qui tient ses renseignements on ne sait d'où, les racontards [*sic*] extra-ordinaires de la ville habituée depuis trois ans aux Noirs des camps de tirailleurs, sont pour elle des indications troublantes apparemment exagérées... Elle brûle de les contrôler. Ses sens qu'elle croyait endormis en souhaitent confirmer l'exactitude...
>
> Lui ne voit pas si loin. La femme blanche est dispensatrice de friandises et de douceurs; il l'accueille avec l'émerveillement d'un enfant qui voit venir une fée.

[The Black man's actions and thoughts are dictated to him from the outside, by custom and tradition, by spiritual demands, whose dictates he would never dream of infringing. For Vania, anything other than what takes her fancy is a prejudice that she can ignore, a baseless convention to which it is better not to submit. [...]

For the time being, Vania claims to find in Tiékoro a brother exile, of a lower race, who could be her slave and, for an hour, her toy... But she suspects that this toy is nothing ordinary, and there gradually wells up within her the desire to convince herself of it. The secrets confided to her by her chambermaid, who picked them up one knew not where, the extraordinary tittle-tattle of a town which for three years had harboured Blacks in its barracks, are for her seemingly exaggerated, disturbing indications... She longs to check them out. The senses she had thought dormant yearn to confirm their accuracy...

He is not so far-seeing. The white woman hands out goodies and goodness; he welcomes her like a child seeing a fairy approaching.]

Starting from such psychological premises, neither of the characters could escape the deeply ingrained assumptions of colonialist writers whereby the white woman wants to prove a theory and the Black man raise himself to the level of Whites. The trigger mechanism is operated when Vania takes the initiative by speaking of the invasion of her country by the Soviets and Tiékoro responds: 'Pourquoi nous n'allons pas les tuer, madame?' [Why we not go kill them, lady?].

> Vania dressa subitement la tête. Une flamme luisait dans ses minces yeux noirs. Elle se recula un peu; elle regarda Tiékoro du haut en bas et conçut pour lui de l'admiration. Dans sa simplicité, le Noir venait d'évoquer dans toute sa force la chose que souhaitaient tous les exilés. Tiékoro venait de parler comme un enfant; elle vit en lui un homme, le seul qu'elle eût rencontré depuis longtemps.
>
> Elle lui prit la main, cette grosse main qui débordait entre ses petits doigts, et elle eut la sensation d'un airain fraîchement fondu prêt à frapper le colosse d'argile. Ses sens déjà avaient parlé; la pitié de son cœur l'avait entraînée. En ce moment le Noir acheva de la conquérir.

[Vania raised her head sharply. A flame flickered in her narrow dark eyes. She stepped back slightly, took a look at Tiékoro from top to toe and felt a tinge of admiration. In his simple way, the Black had just evoked what every exile most wanted. Tiékoro had spoken like a child; she saw in him a man, the only one she had met for a long time.

She took his hand in hers, that huge hand which overflowed between her tiny fingers, and had the sense of a newly cast bronze ready to strike a clay colossus. Her senses had already decided; the pity in her heart had carried her away. In that instant the Black completed his conquest of her.]

Only excessive respect on Tiékoro's part delays the inevitable sexual encounter, undertaken at the initiative of Vania, whose fantasies remain intact. No less intact are the authors' presuppositions, here expressed in the suspension points of soft porn:

> Dans le silence, le choc des boutons d'uniforme sur le parquet accompagna le bruit mou des habits.
>
> .   .   .   .
>
> — Sauvage! cria Vania, tendrement...

[In the silence, the clink of uniform buttons on the floor accompanied the muffled fall of his clothes.

.   .   .   .

— You savage! cried Vania, tenderly...]

However, coupling and communion do not rhyme: Vania and Tiékoro remain as fundamentally foreign to each other as they were at the outset:

> Maintenant qu'elle était toute à Tiékoro, elle se sentait, par sa race, par sa naissance, par son éducation, impénétrable à lui, et lui à elle. Les sentiments dont son âme était pleine ne trouvaient pas d'écho dans celle de son amant. [...]
>
> Le bonheur de Vania, du moins ce qu'elle désignait ainsi, eût été certes plus accompli, si elle avait pu canaliser l'humeur de Tiékoro, pénétrer son caractère, surprendre les intentions de celui qui demeurait pour elle plus qu'un étranger. [...]
>
> Tiékoro, de son côté, sentait la confiance lui revenir chaque jour davantage. Rassuré sur les intentions des génies le jour du sacrifice de la poule noire, il se trouvait dans le même temps dégagé de ses scrupules. Ayant constaté que la femme aux cheveux de cuivre n'était point dissemblable des créatures faciles de la

maison voisine du pont, et au demeurant peu différente de Kamassa et de Tatine [filles de son village qui s'étaient librement données à lui], la barrière qui le séparait de Vania et qu'il avait hésité à franchir s'abaissait chaque jour. La crainte des machinations subtiles et perverses d'une fille des Hommes-aux-oreilles-rouges fit place au plaisir qu'il prenait à cueillir un fruit si aisé.

[Now that she belonged completely to Tiékoro, she felt, through her race, her birth and her education, impenetrable to him, and him to her. The feelings crowding into her soul found no echo in her lover's. [...]

Vania's happiness, or what, at any rate, she gave that name, would have been more complete if she had been able to channel Tiékoro's moods, get under the skin of his character, surprise the intentions of someone who remained more than a stranger to her. [...]

Tiékoro, for his part, felt increasingly confident with every passing day. Reassured about the intentions of the spirits on the day when the black hen was sacrificed, he found himself also freed of his scruples. Having established that the copper-haired lady was in all respects like the women of easy virtue in the brothel by the bridge and furthermore scarcely different from Kamassa and Tatine [girls from his village who had freely offered themselves to him], the barrier which separated him from Vania and which he had hesitated to cross got lower each day. Fear of the subtle and perverse machinations of a daughter of the Men-with-Red-Ears gave way to the pleasure he took in picking so ready a fruit.]

It is clear from these extracts that the analysis of psychological motivation is at least more developed than the platitude of the scenario, but at root it reiterates the crass Romantic assumption of a gulf between Black and White.

Tiékoro's repatriation is announced, and Vania decides to go ahead so as to welcome him to Dakar and continue to live out her dream there. It turns into a nightmare. Already, in Saint-Raphaël, the ill-assorted couple had been subjected to soldiers' gibes.[137] In the capital of French West Africa, the rebuffs and insults are even more blatant. Hounded out of a restaurant and successive hotels, with the white elite snapping at their heels, rejected even by a nun devoted to charitable work—'Tu parles, fit-elle en caressant sa mâchoire rasée, une *poule* avec un nègre!...' [You must be joking, she said, stroking her shaven chin, a *hooker* with a Negro!...]— they end up finding lodgings in a suspect area near the railway station.

Each member of the couple becomes aware of the aggression threatening them. Under a respectable surface as draper and hatter, the Frenchwoman Madame Philibert is a persistent pimp and busybody, giving Vania unsolicited advice on everything and nothing:

> — Ah! ma petite dame, vous suivez un mauvais chemin. On vous voit tous les jours avec un nègre... C'est votre affaire, ça, madame... Pas la mienne... Non pas, certes... Ces gens sont nos domestiques... pas nos amants... Ou alors... on se cache... vous comprenez... Mais vivre avec lui, vous promener en ville... ça ne se fait pas... Tandis que...

> ['Oh dear, you're on a downward path, young lady. You're seen every day with a Negro... That's your business of course... Not mine... Of course not... Such people are our servants... not our lovers... Or else, in secret, you understand. But living with him, walking in town together... that's not done... Whereas...']

Tiékoro's arrival interrupts her flow, but it turns into a flood:

> — Vous ne savez pas ce que vous faites, fit Mme Philibert—la colère faisait trembler sa voix—vous vous en repentirez, vous verrez. Ah! vous croyez que vous allez nous salir toutes ici, nous faire passer pour des...
> Le dernier mot se perdit dans le grincement de la porte du jardin.

> ['You don't know what you're doing,' Madame Philibert said, her voice trembling with anger, 'You'll live to regret it, you'll see. Oh! you think you're going to blacken all of us here, have us taken for...'
> The last word was lost in the squeaking of the garden gate.]

Tiékoro, for his part, recounts the petty things done to him at the barracks, and once again the authors display a realism which masks a prejudice when they add:

Inaperçu à son arrivée, le bruit de son aventure était parvenu aux oreilles des sous-officiers et des officiers. Chacun voyait en lui l'usurpateur d'une femme isolée qui, par le droit des Tropiques, pouvait appartenir à tous.

[Unnoticed when he arrived, echoes of his affair had reached the ears of NCOs and officers alike. Each one saw in him the usurper of a solitary woman who, by rights in the tropics, could belong to everyone.]

The couple's fragile happiness prompts a racial division whose Manicheism Mille and Demaison denounce:

ce que Tiékoro oubliait dans sa naïve outrecuidance, c'était les menées ténébreuses des esprits souterrains... Sa présence et son bonheur étaient, à son insu, en train de soulever la ville entière, ou du moins, parmi ses habitants, les seuls dont l'opinion comptait. L'aventure de Vania et de Tiékoro dressait tout simplement l'un contre l'autre le parti des Blancs, gardien jaloux de la race supérieure, et la [sic] parti des Noirs lettrés ou affranchis par la guerre, férus d'égalité, réclamant impérieusement l'abolition des préjugés de couleur.[138] [...] Comme [...] les Blancs détenaient l'argent et l'effective puissance, tous les Noirs conscients de leurs droits de citoyen faisaient bloc en faveur de Tiékoro et de Vania. Mais tout cela était ignoré de Tiékoro lui-même, qui n'inspirait d'ailleurs aucune sympathie à ses partisans. Quelle affinité pouvait en effet exister entre un Koniagui sauvage, même habillé par un tailleur de Saint-Raphaël et coiffé d'un casque de liège enrubanné, et des Ouolofs, des Lébous, des Toucoulaures [sic], des Sérères christianisés [...].

[what Tiékoro forgot in his naive presumptuousness were the shadowy plots of the underground spirits... His presence and his happiness were, unknown to him, provoking the whole town, or at least, those of its inhabitants whose opinion counted. The adventure of Vania and Tiékoro quite simply ranged against each other the White party, jealously guarding its racial superiority, and the party of Blacks either educated or freed by the war, intent on equality and clamouring imperiously for the abolition of racial prejudice. [...] As [...] the Whites held the money and effective power, all the Blacks conscious of their rights as citizens formed a block in favour of Tiékoro and Vania. But of all that Tiékoro himself was unaware: he inspired no sympathy in his partisans. What possible affinity could there be between a wild Koniagui, even dressed by a tailor from Saint-Raphaël and

78

wearing a pith-helmet with a ribbon, and Wolofs, Lebous, Tokolors, or Sereers converted to Christianity [...]?]

Things turn sour. Tiékoro, attacked by a gang of Blacks whose racial affinity fails to outweigh the money offered by their anonymous backer, is taken in by a Manding woman, Moussouba, whose gods and charms prove more powerful than Vania's. According to the authors, a deeply atavistic response leads him to prefer making love to a black woman, even one from a different tribe:

> Vraiment cette Moussouba—protégée du Serpent—mettait dans l'amour plus de dignité que la femme aux cheveux de cuivre... L'impassibilité de ses embrassements même lui paraissait agréable et décente. Son silence également: que la femme blanche, abondante en paroles et fertile en gestes, ne savait-elle imiter en cela sa rivale noire?...

> [Really, Moussouba—protected by the Snake—put into love more dignity than the copper-haired woman. Even the impassive nature of her embraces struck him as agreeable and decent. Her silence too. Why did the white woman, plenteous in word and profuse in gesture, not know how to imitate her black rival in that respect?...][139]

Vania will discover Tiékoro only to lose interest in him again for ever, discarding him like an old toy which has served its purpose. She returns to Europe, moved to hear some Russian songs of her childhood sung on the quays at Dakar. She recounts in her own way what she sees as no more than a 'fantaisie passagère' [fleeting fancy] helping her to keep her 'auréole de légende' [halo of legend] in place: she can dine out on tales of exotic difference. As for him, he returns to his village, responding to the call of his tutelary spirits: documentary ethnography takes over the fourth and last section of the novel, which Vania's absence deprives in consequence of narrative tension. Neither Tiékoro's atavistic preoccupations, nor his election as village chief, nor even this long episode given over to him alone so as to create a balance with the prologue in which Vania alone appears, can make up for her absence. The weakness of the ending of the novel, when Tiékoro, in a stupefying cloud of alcohol, replies to a question about white women, is all too apparent: 'Elles sont là-bas... dit-il enfin. Il y en a...' ['They are over there...', he said at last. 'There are some...'].

Such rare women's voices as were heard in the 1820s—that of Sophie Doin prepared to envisage a positive outcome to a *Blanche/Noir* relationship or that, pre-eminently, of Madame de Duras penetrating the torment of otherness in an inflexible society—are for a century drowned out by the foghorns of masculine imperialism. It will take a new generation of women writers to question the political and literary stereotypes and shibboleths of colonialism.

CHAPTER 4
OPPOSITE GENDERS, OPPOSITE AGENDAS

'Black men are pearls in beauteous ladies' eyes.'
Shakespeare, *The Two Gentlemen of Verona*, V, ii, 12.

'LA COLONISATION n'est pas une entreprise humanitaire, elle est un régime d'oppression politique ayant pour fin l'exploitation économique des peuples soumis' [Colonisation is not a humanitarian enterprise: it is a regime of political oppression whose purpose is the economic exploitation of subject peoples].[140] Colonial discourse has always given rise to its counter-discourse. Colonisers, like the slave-traders before them, got on with their job, rather as Wole Soyinka, in his cutting critique of Negritude, suggested that a tiger pounced on its prey rather than talk about its 'tigritude'. France's 'mission civilisatrice' [civilising mission] certainly had its theorists, but everything was directed towards practical ends. The First World War called a great deal into question, but had a particular impact in France's relations with Blacks, since it brought over 150,000 West African infantrymen to her shores. At least twenty-five thousand died as cannon-fodder—a figure of 22 per cent has been suggested—while many others went missing.[141] Never had the average French person seen so many Blacks in flesh and blood.

Almost more successful, in the long run, than political colonisation was the entrenchment of its psychological counterpart which the arrival of jazz and the fashion for negro art, song and dance could not mask. The Manichean, demonising binary model was accepted, even to their cost, by those who were colonised, and largely persists to this day. I have already warned that the polarity adopted for this book carries its own distortions and over-simplifications.

81

The question of how to escape from it still exercises black intellectuals and rightly too preoccupies us here.

In the 1920s, women writers found a third way between colonialist and anticolonialist discourses, with their mutual incomprehension and antagonism. Marginalised within a patriarchal system, they offer their sympathy, but can only gesture towards the abolition of European socio-cultural barriers. For men and women alike, empowerment within a foreign society is a lure and can be a delusion, but its attraction is double for women. The latter part of this chapter focuses on two texts, by Lucie Cousturier and Louise Faure-Favier, which subvert the traditional discourse and explore possible ways of promoting understanding between Blacks and Whites.

Colonialism is fraught with paradox:

> œuvre civilisatrice mais qui s'accomplissait dans la violence et les destructions, œuvre de régénération nationale mais qui détruisait tant de Français, épopée aventureuse mais qui sombrait dans l'ennui et la monotonie, découverte des autres mais regrets qu'il ne soient pas nous,

> [a civilising undertaking which depended on violence and destruction, a work of national regeneration but which destroyed so many Frenchmen, an adventure epic but which fell into tedium and monotony, a discovery of others full of regret that they are not us],

as Martine Astier-Loutfi neatly encapsulates it.[142] Colonial novels were caught in the same vice, reassuring only to deceive. Fleeing from the Old World sometimes for negative reasons, their heroes were bound to praise it to indigenous populations who were invariably perceived as stupid and sometimes as dangerous as well. Fleeing the post-Romantic exoticism of a Loti, their authors turned to a naturalism whose scientific nature was at odds with novelistic inventiveness. All too often, to the cost of both kinds of writing, creative and documentary, there is no gap between novels and reports, short stories and essays.

In the writings of Lucie Cousturier and Louise Faure-Favier, there is no such confusion. Both write about the provincial France with which they are familiar, and when, in reality or in imagination, they travel to Africa, it is to learn, not to dictate terms. Both dare to view in a favourable light the Blacks they present. The first, a Parisian painter, determinedly free-thinking and with early communist sympathies, displays an appealing naivety and generosity. In her country house at Fréjus, near the same Saint-Raphaël that we came across in *La Femme et l'homme nu*, she has an encounter which for her is capital: that of the *Tirailleurs sénégalais* [West African infantrymen]. The resulting book, *Des inconnus chez moi* (1920), is the inevitably one-sided account of what follows: a revolution in her attitudes towards Blacks in the course of the basic language lessons which she gives them. A *témoignage*, it has no truck with fiction.

Faure-Favier's novel *Blanche et Noir* (1928) is no less unambiguously a novel. It recounts the scandal caused among the provincial bourgeois of Monistrol-sur-Loire by the marriage of a respectable but broad-minded widow, Malvina Lortac-Rieux, bored with living with her son and starchy daughter-in-law, to a Senegalese, Samba Laobé Thiam, who came to represent his country at the Exposition Universelle of 1889. The narrator, Jeanne Lortac-Rieux, Malvina's granddaughter, has as her uncle the biracial son of this *couple domino*'s union. To emphasise the irony of the contrast, the fiction has François Laobé-Rieux and his niece being born on the self-same day. Fascinated by Africa as soon as she discovers a truth long hidden from her by her parents, Jeanne eventually meets her uncle François when, as a pilot exprienced in the First World War, he lands one day literally and metaphorically out of the blue in the field behind her house. There is an immediate empathy between them. Suggestive surmise aside—marriage between an uncle and his niece being precluded by the Church—Jeanne does not hesitate to fly off to Senegal with this married Black man (married to a white woman), into an ambiguous but resolute freedom.

In what circumstances can such a moral revolution have taken place? The broad context need not detain us: the 'twenties have the reputation as madcap years marking the release from the tension and fears of the Great War. The *Tirailleurs sénégalais,* out of their element in the cold mud of battle, talking the *petit nègre* [pidgin French] which so delighted the caricaturists, earned the compassion of the nurses and, as we have seen in Vania, of the *marraines de guerre* who took an interest in their welfare. Recruited by often dubious methods, killed and wounded for a country which they knew exclusively through its camps, trenches and hospitals, they received the uniform and were sent home with thanks and even the occasional medal.[143]

The representation of the *Blanche/Noir* couple makes a modest but significant contribution to the collapse of the colonialist mentality. The point of view represented by women, made increasingly conscious of their own capacities by the absence of their menfolk during the war, and thereby, in some cases, of a traditional subservience parallel to that of Blacks, is all the more potent. Well before Simone de Beauvoir, for whom women and Blacks 's'émancipent aujourd'hui d'un même paternalisme' [are today emancipating themselves from the same paternalism], the phenomenon had not only been known, the metaphor of colonisation common to the two conditions had also been recognised.[144] Houssain quotes Marthe Bancel, for example, in support of his highly pertinent question:

Comment les coloniaux, avec leurs préjugés, imagineraient-ils d'ailleurs qu'une Blanche puisse tomber amoureuse d'un Noir? La différence de culture semble un obstacle infranchissable, et surtout c'est un sujet tabou car il remettrait en question la supériorité du Blanc et l'égoïsme du mâle. Une coloniale en témoigne avec véhémence:
"Pourquoi, vous qui avez certainement recherché le contact de négresses, d'annamites, de japonaises, vous mettez-vous en colère à la seule idée d'amour entre blanches et gens de couleur? Ne me dites pas que c'est l'horreur du mélange des races, puisque c'est vous, coloniaux célibataires, qui laissez un peu partout vos métis!"

[How could colonials, with all their prejudices, possibly imagine a white woman falling in love with a Black? The cultural difference appears as an insurmountable obstacle, and it is in any case a taboo subject because it would call into question the superiority of the White and the egoism of the male. A woman from the colonies bears fervent witness:

> 'Why do you men, who have certainly sought contact with Negresses, Annamites and Japanese geishas, get angry at the very thought of love between white women and coloured men? Don't tell me it's horror at mixing the races, since it's you bachelor colonists who leave your mulatto children all over the place!']¹⁴⁵

It is true, as Anna Maria Diefenthal recalls, that in the colonial period, as far as lasting relationships were concerned, there were 'très peu de chances pour que des couples Blanches et Noirs se forment' [very few chances of *Blanche/Noir* couples forming].¹⁴⁶ A social and moral revolution was needed—is still needed in some cases—for white women and black men to enjoy a happy, stable, unthreatened relationship. That revolution, as Frantz Fanon was to show, had to come also from within. As far as a white girl was concerned, she risked, in Martine Bauge-Gueye's words, to be 'plus attirée par le mystère africain que par la personnalité de l'homme' [more attracted by the mystery of Africa than by the personality of the individual man].¹⁴⁷ As for the Black, according to Fanon,

> il s'agit de déterminer dans quelle mesure l'amour authentique demeurera impossible tant que ne seront pas expulsés ce sentiment d'infériorité [...], cette surcompensation.

> [you have to determine the extent to which authentic love remains impossible so long as a sense of inferiority, with its associated overcompensation, has not been surmounted.]¹⁴⁸

Bauge-Gueye's embarrassment is manifest:

> il y a comme un reniement de sa race dans son choix d'une femme blanche. Il a gardé d'elle une certaine image de supériorité par rapport à la femme noire. [...] Il cherche à se valoriser plus ou moins inconsciemment en devenant un objet digne de l'amour d'une Blanche.

> [there is, as it were, a denial of his race in his choice of a white woman. He has kept a certain image of her superiority compared

with black women. [...] He is seeking, more or less consciously, to make the most of himself by becoming worthy of the love of a white woman.][149]

The result is inevitable:

> On a l'impression qu'il s'agit moins de mariages d'inclination que d'une manière de s'affirmer pour le Noir, de réaliser une théorie pour la Blanche.

> [We have the impression that it is less a matter of marriages of true minds than a way for the Black to assert himself and for the white woman to put a theory into practice.][150]

A personal revolution is still not enough. Society exerts pressures more or less acknowledged, more or less direct. The colonial novel, by its very nature, takes place in a colonial setting. But one tautology can hide another: the anticolonial French novel, in which a white woman and a black man can perhaps love one another, takes place almost by definition in metropolitan France, but only in a setting where the prevailing mentality is subject to dissent. The earliest analysis of *Blanche/Noir* couples in Black African literature, that of Mineke Schipper-De Leeuw, underlines the radical difference between those who choose to live in Europe and those who set up house in Africa. She also points out the difficulty of success for what Ouologuem would call these 'damnés de l'amour' [damned in love],[151] judging from the fictional cases, in either continent:

> Un mariage entre Blanches et Noirs s'avère pratiquement impossible en Afrique coloniale. Si la société africaine tradition-nelle s'y oppose, la société blanche le combat par tous les moyens, afin de maintenir sa position de prestige et de supériorité. [...] On dirait qu'en Europe les obstacles s'interposent moins nombreux entre femmes blanches et hommes noirs [...] mais la société occidentale y est hostile encore bien des fois.

> [A marriage between white woman and black men is practically impossible in the African colonies. If traditional African society is opposed to it, white society fights it tooth and nail so as to maintain its position of prestige and superiority. [...] In Europe the obstacles between white woman and black men would appear

to be less numerous [...] but western society is still frequently hostile.][152]

Should we then conclude, with Diefenthal, that 'le mariage mixte réussit difficilement en Europe comme en Afrique' [it is as hard to make a success of a mixed marriage in Europe as it is in Africa]?[153] In saying that, we would say no more than that every intimate partnership has its attendant problems, even if biracial mariages suffer from special social pressures. It also overlooks the fact that a work of fiction is not a sociological treatise.[154] Schipper-De Leeuw reminds us in passing:

> Il est vrai qu'un bonheur durable comme thème n'est pas aussi intéressant que des péripéties dramatiques, mais la fin abrupte qui intervient chaque fois dans l'amour entre Blanches et Noirs des romans négro-africains suggère tout de même que les auteurs se voient dans l'impossibilité de faire survivre cet amour aux vicissitudes de la vie.

> [It is true that lasting happiness is not as interesting a topic as dramatic vicissitudes, but the abrupt ending of *Blanche/Noir* love in black African novels suggests all the same that the authors see this love as unable to survive the ups and downs of life.][155]

An open acknowledgement of the difficulties and pressures, both social and literary, will allow a more accurate assessment of the literary qualities of a given work.

For the requirements of his thesis, Houssain pays more attention to Lucie Cousturier's travel writings than to the text in which she recounts her first discovery of black Africans. It is true that the two volumes of *Mes Inconnus chez eux* (1925; 1: *Mon amie Fatou, citadine* and 2: *Mon ami Soumaré, laptot*), are perspicacious accounts which warrant the author's classification, alongside André Gide and Félicien Challaye, among the 'inquiéteurs' [disturbers].[156] Houssain observes:

La sympathie envers les Noirs n'exclut pas l'esprit critique, et Lucie Cousturier voit l'Afrique plus encore en féministe qu'en artiste (elle peint des aquarelles). [...] Sensible et cultivée, douée pour la polémique et en avance sur son époque, Lucie Cousturier mérite d'être relue, malgré quelques erreurs d'interprétation.

[Sympathy for Blacks does not exclude a critical sense, and Lucie Cousturier sees Africa more as a feminist than as a painter of watercolours. [...] Sensitive and cultured, with a gift for polemic and ahead of her time, Lucie Cousturier deserves re-reading, in spite of some errors of interpretation.][157]

By focusing rather on her first book, we shall see that these errors of interpretation simply do not exist: she is on her home ground, welcoming increasing numbers of *Tirailleurs sénégalais* from Fréjus wanting to learn to read and write French. Her account, written with a delicious sense of irony, is all the more powerful in that she admits at the outset her total ignorance of Blacks and furthermore 'une colère peu patriotique' [somewhat unpatriotic anger] towards them when the construction of their barracks involves the destruction of a four-hundred-year-old olive grove.[158] Such a massacre would have generated in many a witness, beyond the commonplace 'not-in-my-back-yard' syndrome, an ineradicable prejudice.

This open-mindedness allows Lucie Cousturier to run counter to the prevailing colonial discourse by affirming: 'Je ne conquiers rien, je suis plus ou moins conquise' [I am conquering nothing; I am more or less conquered].[159] With no religious or political axe to grind, and refusing the linguistic deception that turns domination into 'pacification' or 'assimilation', she shows a missionary spirit only insofar as she seeks to provide—learning as she goes along—basic literacy skills without asking anything in return. Yet she is trapped within the colonialist dichotomy and faces the difficulty of well-intentioned Whites discovering colonised peoples that Memmi was to analyse in his *Portrait du colonisateur*.[160] Before travelling to Africa, it is as if her very naivety, sustained to the last—'croyez-en un peintre,—vous qui possédez l'inégalable génie d'être noir!' [believe a painter—you who have the unrivalled genius of

88

being black!] are the closing words of her travel diary[161]—
protects her against an attitude of rejection in favour of
generosity. In her first book she is not overtly anticolonialist, but convivial in a way no tract could be.

Relegated to a footnote, the following remark by Houssain deserves more prominence in our present reflections:

> Par son double rôle de "franc-tireur" et d'"inquiéteur", l'écrivain
> anticolonialiste apporte à la fois une réponse (attaques contre un
> régime donné) ET une question (comment a-t-on pu mépriser la race
> noire? comment peut-on mépriser l'homme?).
>
> Or, selon la belle formule de Serge Doubrovsky, la littérature
> n'est-elle pas "toujours une question à travers une réponse, une
> réponse à travers une question"?

> [In the double role of 'sniper' and 'disturber', the anticolonialist
> writer offers both a response (attacks against a given regime)
> AND a question (how can the black race have been despised? how
> can one despise men?)
>
> Now, in Serge Doubrovsky's neat formulation, is literature not
> always 'a question via a response and a response via a
> question'?][162]

If Cousturier softens her direct attacks, she disturbs
constantly by putting questions which embarrass the
colonialist mindset, certainly, but also all those who, when
not mindlessly indifferent, went along with it, in other
words the vast majority, including even from among the
proletariat (to be forgiven no doubt because of their lack of
education) and from among left-wing intellectuals (for
whom this alibi is invalid). The communists would not
organise their hostility to colonialism for another decade,
prompted by the jingoistic Exposition Coloniale of 1931.

Cousturier summarises the nature and value of her
experience as follows:

> Moi, je ne cherche pas comment les hommes sont vernis: je
> cherche comment ils aiment, pensent et souffrent. J'ai mêlé
> pendant trois années mes rires et mes larmes avec ceux des noirs et
> je serais flattée de pouvoir dire que les miens ressemblaient aux
> leurs.

[I do not strive to see how men are painted: I strive to see how they love, think and suffer. Over three years I have mingled my tears and laughter with those of Blacks, and I should like to believe that mine resembled theirs.][163]

Under the rubric 'how they love', we find passing references to the *Blanche/Noir* couple. One such, evoked with infinite delicacy, is tentatively formed between Damba Dia, 'gracieux sentimental de vingt ans' [a lissom, sentimental twenty-year-old], who misses more and more of his lessons with Cousturier, and a local grocer's daughter. They become the butt of French NCOs' jokes and are exposed to the disapproval both of the grocer and of the officer who is the girl's approved fiancé.[164]

The very sensitivity of the painter turned teacher leads to the *Tirailleurs* confiding willingly in her: more than once she assumes a quasi-maternal role. Living with her husband and son, she avoids any more intimate relationship. Yet she muses at one point on the welcome that one of her pupils would offer her if one day she turned up on his threshold. Is it because Macoudia M'Baye shows special talent as a draughtsman that Lucie Cousturier admits to an inadmissible thought?:

j'avais pris l'habitude de prévenir tous ses désirs comme il est naturel de le faire à l'égard des personnes que l'on reçoit. Je lui demandais toujours:
"As-tu chaud? as-tu soif? as-tu faim? es-tu fatigué?" Il attendait sans doute que [je] lui demande encore: "Es-tu content tout à fait?... Veux-tu manger ce gâteau? Veux-tu m'embrasser? Veux-tu dormir un peu avec moi?"
Il attendait, par sentiment du rythme; mais il devait à la fin trouver bizarre ma conception de l'hospitalité, laquelle proposait tant de choses dispendieuses et médiocres et omettait les plus magnifiques et qui ne coûtent rien.
Il devait être attristé de ma bêtise, et sans doute se disait-il que, si les rôles s'étaient renversés et qu'il eût à me recevoir, il m'aurait offert de l'amour, aussi simplement qu'une boisson fraîche.

[I had made a habit of anticipating all his desires as any good hostess would. I always asked him: 'Are you hot? Are you thirsty? Are you hungry? Are you tired?' He no doubt expected me to add: 'Are you completely happy?... Would you like to eat this cake? Would you like to kiss me? Would you like to go to bed with me?'

He stood waiting, out of a sense of rhythm, but he must have found my sense of hospitality odd in the end, offering so many superfluous and second-rate things but omitting the most splendid which cost nothing.

He must have been saddened by my stupidity; and no doubt he said to himself that if the roles were reversed and he were welcoming me, he would have offered me love as simply as a cool drink.][165]

The idea attracts her sufficiently for her to relate, at the beginning of her next book, the experience of 'Mme X..., femme d'un administrateur colonial en congé' [Madame X, the wife of a colonial administrator on furlough] who, left alone in the bush, is offered exceptional hospitality. Entrusted by the local chief, at his departure, to his younger brother, the latter protests:

> Mais tout cela n'est pas assez pour toi... Moi j'ai pensé beaucoup à te donner aussi de l'amour qui est le mieux de tout pour une personne qui est forte comme notre roi... mais tu es restée tous les jours et toutes les nuits à marcher, à parler avec tout notre village.

> [But none of that is good enough for you... I have long thought of giving you love as well, best of all for someone who is as strong as our king... but you spent all your days and nights walking, conversing with our village people.][166]

In anticipation of postcolonial theory, everything is not measured by the European yardstick, but Cousturier was no more capable than anyone else of escaping from her own subjectivity. The artist lets her eye be trained by her close contact with Blacks. At the start, she readily admits to her failure to escape from the myth of the noble savage in which, since Oroonoko, Greco-Roman aesthetic norms are the measure of beauty:

> Nous nous rappelons bien les yeux intelligents de Saër, sa bouche puissante sans lourdeur, sa peau mate, son visage mince aux joues longues et fines, avec assez de front et de menton pour ne pas

déconcerter notre esthétique européenne. Nous ne savions encore dire, en 1917, qu'un noir est joli; mais si ce mot signifie relations affables des traits, accord, musique, Saër Gueye était joli. [...]

En février 1917 je disais, ma famille disait, nous disions habituellement: "Ce nègre-là a du caractère... Il a un masque intéressant." Mais ce n'est qu'en 1918 que nous oserons articuler devant Dieu et nos compatriotes: "Ce nègre-là est joli... de toutes les manières."

[We well remember Saër's intelligent eyes, his powerful but not heavy mouth, his matt skin, his slender face with its long, fine cheeks and with enough forehead and chin not to disconcert our European concepts of beauty. In 1917, we were as yet unable to say that a Black was beautiful; but if this word implies an agreeable relationship between features, harmony, music, Saër Gueye was beautiful. [...]

In February 1917 I said, my family said, we all regularly said: 'That Negro has character... He has an interesting mask.' It was only in 1918 that we dared to state before God and our fellow-countrymen: 'That Negro is beautiful... by any standard.']¹⁶⁷

Subsequently, she will learn to detach herself to an extent from western norms:

Ahmat n'est pourtant pas aussi noir que Baïdi et, en l'observant auprès de ce dernier, on songe que c'est par timidité peut-être qu'il s'est arrêté devant nous dans la voie de la complète saturation. De même sa tête est trop petite et trop ronde pour sa taille de près de deux mètres et ses traits, d'une indécision à décourager les ethnologues, encore émoussés par quelques marques de la petite vérole, semblent de fortune, comme provisoires.

Seul, dans cet appareil négligé de la face, un détail essentiel est bien aménagé: son sourire.

[Yet Ahmat is not as black as Baïdi and, looking at them together, I reflect that it may be out of shyness that, in our presence, he has stopped short on the path to complete colour saturation. Similarly his head is too small and round for his height, nearly two metres, and his features, with an indeterminacy to discourage any ethnologist, and blunted by pock-marks, appear haphazard, as it were provisional.

One thing alone, in this random system of a face, one essential detail is firmly anchored: his smile.]¹⁶⁸

In the end, she goes so far as to turn the European viewpoint on its head:

> Si nous avons substitué aux dieux les jolies femmes; si les Grecs leur avaient déjà substitué d'orgueilleux athlètes, ce n'est pas tant mieux, ainsi qu'on l'a dit, c'est tant pis! La beauté-type, dans les arts, n'est qu'un idéal d'empailleurs; les Dieux égyptiens, les Moines de Giotto, les baigneuses de notre Renoir ne comptent que par ce qui les lie à l'art nègre et non par ce qui les lie aux canons.

> [If we have substituted pretty women for the gods; if the Greeks had already replaced them by haughty athletes, it is not so much the better, as is generally said, but so much the worse! Archetypal beauty, in art, is the ideal of taxidermists; the Egyptian gods, Giotto's monks, our Renoir's bathers are to be valued for the way they relate to Negro art, not for their link with the established canons.][169]

This declaration is all the more extraordinary in that the Fauves and Cubists had drawn inspiration from Negro art only to assimilate it into their own aesthetics, not to recognise its intrinsic merit.[170]

Naturally, for a more scientific and systematic rehabilitation of Blacks during this period, one has to look elsewhere. But most of the work of a pioneer such as Maurice Delafosse, for example, post-dates *Des inconnus chez moi*.[171] Similarly, the systematic collection of African oral traditions, sporadic and random in the nineteenth century, begins to bear fruit only in the course of the 1920s.[172] It is partly for that reason, no doubt, that more than one colonial novelist assumed an ethnographical role which, as we have seen, often mars the balance of the fiction.[173]

That at least is not true of Claire Goll's *Le Nègre Jupiter enlève Europa* (1928, first published in German, 1926). It falls, however, into stereotypical mode by juxtaposing Alma, an archetypal Franco-Swedish blue-eyed blonde, with Jupiter, a handsome black government official very much in the princely mould of Anniaba and from an Africa scarcely less fanciful. His hypersensitivity is attributed to the 'neurasthénie des humiliés' [neurasthenia of humiliated people]; his desire is said to be that of all black immigrants:

> Epouser une femme blanche et, par là, prendre rang dans cette race bénie, tel est le rêve qu'il fait annuellement en 365 épisodes.

> [To marry a white woman and thereby take his place in this blessed race, such is the dream he has every year in 365 episodes.]

The one-track dream attributed to Jupiter is realised:

> Ainsi le désir ardent de tous les nègres expatriés était exaucé pour lui: il épousait une blanche. Ses enfants seraient délivrés des stigmates de sa race.

> [So the burning desire of all expatriate Blacks was fulfilled for him: he was marrying a white woman. His children would be liberated from the stigmata of his race.]

The author's view of Blacks is locked in a time-warp. The following could almost come from the pen of Président des Brosses in *Du culte des dieux fétiches* of 1760:

> La philosophie et en général toute réflexion abstraite, ne sont pas l'affaire des nègres, chez qui la simple représentation d'un dieu prend une forme et devient une figurine de bois.

> [Philosophy and abstract thought in general are not the concern of Blacks, for whom the simple representation of a god takes on a specific shape and becomes a wooden statuette.]

The pity is that Negritude would also promote such a view. Goll's own philosophy is no more than homespun:

> Seul un puissant prince exotique pouvait posséder une femme d'un blond aussi rare. Car si l'on voit parfois des mariages mixtes, entre blancs et noirs, la femme blanche présente presque toujours quelque tare: ou elle louche, ou elle a vingt ans de plus que son sombre époux, si fier de cette peau claire quoique fanée. Le plus souvent elle sort du peuple et fait cette "mésalliance" par calcul, car parmi les nègres qui viennent en Europe il y en a qui ont de la fortune.

> [Only a powerful foreign prince could possess a wife so outstandingly blonde. For if you sometimes see mixed marriages

94

between Whites and Blacks, the white woman almost always has something wrong with her: either she squints, or she is twenty years older than her dusky husband, so proud of her pale if faded skin. Most often she is lower-class and forms this 'misalliance' out of self-interest, as some of the Blacks who come to Europe are really wealthy.]

The period view takes on greater likelihood of accuracy when it is echoed by a black writer: in *Banjo*, Claude McKay has his alter ego, the aspiring writer Ray, observe:

> The successful Negro in Europe always marries a white woman, and I have noticed in almost every case that it is a white woman inferior to himself in brains and physique. [...] You know what class of white women marry colored men. [...] There *are* exceptions—white women with money who are fed up.[174]

Little seems to have changed since Edward Long, in 1772, voiced the opinion that

> The lower class of women in *England*, are remarkably fond of the blacks, for reasons too brutal to mention; they would connect themselves with horses and asses, if the laws permitted them.[175]

As a woman of the world presenting a fashionable diplomatic milieu—glossy magazines send photographers to cover Jupiter's marriage to Alma—Goll is aware that a handsome Black would be courted 'par curiosité exotique, par snobisme ou par luxure!' [out of exotic curiosity, snobbery or lust!]. Jupiter bides his time before coition, when a note anticipating Fanon is struck:

> Sous les traits d'Alma, il tenait dans ses bras toutes les blanches de la terre, toutes celles qui osaient insulter, ridiculiser, mépriser et tromper ceux de sa race.

> [In the shape of Alma, he held in his arms all the white women in the world, all those who dared to insult, ridicule, despise and deceive those of his race.][176]

As to the motivation for the breakdown of their marriage, it is borrowed entirely from Othello, with explicit references—complete with suspect handkerchief—and taken to a similar extreme, since Jupiter stabs to death his wife, who has alienated their daughter from her father and taken up with a Swedish friend. The novel's 'real focus', as Moray McGowan observes, 'is not empirical reality but a sustained play with stereotypes'.[177] Racial difference provides the alienating motif for all the parties concerned, and the novel's setting in Paris (as distinct from the provincial setting of the Cousturier and Faure-Favier books) serves almost to emphasise its conventionality. There is none the less some anticipation of Fanon, and McGowan's astute analysis of 'colonised' female alongside 'colonised' Black tends to highlight this:

> the power structure of gender, namely the internalised, involuntary, female constitution of self via the male gaze, is not contradicted or even suspended, but exists in the same narrative space as and runs in the opposite direction to, black subjection to the white gaze.[178]

We have seen something very similar at work in *La Femme et l'homme nu*, and it would be difficult to imagine a more striking contrast between its ending, quoted towards the end of the last chapter, and that of Louise Faure-Favier's *Blanche et Noir*. Other contrasts between the two novels— and with Goll's unhappy exercise in stereotyping—have even profounder resonances.

Faure-Favier's novel, an *éducation sentimentale* rather than an *exploitation sentimentale*, is set in the Upper Loire, Velay and Forez regions of France, which might lead us to expect a regionalist work, with the charm but also the limitations and foibles of the genre. Nothing could be further from the case. On the contrary, it is *La Femme et l'homme nu* which falls into the category, its detailed ethnology corresponding to parish-pump sociology bathed in an atmosphere of timeless prejudice, characterised by the racist gossip which Faure-Favier attributes to precisely the prim bourgeoisie that would relish colonial novels:

Un nègre! quelle horreur! S'amouracher d'un nègre, quelle aberration! Je n'y puis croire encore de la part d'une femme fine, délicate, je dirai presque d'esprit cultivé...

[A Negro! How awful! Falling in love with a Negro, what an aberration! I still can't believe it of such an intelligent, sensitive, I would almost say cultured woman...]

A moment spent with *Tirailleurs sénégalais*, seemingly almost obligatory in such a novel, finds them convalescing in Brittany. They certainly make a striking contrast with the 'blanches Bretonnes' [fair Breton girls], but Jeanne, the narrator, is less inclined to pity their plight than, with wit and irony, to anticipate the apparently nonsensical but in fact profound question that Jean Genet was to pose thirty years later in his epigraph to *Les Nègres*: 'Qu'est-ce que c'est donc un noir? Et d'abord, c'est de quelle couleur?' [What is a Black? And first and foremost, what colour is he?]:[179]

Un blanc, d'ailleurs, est-ce si beau? Et d'abord, qu'est-ce qu'un blanc? Est-ce ce collégien dont les pustules multicolores parsèment la barbe naissante? Est-ce ce vieillard bilieux? Est-ce cette jeune femme qui poudre son nez couperosé, ou est-ce son époux pelliculeux et dartreux dont l'occiput chenu forme des bourrelets rouges?...

Vraiment un blanc n'est jamais blanc. [...]

Mais voilà, les blancs ont décrété, dans leur fatuité, qu'ils détenaient la beauté du monde. Fi du jaune, fi du noir! Le blanc est la couleur idéale. Décret vain autant que puéril.

[What is more, is a White really so beautiful? And first and foremost, what is a White? Is it that schoolboy with his multi-coloured pustules dotted among the first hairs of his beard? Is it that bilious old man? Is it that young woman who powders the broken veins on her nose, or else her husband with dandruff and scurf whose hoary pate is puckered with red wrinkles?...

Really, a White is never White. [...]

But there you have it, Whites have decreed, in their self-conceit, that they alone possess the world's beauty. A fig for Yellows and Blacks! White is the ideal colour. Such a decree is as vain as it is puerile.][180]

The taboo inherent in the colonial mentality whereby it is unthinkable for a white woman to fall in love with a Black is deeply ingrained. In her eye-witness account, Lucie

Cousturier would appear not to have crossed the boundary erected by the colonialist's presupposition, whether within a novel or without, but her attitude is tantamount to doing so. Louise Faure-Favier, for her part, does not deny herself the liberating joy of a literary transgression of the taboo. One finds in her novel an echo not of the 'nègre macrophallique' [macrophallic negro],[181] nor of the presumptuous Black showing off by way of overcompensation or else finding in sex with a white woman the revenge envisaged by Fanon, but rather the other panel of the diptych, namely a white girl whose primary fascination is with the mystery of Africa. Yet that attitude, more evident in the character of Jeanne, the narrator, than in that of her grandmother, whose story we learn only indirectly, gives way in both instances to friendship with and love for an individual. It is in Mille and Demaison, not in Cousturier or Faure-Favier, that we find the over-endowed Black and the racial stereotyping. Tiékoro may not be a wholesale stud, but he nevertheless engages widely in love-making with the nubile girls in his village, with a prostitute in Saint-Raphaël, and with the Manding woman in Dakar, as well as with his *marraine de guerre* in search of exotic sexual adventure.

It is not women in general who attract Samba Laobé, it is Malvina Lortac-Rieux, and vice versa. They fall in love; they get married. What could be more natural? Social prejudice alone, embodied in colonial writings and attitudes, stands in opposition. Houssain recognises that

> ce roman est un document accablant sur le mythe du nègre dans une certaine bourgeoisie française des années 1900–1920. [...] Ce roman est en même temps un essai de réhabilitation à la manière de Lucie Cousturier, parfois un peu naïf mais touchant.

> [this novel is a damning indictment of the myth of the Negro as peddled around certain bourgeois milieux in 1900–1920 France. [...] This novel is at the same time an attempt at rehabilitation in the manner of Lucie Cousturier, sometimes a little naive, but touching.][182]

The same critic also believes that it does not go far enough in its treatment of the *Blanche/Noir* couple:

Louise Faure-Favier ose aborder ce thème, mais de manière indirecte et superficielle. [...] Les vrais problèmes sont éludés: une Blanche ne peut-elle aimer un Noir que s'il est particulièrement beau, intelligent, et cultivé? N'y a-t-il aucun problème entre un Noir dit "évolué" et une Blanche?

[Louise Faure-Favier dares to tackle the theme, but in an oblique and superficial manner. [...] The real problems are avoided: can a white woman love a black man only if he is outstandingly handsome, intelligent and cultured? Does no problem arise between a westernised Black and a white woman?][183]

The second part of this quotation, apparently in contradiction with the first, does not seem to me to take sufficient account of the considerable step taken by Faure-Favier towards a reading of the *Blanche/Noir* relationship which is both optimistic and well-grounded.

Most literary couples of the sort are doomed to suffer a tragic or negative ending. Malvina dies of a fever before marrying Samba Laobé according to Church rites, but after a recognised indigenous marriage and after their child is born. Not for a moment does she regret her choice. Given the conjunction of bourgeois and colonialist mentality in the 1920s, it would be difficult to go further, and as we have seen, Claire Goll went much less far. Faure-Favier pointedly sets Malvina's 'abduction' at the height of colonial expansionism, in 1889, and, symbolically, in the context of the Universal Exhibition, that show of jingoistic triumphalism, held that year. The coincidence of white niece and black uncle being born on the same day may be considered facile—the author laughs disarmingly at her own device: 'Ma généalogie n'est bicolore que par accident. Mais quel accident!' [My genealogy is two-coloured only by accident. But what an accident!]—but we know that twins have always played a special role in literature and we note that this unlikely couple is not what primarily fascinates the good people of Monistrol: that honour is reserved for Malvina and Samba Laobé. What is more, the friendship between Jeanne and François, mirroring the central *couple domino*, clearly signals, against bourgeois convention, the author's extended approval of their union. An ironic twist of fate is echoed in implicitly ironic language when Jeanne marries a pilot who is killed in the war six months later: her *mariage blanc* to a White is symbolically unconsummated. The treatment of the theme can scarcely be dismissed as oblique or superficial: it lies at the heart of the novel and resonates from generation to generation.

Can a woman be reproached for being attracted to a man who is 'particulièrement beau, intelligent, et cultivé' [particularly handsome, intelligent, and cultured]? Surely not, either in life or in fiction where such options are freely decided by the author. But in fact Faure-Favier, through her narrator, does not insist on Samba Laobé's physical beauty. She mentions his beauty, but insists rather on his courage, his presence and his distinction, calling him powerful, intelligent and enterprising:

> Samba Laobé fut le premier chef nègre qui utilisa, pour son commerce, le chemin de fer de Saint-Louis à Dakar. Il contribua ainsi à faire de la région jusqu'alors désertique du Cayor une des plus fertiles de l'Afrique Occidentale.

> [Samba Laobé was the first black chief to use the Saint-Louis–Dakar railway line for trade. He thus contributed to making the previously barren Cayor region one of the most fertile in West Africa.][184]

But we learn about these personal qualities only from page 188 onwards. The author's discretion in the matter is remarkable: by reversing the myth of the Black's ugliness when seen close up, Faure-Favier may go too far and fall into the trap of the idealising counter-myth, but at least she tends towards a more sensible balance. Explicitly, she takes her distance from the caricatures prevalent in children's books and colonial novels: it is young Jeanne, not the author herself, who exclaims:

> Je me souvins d'un nègre de mon album d'images. Il était couleur chocolat avec une couronne de plumes multicolores, le torse nu, les jambes nues.

[I remembered a Negro from my picture-book. He was chocolate coloured with a crown of multicoloured feathers, a bare chest, and naked legs.]

Implicitly, in her presentation of Samba Laobé and his son, she denounces the infantilising myth of the Negro, which was the dominant caricatural image of the time.[185]

As for Houssain's last reproach, regarding the lack of problems arising from a *Blanche/Noir* relationship, it is better founded. The author chooses to use a young narrator held in total ignorance until the age of ten about her grandmother's 'shameful' escapade and her black uncle's existence. Subsequently, she is fascinated by the puzzle which she endeavours to reconstruct from distorted or hidden pieces of information: only when her uncle François appears does she—do we—learn the full picture. The decision to emphasise the non-conformist aspect of Malvina and Samba Laobé's affair must be considered deliberate on the author's part. Comment on any difficulty within the marriage would have reduced its impact on the small-minded people of the country town and on the average reader of the time. The authorial decision is further underlined by having Jeanne fly off with François. 'Viol' [Rape] followed by 'vol' [flight/theft], no doubt, in bourgeois minds, but as Fanon remarked, 'une Blanche qui accepte un Noir, cela prend automatiquement un aspect romantique. Il y a don et non pas viol' [A white woman accepting a Black, that automatically assumes a Romantic coloration. It is giving rather than seizing].[186]

We have already mentioned that François Laobé-Rieux was married. It emerges only very late in the novel that his wife is white. The author does not insist on it, but this relationship adds a further thread to the already complex skein of *Blanche/Noir* couples in the novel. François had to face the racial prejudice of Yvonne's father, a French industrialist based in Dakar. Jeanne protests:

> Se peut-il qu'un homme intelligent ait pu refuser sa fille à un homme tel que vous? dis-je avec élan. Il ne savait donc pas discerner la valeur des êtres?'

['Is it possible for an intelligent man to refuse his daughter to a man like you?', I said with some passion. 'Was he incapable of seeing people's real value?]

Only Samba Laobé's intervention, shortly before his death, had persuaded Yvonne's father to relent, but the latter's shame had driven him back to France with his wife when their mulatto granddaughter was born. The author underlines the continuing nature of the struggle for justice and denounces the contradictions:

> Vous le voyez, François Laobé-Rieux recommence, pour ses enfants, la rude lutte de son père. C'est en vain qu'à Dakar, à Saint-Louis, à Rufisque, les frontons de nos monuments en ciment armé portent la grande devise: *Liberté, Egalité, Fraternité!* Des mots seulement et qui ne retentissent pas au cœur des hommes blancs. Ah! qu'ils sont peu fraternels aux nègres ces fonctionnaires que le gouvernement de la République multiplie dans ses colonies. Mais qui nous sera jamais fraternel?

> [You see, François Laobé-Rieux is beginning all over again for his children the struggle his father had. It's no good the façades of reinforced concrete monuments in Dakar, Saint-Louis and Rufisque being inscribed with the great motto: *Liberté, Egalité, Fraternité!* Such words are hollow, with no resonances in white men's hearts. Oh! how lacking in fraternity towards Blacks are all those civil servants scattered across its colonies by the Republic. Who will ever be fraternal towards us?][187]

To this last question, Jeanne's reply, however rapid and simplistic it may appear, echoes Cousturier and anticipates later feminists:

> — Les femmes, lui répondis-je. Les femmes reprendront, un jour, le beau rôle de médiatrice qui fut celui de Malvina Rieux, en 1890, dans le Sénégal encore insoumis. Les femmes, avec leur cerveau élargi et leur cœur meilleur: Voilà les véritables civilisatrices! Ce sont elles qui feront cesser ce terrible antagonisme de races et qui empêcheront les hommes, après s'être battus pour des territoires, pour des religions, pour de l'argent, de s'entre-tuer pour des couleurs...
> "Il leur suffira de décréter que la race noire vaut la race blanche et que la beauté réside là autant qu'ici, qu'un cerveau de noir est constitué de blanc et qu'il n'est qu'une humanité.["]

['Women', I answered. 'Women will one day assume the role of mediation played by Malvina Rieux, in 1890, in an as yet incompletely conquered Senegal. Women, with their larger brains and bigger hearts. They are the real civilisers! It is they who will bring an end to this terrible antagonism between the races and who will stop men, after their fights over territory, religion and money, killing each other over colours...

They will need do no more than decree that black people are equal in worth to white people, that beauty resides as much in you as in us, that a black brain is white, and that there is only one humanity.']188

Is this 'ébauche du thème [Blanche et Noir] chez une romancière' [sketch of the *Blanche/Noir* theme by a woman novelist] naive, as Houssain thinks?189 In some respects, yes, though Houssain seems as unaware of earlier instances as Faure-Favier is. Disarming innocence is a powerful weapon. François says about colonisers: 'Vous nous avez apporté votre civilisation, mais vous nous refusez votre affection' [You have brought us your civilisation, but you have refused us your affection]. Alain Ruscio considers this novel an 'étonnant ouvrage' [astonishing work], while adding his own caveat:

Ce n'est sans doute pas de la grande littérature, mais c'est écrit en 1928, et les bons sentiments, en ce domaine, ne sont pas alors légion.

[This is not great literature, perhaps, but it was written in 1928, and fine sentiments, in this area, were not then two a penny.]190

Gide's view of fine sentiments making bad literature seems to inform this opinion. But we recall, as Paul Morand noted at the time,

en 1928, la France se trouve à la tête de millions de nègres. Des nègres, il y en a, non seulement dans son empire colonial, mais sur le Rhin, sur la Côte d'Azur, dans ses usines, dans ses administrations, dans les ports [...]. Ces gens de couleur remplissent les hôtels meublés, les bars, peuplent nos nuits, donnent le ton à nos plaisirs.

[in 1928, France heads millions of Blacks. Blacks are everywhere: not only in her colonial empire, but also on the Rhine and the Riviera, in its factories, offices and docks [...]. These coloured people are filling the boarding-houses, the bars and our nights; they set the tone for our pastimes.][191]

The Whites who do not look down on them are not, indeed, two a penny, and official attitudes and histories have consistently played down their contribution. In the 1920s, we have to look to black Americans such as Claude McKay, presenting, in *Banjo*, well before Sembene, the dockers of Marseilles, to find in imaginative literature—as distinct from slave-narratives and similar autobiographies —Blacks who are fully rounded characters.[192]

Lucie Cousturier and Louise Faure-Favier nevertheless make a significant contribution and do not deserve the neglect from which they have both suffered, even at the hands of feminists. The velvet revolution they brought about in their different ways anticipates that of Negritude which has enjoyed far more publicity. Houssain sees that

> le temps de la démythification et de la réhabilitation a commencé juste après la première guerre mondiale avec Maurice Delafosse et Lucie Cousturier, insensiblement peut-être mais inéluctablement.

> [the time of demythification and rehabilitation started just after the First World War with Maurice Delafosse and Lucie Cousturier, imperceptibly perhaps, but irremediably.][193]

It seems to me that Louise Faure-Favier contributed to that movement in more ways than one, in that the governing metaphor of her novel, linked to the aviation that was her passion, symbolises the emancipation of the Negro as much as it does that of women.

Félicien Challaye, who started as an ardent colonist, learned from his experience:

> les avantages de la colonisation ne suffisent pas à compenser les injustices, les violences, les crimes de toute sorte qu'elle entraîne. Le passif l'emporte infiniment sur l'actif. On en sera convaincu si l'on essaie d'imaginer avec force toutes les souffrances des

indigènes, méprisés par leurs maîtres, brutalisés, volés, violés, tyrannisés, meurtris dans leur corps et dans leur cœur.

[the advantages of colonisation are not sufficient to compensate for the injustices, violence and crimes of all sorts perpetrated in its name. Its debit far outweighs its credit. To be convinced of that, you have only to imagine vividly all that the natives suffered, despised by their masters, brutalised, robbed, raped, tyrannised, wounded in body and heart.][194]

This is the system which, in its armed insistence on the innate superiority of the White, is reflected in colonial novels. But as Houssain rightly insists, 'on ne fonde pas un "humanisme" sur le mépris de l'autre' [no 'humanism' can be founded on contempt for others].[195] Lucie Cousturier and Louise Faure-Favier would agree wholeheartedly. But a lack of contempt is not adequate either. Demaison does not openly despise Tiékoro; on the contrary, he takes seriously the beliefs and social milieu which weigh upon him in so positivist a manner. But treating him as a specimen does not amount to treating him as a man, whereas the *Tirailleurs* presented by Cousturier are men, and she treats them as such. Similarly, despite the occasional drops of rose-water in Faure-Favier's novel, she draws her black characters as fully as her white.

The very fact of presenting a normal relationship between Blacks and Whites is a challenge to colonialist thinking. Just as Doin and Duras had, in the 1820s, called into question the prejudices of their society, so Cousturier and Faure-Favier do likewise, but against a new background: the intervening century had replaced slavery by colonialism. It also paraded a literature which approvingly and ostentatiously entrenched enduring prejudices against Blacks. Against this general lack of consideration, might would clearly not be right: example is more powerful an argument. So Cousturier and Faure-Favier bear witness, allowing their radical critique to emerge through explicit and implicit observations. Cousturier's closing comment and question have lost none of their force:

Si entre Blancs et Noirs, [...] existe une attraction de couleur et de formes, une attraction sexuelle, le grief de race est dénué de sens. Tel serait le reproche entre amants et maîtresses d'être de sexes différents. Ce serait d'idiots. Les Blancs le seraient-ils?

[If, between Blacks and Whites, [...] there exists an attraction of colours and forms, a sexual attraction, then racial grievance is meaningless. It would be like lovers and their beloved complaining of being of different sexes. They would be stupid. Is this what Whites are?][196]

Two years later, Gide's celebrated formula was to sound like a confirmation of this sad assessment: 'Moins le blanc est intelligent, plus le noir lui paraît bête' [The less intelligent the White is, the more stupid the Black appears to him].[197]

CHAPTER 5
THE FRENCH EMPIRE WRITES BACK

'Jusqu'à ce jour, l'homme blanc seul a parlé.
L'homme blanc, c'est le maître.
Le moment est venu de donner la parole à l'esclave.'
[So far, only white man has spoken.
The white man is master.
The time has come to give the slave a voice.]
Victor Hugo[198]

WHETHER the *Tirailleurs sénégalais* returned to West Africa or stayed on in France after the war, a huge number of Blacks had lived through an experience scarcely less profoundly alienating than that of earlier generations who had been subjected to the 'middle passage' of the now infamous triangular trade and transported to the New World. 'Quand on a connu la Blanche, on n'est plus tout à fait noir' [When you have known a white woman, you aren't completely black any longer].[199] *Tirailleurs sénégalais* were recurrent stereotypical figures in the writing and popular imagery of the period, but other Blacks were also making their mark.[200]

Administrators or intellectuals, *assimilés*, *nègres blancs* [white Negroes], well or ill white-washed, *négropolitains*, 'lactifiés' [dipped in milk] as Fanon would say, they also began to express themselves. The shift from being objects to subjects is a critical one. Increasingly aware of their condition, Blacks started 'writing back to the centre', in Salman Rushdie's memorable phrase.[201] Writing was by definition therefore a political act and, almost by definition up to the time of independence and sometimes beyond, reflected (to put it at its most neutral) relations with the French. While sociological considerations are sometimes

107

tinged with ideology, however, there is no evidence, such as one finds in equivalent English-language writing, of nationalism as such being a factor in African rejection of a white wife brought from Europe.[202]

The controversy stirred up by the Prix Goncourt being awarded to René Maran for *Batouala, véritable roman nègre* in 1921 had essentially extra-literary pretexts: could one or could one not allow a prize to be awarded to a swingeing critique of the colonial system made by a Black? While the novel was less hard-hitting than its preface, it set a pattern for the social and political protest which writers would treat in their different ways in the quest not just for tolerance— that leaves the tolerated in a position of inferiority—but for equality of respect.

What is clear is that Black writers take an interest in the *Blanche/Noir* couple as an emblematic nexus of the fraught relationships between coloniser and colonised. Yet in the early stages, an assumption of cultural inferiority is built in. Ousmane Socé's 1937 novel *Mirages de Paris*, to which I shall return shortly, has a debate focusing on miscegenation which shows the link between individual mixed-race relationships and a whole continent pulling itself out of its benightedness:

> Or, de nos jours, il se forme en Afrique noire, comme cela s'est fait chez tous les peuples, à une époque donnée de leur histoire, un véritable accouplement avec un pays plus avancé en civilisation, et d'où naîtra l'Afrique nouvelle.

> [Nowadays, in black Africa, just as in every nation at some stage of its history, a veritable coupling is taking place with a country whose civilisation is more advanced , and from which a new Africa will be born.][203]

One applauds the notion of cultural interaction while deploring the cap-in-hand stance engendered by centuries of acculturation. It scarcely seems the best basis for a marriage of true minds, whether at the individual or the collective level.

Oruno Lara's 1923 novel *Question de couleurs* evokes the author's fellow-Guadeloupeans in Paris and their preoccupation with skin-colour and racial subclassification. The principal friendship between two mulattos, René Frault and Nelly Guérin, has the former finally persuade the latter of the dignity of being a Black, and specifically 'un nègre', so anticipating Césaire's stance of a decade later:

> ... mieux valait se montrer tel qu'on était, se dire noir puisqu'on l'était, revendiquer le mot nègre, et travailler à s'instruire, à se perfectionner, pour arriver à faire respecter, dans les droits acquis, et le mot et la chose.

> ... un sentiment a grandi en moi. Une fierté, une conviction d'Humanité... J'étais un homme! Le mot nègre, était-ce un outrage? je l'acceptais. Mieux! je le réclamais. Et dès lors, la lutte commença.

> [... it was better to present oneself as one was, call oneself black because one was, to lay claim to the word Negro, and work to improve one's knowledge, perfect one's being, and inspire respect, through rights acquired, both for the word and for the thing.

> ... a feeling grew within me. A kind of pride, a conviction of being Human... I was a man! Was the word Negro an outrage? I accepted it. More than that! I claimed it. And thereafter the fight began.][204]

Replying to questions, Frault expresses opinions on *Blanche/Noir* relations which confirm the author's view, stated in the preface, of 'la grande influence de la femme, quelle que soit sa race, par sa collaboration aux mœurs, dans l'œuvre de progrès social et d'égalité humaine' [the great influence of women, of whatever race, through their moral contribution to the work of social progress and human equality]:

> — Pourquoi certaines blanches préfèrent-elles les noirs?
> — Ce n'est pas une préférence, c'est une tendance généreuse d'aimer ceux qui sont méconnus. Elles bravent les préjugés, et ouvrent les voies à l'avenir. Les blanches qui fréquentent les noirs sont les vraies messagères du Progrès.
> [...]
> — Pourquoi préfères-tu les femmes blanches?
> — Je ne les préfère pas, je les admire, je leur suis reconnaissant de nous faciliter la vie.

— Dis que tu les aimes!
— Ce sont des femmes.

['Why do certain white women prefer Blacks?'
'It isn't a preference, it's a generous tendency to love those
who are insufficiently known. They stand up to prejudice and open
avenues into the future. White women who frequent Blacks are
the real harbingers of Progress.'
[...]
'Why do you prefer white women?'
'I don't prefer them, I admire them, I'm grateful for the way
they make life easier.'
'Admit that you love them!'
'They are women.']

Unfortunately, all trace has been lost of a significant
short story of which Pierre Klein has written:

la première Nouvelle sénégalaise a, m'a-t-on dit de différents
côtés, été écrite en 1923 par Massyla Diop. Elle était intitulée "Le
Chemin du salut". Je n'ai pas réussi à la retrouver—Birago Diop,
frère [cadet] de Massyla, non plus; mais Birago m'a confirmé que
"Le Chemin du salut" traitait du tabou de la mixité raciale dans
le couple—on dit maintenant "le couple domino"—, plus fort selon
lui, à l'époque, que le tabou religieux.

[the first Senegalese short story, I am widely assured, was written
in 1923 by Massyla Diop. It was called 'The Road to Salvation'. I
have not been able to find a copy—Birago Diop, Massyla's
[younger] brother neither; but Birago has confirmed to me that
'The Road to Salvation' dealt with the taboo of the racial mixing
of couples—now called the *couple domino*—stronger at the time
than any religious taboo.][205]

Within the same decade, Bakary Diallo touches passingly
on the subject in his 1926 novel, *Force-bonté*. The innocent
eye of the already—by West African standards: remember
Anniaba?—pale Fula registers his first sight of a white
woman in his native town on the Senegal river:

Je rentre chez le traitant que l'on appelle Hache, le plus grand
commerçant de Podor, et j'y vois une personne jeune, aux cheveux
blonds dorés, aux yeux bleus. C'est la première fois que je vois une
femme blanche. Je me trouve devant des gens plus blancs que les

Foulbés. Je suis étonné, je les regarde et les entends parler; comme je ne les comprends pas, je me sens plus étonné encore.

[I went into the shop of the trader called Hache, the largest retailer in Podor, and I saw a young person with golden blond hair and blue eyes. It was the first time I saw a white woman. I'm facing people even whiter than the Fulbe. I'm astonished, look at them and hear them talk; as I don't understand what they say, I feel even more astonished.]

Bakary's subsequent experience in France as a *Tirailleur sénégalais* makes him boast: 'Bonheur à moi, j'ai une sœur en France... Je ne croyais pas trouver l'amitié des blancs pour les noirs' [How happy I am, I've a sister in France... I never expected to find white people befriending Blacks]. But the object of his excitement is Simone Baudry, some six or seven years old: his very naivety suggests that she was his only friend there.

In the 1920s, however, literature by Blacks attracted far less attention (Negritude had its beginnings only in the 1930s and its time of glory only after the Second World War) than Negro art. 'Discovered' in 1905 by the Fauves, who in turn inspired the Cubists—despite Picasso's *boutade*: 'l'art nègre, connais pas!' [Negro art, don't know it]— welcomed by the Surrealists who then rejected it *en bloc* to mark their disapproval firstly, in 1925, of the French intervention in Morocco and then of the Colonial Exhibition in 1931, Negro art exerted its influence on a whole generation of French writers.[206]

It is among the popular arts, however, that the extent of contemporary 'negrophilia' can be measured. Paul Morand writes of 'l'engouement nègre' [the Negro craze], declaring that 'notre âge est un âge nègre' [our age is the age of the Negro].[207] It would be difficult to overstate the impact of jazz, the Revue nègre, the Bal nègre in the rue Blomet, of Josephine Baker, even of Al Jolson blacked up in *The Jazz Singer* of 1927, firstly on the fashionable youth of Paris, then gradually spreading like a bush-fire through 'un public avide de dépaysement et d'exotisme' [a populace hungry for escape and exoticism] after the privations of war.[208] Posters, in which Apollinaire, in 'Zone', had seen a kind of poetry, but which perpetuated stereotypical distortions, invited passers-by to savour the delights of the Bal nègre or a chocolate drink proposed by *Tirailleurs sénégalais* wreathed in those 'rires Banania' [Banania smiles] which would so outrage Senghor.[209] The decorative arts and publicity reflected the fashion while helping to set it.[210] The popular imagination was also stimulated by new means of contact with Africa. Mermoz and Saint-Exupéry were among the heroes of the Aéropostale which linked France with South America, stopping over at Saint-Louis in Senegal. The present-day Paris–Dakar rally is the offspring of the first crossing of the Sahara by automobile in 1923 and of central Africa in 1924–25.[211]

The fame of André Gide—he occupied a place in French intellectual life that Sartre would fill later—was sufficient for his *Voyage au Congo* of 1927 and the sequel, *Retour au Tchad*, of the following year to enjoy a wide readership. Was it enough to counterbalance the considerable influence of Lévy-Bruhl's racially supercilious *Les Fonctions mentales dans les sociétés inférieures* (1910), *La Mentalité primitive* (1922) and *La Mythologie primitive* (1925) before he recanted? It may be doubted, since Gide explicity acknowledged his debt. Even so, some of his denunciations of the ravages of France's *mission civilisatrice*, echoed by Denise Moran's *Tchad* (1934) and, even more polemically, by the journalist Albert Londres in articles printed in *Le Petit Parisien* and collected under the title *Terre d'ébène* in 1929, trounced some of the reassuring stereotypes of colonialism. Against that, the picturesque exoticism of Paul Morand in *Magie noire* and *Paris-Tombouctou*, both published in 1928, tended to reinforce prejudices, while in their own zany way the Surrealists continued to sabotage received opinions.[212] There was no lack of people to defend the system, however, but its official apotheosis at the 1931 Exposition Coloniale can also be seen as its swan-song.[213] Voices such as Céline's and Césaire's would soon arise to spoil the self-satisfied harmony, and the Second World War would add a cacophony which could only bring the end of colonialism nearer.

112

The *Blanche/Noir* couple is clearly fascinating for Black writers, but it should not be assumed that they readily escape from the pervasive stereotypes. Even so, the fact that for the first time the question is seen from the angle of black authors is significant. However timid their initial explorations, a body of work will gradually accrue to counterbalance and challenge the prevailing dominance and assumptions of white writers, even of those most sympathetic to their case (sometimes the most prone to stereotyping).

Ousmane Socé Diop places a *Blanche/Noir* couple at the heart of his novel, *Mirages de Paris*, first published in 1937, and sets down an important marker in several respects. A bright young Senegalese, Fara, steeped in idealised images of France drawn from his schoolbooks, travels to Paris to attend the 1931 Colonial Exhibition. There he meets, woos and marries Jacqueline Bourciez, cut off by her racist father but enjoying her mother's discreet and limited support. Not only will a thinly veiled autobiographical narrative basis of travel to France (usually for the purposes of study) recur time and again in writings by French-speaking Blacks: this novel inaugurates a series of *romans à thèse* spelling out the different interracial positions adopted, complete with their hypocrisies and self-contradictions, and the constant danger of falling between two cultures.

The initial description of Fara, with 'le front fuyant et le nez aux ailes larges' [a receding forehead and flared nostrils], escapes from the Oroonoko syndrome of reference to European Classical models. In a similar vein, when he leaves the Koranic school for 'l'école des blancs' [the white man's school], he confronts the French teacher:

> Ils se rendirent dans une maison où une femme "aux oreilles rouges" faisait répéter, à de petits noirs, des mots absolument vides de sens. Une femme haute, mince et qui avait des yeux bleus comme ceux des chats. Elle portait un vêtement semblable au cafetan et sur la tête une sorte de calebasse, à larges bords, pareille aux chapeaux des bergers de la brousse; autour de la calebasse s'enroulait un ruban noir.

[They went into a house where a woman with red ears was making black boys repeat words totally devoid of meaning. A tall, thin woman, with blue eyes like a cat's. She was wearing a garment like a caftan and a kind of calabash on her head, with a wide brim, like the hats that shepherds wear in the bush; around the calabash was tied a black ribbon.]

The point of departure for comparison is local experience. Yet such projections had proved possible in European imaginations: in the wake of the ironic stance famously inaugurated by Montesquieu's *Lettres persanes*, Bernardin de Saint-Pierre speaks through Annibal, head of the black slaves in *Empsaël et Zoraïde* (II, v), to describe the European dress of the time:

> J'ai quelquefois ri en les voyant débarquer de leur pays. Il y en avait qui avaient sur leur tête de grands paquets de cheveux qui n'étaient pas à eux. Ils les avaient couverts de graisse de porc et de farine, et d'une coiffure noire à trois cornes. J'en ai dépouillé un, un jour, dans un vaisseau que nous prîmes. Je trouvai dans son habillement, de la tête aux pieds, vingt-sept pièces différentes, cinquante-deux boutons, six boucles, et douze poches remplies d'une multitude de choses dont ils ne sauraient se passer.

> [I've sometimes laughed when they disembarked from their country. Some of them were wearing on their heads great bunches of hair which didn't belong to them. They had smeared them with dripping and flour, and covered them with a black headpiece with three horns. I stripped one of them one day in a ship we took. I found in his garments, from head to toe, twenty-seven different items, fifty-two buttons, six buckles and twelve pockets filled with a host of things they couldn't do without.][214]

Fara's French schooling nourishes both his introspection and his view of France as a distant world of wonders. Travelling there by ship exposes him to stock attitudes struck by his fellow-passengers, some insidiously favour-able—'Je vous assure que les Noirs sont capables d'assimiler notre culture aussi bien scientifique que littéraire' [I assure you that Blacks are capable of assimilating our culture, both scientific and literary]—with French culture the measure and goal of such efforts, and others archetypally hostile but in some ways more empowering in prompting reaction to their brutal bluntness: 'vos sujets doués pourraient n'être que d'habiles perroquets qui vous récitent des choses auxquelles ils n'ont rien compris' [your best pupils could be just clever parrots, reciting back to you things that they haven't understood]. For the purposes of continuing trade and political domination, such people think the less learning the better:

> il ne faut pas trop leur ouvrir les yeux, car vous n'en feriez que des "éléments dangereux" et le jour où ils verront très clair, ils nous f... à la porte!

> [you mustn't open their eyes too much, or they'll become 'dangerous elements', and the day they see things clearly they'll kick us out!]

'On ne peut plus rien faire à la colonie avec des Noirs émancipés' [You can do nothing more in the colony now the Blacks are emancipated]. A heavily emphasised shift from the belittling 'tu' to the polite 'vous' and on to addressing Fara as 'Monsieur' plots the course in hypocrisy which those holding such views adopt when, finding Fara intelligent, courteous and well-spoken, they proudly show him round their home ground of Bordeaux.

What would spark off in Fanon a tormented psychoanalysis of black identity, the innocent remark of a child about his colour, is handled with greater aplomb and balance by Socé:

> Maman, regarde le monsieur! Il a oublié de se débarbouiller, disait à sa mère, en levant un petit index timide, un blondinet aux cheveux dorés et au teint de maïs.

> ['Mummy, look at that man! He's forgotten to wash himself,' said a little boy with golden hair and maize-coloured skin, raising his finger timidly.]

Fara does the sensible thing and offers the child his hand, leaving not a trace on the tiny fingers and only indifference in his mind: 'il se désintéressa du monsieur' [he took no more interest in the man]. It is at least a beginning.

115

As to the love between Fara and Jacqueline, it burgeons despite the latter's hesitations, burdened as she is not only with an awareness of ambient hostility but also, and more specifically, with that of her father:

> dans leurs sorties, des gens les dévisageaient d'étrange façon; chez les uns c'était un peu de surprise [...]; d'autres manifestaient de la tolérance; chez tel spontané, on remarquait une réaction non dissimulée qui le mettait en arrêt comme un chien qui découvre un objet intéressant.

> [on their outings, people looked at them strangely; some registered a degree of surprise; others showed tolerance; in one case, they saw a spontaneous reaction when a man stopped short like a dog finding something interesting.]

When Jacqueline broaches the subject of her love for Fara, 'son père manqua d'étouffer de colère' [her father nearly choked with anger]. After she has left the house, he bursts with indignation: 'La sal...! s'écria M. Bourciez. Dis-moi immédiatement où elle est allée avec ce nègre! Je crois que je vais la tuer!' ['The hus...!' shouted Mr Bourciez. 'Tell me immediately where she's gone with that nigger! I think I'm going to kill her!']

Powerless and increasingly penniless, the couple live on love and dreams, the latter fed by reading novels in both cases (see pp. 14, 97), in the manner of Emma Bovary. But there is also realism about any hypothetical return to Africa:

> — En Afrique vous seriez malheureuse, fit observer Fara, c'est un climat incommode pour vous et vous y rencontreriez de l'hostilité.
> — De la part des indigènes?
> — Et des blancs aussi qui vous regarderont de travers pour des raisons de prestige de leur race en terre coloniale.
> — Et les indigènes n'aiment pas les Français? Vous m'avez pourtant dit qu'ils étaient citoyens français?
> — Oui, mais en matière matrimoniale ils ont, comme vos parents, leurs préjugés.

> ['In Africa you would be unhappy', Fara remarked, 'It's a difficult climate for you and you'd encounter hostility.'
> 'From the natives?'

'And from Whites looking askance at you for reasons of racial prestige in a colonial territory.'

'Don't the natives like the French? You told me that they were French citizens.'

'Yes, but where marriage is concerned, they, like your parents, have their prejudices.']

The fullest reflection on mixed-race relations comes in chapter XII, when Fara goes to tell his Senegalese friend Sidia, a philosophy student, about the impending birth of his child. While Sidia's arguments are rational and plausible, he speaks strongly in favour of racial purity. We are clearly intended to side with Fara who, implicitly following Pascal—'Le cœur a ses raisons que la raison ne connaît point' [The heart has its reasons which reason knows nothing of]—allows an emotional dimension to colour his position: 'Deux êtres qui s'aiment se moquent bien des théories et même des interdictions' [Two people who love one another pay no heed to theories or even to a ban]. Countering Sidia's adverse views on miscegenation, Fara points to his friend's inevitable cultural and intellectual *métissage* by the very fact of studying in Europe:

c'est encore du métissage et du véritable car ce qui fait un homme c'est encore plus sa culture et ses idées que la coloration de sa peau.

[that's still miscegenation, and the real sort, for what makes a man is far more his culture and ideas than the colouring of his skin.]

No more than Ourika can Sidia return to Senegal and marry within his religion or intellectual class. The dialogue of opposing ideas, political versus cultural, propounded here by the author closely mirror those being developed at the time on the one side by Hitler, here adumbrated by Sidia, and on the other by Socé's friend Senghor, represented by Fara. What is added is a specific call for Senegalese women to be educated.[215]

The narrative turns to unalleviated tragedy: privations contribute to Jacqueline's death in childbirth. The baby boy is adopted by her parents, and while M. Bourciez extends a stiff hand of sympathy to Fara, he lectures him, his moral blinkers still firmly in place:

> les "convenances" veulent qu'on ne sorte pas de sa race pour se marier et même de sa sphère sociale; [...] il faut épouser une femme de votre race et de votre pays... cela vaut mieux à tous les points de vue; ceux qui agissent contre l'ordre naturel des choses en pâtissent toujours...

> [the 'proprieties' expect people to marry within their race and even within their class; [...] you should marry a woman of your own race and country... it's better from every point of view; those who go against the natural order of things always suffer...]

Fara reflects: 'Il ne s'obstinerait plus à demeurer sur cette terre d'Europe où il ne serait qu'un étranger' [He would not insist on staying in Europe, where he would always be a stranger]. Sidia encourages him to return with him to Senegal, and the passage is booked. Staring into the water from a bridge over the Seine, he sees an apparition of Jacqueline reminiscent of the Lady of the Lake. But for him there is no Excalibur: to embrace his insubstantial vision he plunges into the beckoning water, and the novel's closing words lead us to suppose that it is to a pointless death.

Symbolically, his suicide encapsulates the impossibility at the time of bridging the socio-cultural gap between Blacks and Whites, and there will be many more protagonists in novels by black Africans who confront the difficulties and are bruised by their experiences. The rooted racism of a M. Bourciez is in many ways easier to cope with than displays of kindness. Fara, hypersensitive, interprets smiles in his own way: 'Dans la rue il retrouvait sur le sourire des passants cette même ironie protectrice qui le criblait de flèches!...' [In the street he read into the smiles of passers-by that same irony which pierced him with arrows!]. He is in a no-win situation, damned either by overt conservatism or by the self-doubt generated by years of oppression and acculturation. Until individual confidence can grow within a context of racial and social confidence, the Black is trapped in a mesmerising hall of mirrors. The historical importance of Negritude is that, whatever its limitations, it provides, against the background of French exploitation and paternalism, a platform for confidence.

Negritude will enjoy its full flowering only after the Second World War, with the launch of *Présence Africaine* and the first Paris edition of Césaire's *Cahier d'un retour au pays natal*, including André Breton's eulogy, in 1947, and the publication of Senghor's ground-breaking *Anthologie de la nouvelle poésie nègre* in 1948. Its seminal preface by Sartre, 'Orphée noir' [Black Orpheus], gave it exceptional publicity. He had already explored a *Blanche/Noir* relationship in his 1946 play, *La P... respectueuse*. While its setting in the U.S.A. puts a different slant on the attitudes explored, as they shift from the white prostitute's denunciation of the black escapee to sympathy with him, its focus on racism there is not without its implications for French audiences. While one expects black writers to invite them to reflect in a new way on their racial prejudices and the traditional representation of the Negro, it is sufficiently unusual in white writers to be worthy of note. The culmination of the type will be Genet's *Les Nègres* of 1959.

André Roussin's *La Petite Hutte* (1947), however different in tone, with its fantasy and badinage, has a black protagonist and in its way calls his status into question. The archetypal *ménage à trois* is reduced to its emblematic essentials by having the trio shipwrecked on a desert island. A no less emblematically mute Man Friday appears in the guise of 'un jeune Noir superbe, statue vêtue d'un simple pagne' [a superb young Black, a statue dressed in a simple loincloth], otherwise wearing only feathers in his hair and a lei round his neck. Archetypes are exploited for amusement: with the two Whites roped to a tree, the white woman takes delight in making stereotypical assumptions, firstly that the Black is a prince and secondly that he wants her favours in return for the release of her husband and lover. The pantomime bubble is burst when the Savage turns out to be none other than a French cook from the ship's galley, when, as Chalaye puts it, 'le prince charmant

119

redevient crapaud' [Prince Charming turns back into a toad]. Suzanne's reaction is to want him lynched, coupling racism with class prejudice, as is also the case in *La Reine blanche*, by Pierre Barillet and Jean-Pierre Grédy (1953).[216]

Our focus in this chapter is rather on black writers, however, and two novels from the late 1940s deserve particular attention. In 1947, René Maran, the author who made his name with *Batouala* in 1921, controversially winning the Prix Goncourt, published *Un homme pareil aux autres*. The allied position against Hitler in the Second World War presupposes hostility to racism. Even if not universal, the rapid evolution of enlightened social attitudes, the spread of tolerance along with increased contact, the recognition that miscegenation is not necessarily a *pis-aller* nor its offspring monsters, these were welcome developments which the *prise de conscience* of Negritude had, in its intellectual sphere, fostered and recorded to some degree.

Fanon argues that, as a response to acculturation, 'le Noir veut être Blanc' [the Black wants to be a White], and no more so than when with a white person. The process of enwhitenment is characterised in a nutshell at the opening of chapter 3 of his *Peau noire, masques blancs*:

> De la partie la plus noire de mon âme, à travers la zone hachurée me monte ce désir d'être tout à coup *blanc*.
>
> Je ne veux pas être reconnu comme *Noir*, mais comme *Blanc*.
>
> Or—et c'est là une reconnaissance que Hegel n'a pas décrite— qui peut le faire, sinon la Blanche? En m'aimant, elle me prouve que je suis digne d'un amour blanc. On m'aime comme un Blanc.
>
> Je suis un Blanc.

> [From the blackest part of my soul, through the hatched zone, wells up this sudden desire to be *white*.
>
> I don't want to be recognised as a *Black*, but as a *White*.
>
> Now—and this is something Hegel did not describe—who can do that, other than a white woman? By loving me, she proves that I am worthy of 'white' love. I am loved as a White.
>
> I am a White.]

This suspect syllogism is denounced lengthily by Fanon through the fictional case of Jean Veneuse in Maran's *Un homme pareil aux autres*, in whom Fanon sees 'une structure d'abandonnique du type négatif-régressif' [an abandonment syndrome of the negative-regressive type]. As a literary critic rather than a pyschiatrist, I see the book in a different light, for its naive optimism. On the human plane, I subscribe fully to Fanon's declaration: 'notre but est de rendre possible pour le Noir et le Blanc une saine rencontre' [our aim is to make a healthy encounter between Black and White possible], but as the present book shows, neither of us is the first to envisage that possibility.[217]

Like some earlier and many later novels investigated here, *Un homme pareil aux autres* establishes a plausible naturalistic framework within which a black man and a white woman, exercising a free choice, can fall in love and marry. Veneuse was brought up and schooled in France, though we are given no details as to his exact colonial provenance, his age on arrival in France, or his precise personal and family circumstances. They none the less appear remarkably like Maran's own, born as he was in the West Indies, educated at Bordeaux and, after joining the Colonial Service, posted to Africa. In the opening three-page section, set in italics to indicate its status as a preface, the fictional Jean Veneuse, the focalising narrator of this programmatic novel, presents the work as a 'récit, qui constitue moins un livre à thèse ou un état de race qu'un état d'âme' [narrative constituting less a philosophical novel or an overview of race relations than a state of mind]. What is seen here as the lesser might well be perceived by the reader as the greater. Indeed, the last paragraph of the introduction both legitimises such a view and calls for the page to be turned on pseudo-scientific 'proofs' of racial inferiority:

> *Le livre que voici n'est, au fond, que le voyage d'une race à une autre et d'un cœur à un autre cœur. Puisse-t-il, par sa simplicité sans apprêt et son dépouillement, imposer silence aux préjugés, aux sophismes et aux partis pris, qui cherchent à transformer les arrêts changeants de sciences trop souvent faillibles en autant d'impératifs ethniques.*

> [The present book is basically no more than the journey from one race to another and from one heart to another heart. May it,

in its very artless simplicity and its spareness, silence the prejudice, sophistry and partisanship which seek to transform the shifting and all too fallible decrees of science into so many ethnic imperatives.]

Veneuse presents himself:

je ne suis qu'un nègre, un nègre qui, par son intelligence et son travail assidu, s'est élevé à la réflexion et à la culture de l'Europe.

[I am merely a Negro, a Negro who, thanks to his intelligence and hard work, has raised himself to the level of European thinking and culture.]

Working in the colonial service, one of the standard aspirations of educated Blacks in the French Empire, he sails from Bordeaux for the Congo, charged by a friend to look after the newly-wed Clarisse Demours while on board. In identical terms, he is presented first in general and then to her as 'un nègre comme on voudrait qu'il y eût beaucoup de blancs' [a Negro such as you would like many Whites to be], a distant echo of the title of Joseph de La Vallée's 1789 novel, *Le Nègre comme il y a peu de blancs*. More generally, the comment underlines the necessary distinction between skin-colour and moral calibre. We recall that Shakespeare, through the Duke of Venice speaking to Brabantio, Desdemona's father, makes just that distinction in respect of Othello:

If virtue no delighted beauty lack,
Your son-in-law is far more fair than black.
(I, iii, 289–90)

Just as the deeds of the Moor of Venice single him out as an exceptional captain, so Veneuse stands out as remarkable to his European friends, but in an ironic way reminiscent of Montesquieu's question 'Comment peut-on être persan?' [How can anyone be Persian?]. That Veneuse should be a thinly veiled autobiographical projection suggests that Maran relishes that irony at the expense of the White speaking:

Etre nègre, a-t-on en effet idée d'être nègre? Voilà qui est déjà singulier, à une époque où les blancs ont envahi toutes les parties du monde. Mais être nègre, et fonctionnaire colonial, et cultivé par-dessus le marché, voilà qui est prodigieux, renversant, miraculeux!

[To be black, could anyone ever think of being black? That's peculiar enough, when Whites have invaded every part of the world. But to be black, and a colonial administrator, and cultured into the bargain, that really is extraordinary, staggering, miraculous!]

An early *tête-à-tête* between Veneuse and Clarisse refers specifically to Othello's jealousy. Thus far, they have met largely in the company of others, and Veneuse's colour-sensitivity to the fact that she has left them to talk to him alone masks both an inferiority complex and a degree of vanity tinged with pride:

— Vous êtes venue trouvez [*sic*] l'ours que je suis! Prenez garde, petite madame. C'est beau d'avoir du courage! Mais vous allez vous compromettre, si vous continuez à vous afficher de la sorte. Un nègre, fi donc! Ça ne compte pas! C'est déchoir que frayer avec quelque individu que ce soit de cette race.

['You have come back to see what a bear I am! Take care, young lady. It's all very well being brave. But you are going to compromise yourself if you carry on doing such things in public. A Negro, watch out! That doesn't count. It is demeaning to go around with anyone of that race.]

Going on banteringly to list the European travellers who would be wittier and more respectable company for her, Veneuse prompts the following riposte:

— Je comprends maintenant. Monsieur est jaloux, il me fait une scène rentrée. Othello, va! Laissez-moi cependant vous dire que vous avez tort de me chanter pouilles. S'il me fallait choisir entre les gens que vous avez nommés et vous, malgré votre... couleur, je vous affirme que c'est vous que je choisirais sans hésitation.
L'aveu, direct, me flatte infiniment.

['Now I understand. You are jealous, and want to hide your game. You Othello, you! Let me tell you that you're wrong to jeer

at me. If I had to choose between the people you've mentioned and you, despite your... colour, I can assure you that I would choose you, without any hesitation.'
This blunt confession is infinitely flattering to me.]

That this is the start of a shipboard romance will surprise nobody. But Veneuse avoids jealousy (as well as the more overt reference to Othello that Goll had favoured) and uses this relationship and another social friendship (with Madame Coulanges) to understand better the more profound and lasting love that he has for one Andrée Marielle in Paris. The intriguing psychology expressed at this point has nothing to do with skin-colour:

> Le comble, c'est que j'aime moralement Andrée dans Mme Coulanges et physiquement avec Clarisse. C'est insensé. Mais il en est ainsi. J'aime Clarisse, j'aime Mme Coulanges, bien que je ne pense ni à l'une ni à l'autre. Elles ne sont pour moi qu'un alibi me permettant de me donner à moi-même le change. J'étudie Andrée en elles et apprends à la connaître par cœur.

> [What is extraordinary is that I love Andrée morally in Madame Coulanges and physically in Clarisse. It's crazy. But that's the way it is. I love Clarisse, I love Madame Coulanges, although I think of neither of them. For me they are just an alibi letting me pull the wool over my eyes. I study Andrée in them and learn to know her by heart.]

It is on this same page that the title is woven into the texture of the book after the opposite contention—'Un Nègre n'est pas un homme comme les autres' [A Negro is not a man like anyone else]—had been postulated earlier:

> je ne sais plus qu'une chose: c'est que le nègre est un homme pareil aux autres, et que son cœur, qui ne paraît simple qu'aux ignorants, est aussi compliqué que peut l'être celui du plus compliqué des Européens.
> J'aime Clarisse. J'aime Mme Coulanges. Et c'est Andrée Marielle que j'aime. Elle seule, pas une autre.

> [I know only one thing now, and that is that the Negro is a man like any other, and that his heart, which appears simple only to ignorant people, is as complicated as the most complicated European one.

124

I love Clarisse. I love Madame Coulanges. And it's Andrée Marielle I love. She alone, not someone else.]

This love survives the vicissitudes and pressures of arrival in the Congo and the prejudices towards a black-and-white relationship brought to bear by both Blacks and Whites. Moreover, it survives the death on service in Tchad of M. Demours, Clarisse's husband. When Veneuse gives her the news, she merely reiterates her love for him and offers to follow him, something that neither the administration officially nor he personally can accept. And his rebuff turns her brand of loving into an emotional over-reaction, with contempt expressed in explicitly racial terms: 'Sale nègre, va! Sale nègre! Je te hais, toi et toute ta race' ['Dirty nigger! You dirty nigger! I hate you, you and all your race'].

Part II of the novel describes the rounds of a provincial administrator and presents *in extenso* his lengthy correspondence with Andrée in particular, but also with a somewhat mollified Clarisse and other friends. His readings also occupy considerable space, a full list of the books in his luggage having been somewhat disconcertingly given at an early stage. Eight pages are devoted to his enthusiastic reflexions on André Suarès. (Such showing off—encapsulated in a fondness among black writers for the imperfect subjunctive long after its demise as a living tense in France—has been the butt of critical comment.) Finally he returns to Paris, with the reader still uncertain as to the future of his relationship with Andrée, whom we meet only in the last three pages of the book. In reply to Veneuse's proposal of marriage, high-minded unspoken words are attributed to her: 'L'amour est plus fort que la mort, plus fort que les haines de races' [Love is stronger than death, stronger than racial hatred], and her consent is reduced to a nod, a sigh and weakness at the knees in, as the closing maxim has it, 'le silence des gens qui préfèrent se taire, parce qu'ils ont trop à se dire' [the silence of people who prefer to remain silent, because they have too much to say to one another].

While the reader is no doubt intended to feel a warm glow at the happy reunion of the faithful couple and the implied abolition of racial barriers, the programmatic and sententious nature of the novel reduces our sympathy for its tenets, however admirable they may be to the wishful thinking of the liberal mind. For nothing is in fact resolved. The dreamy idealism of the ending, laced as it is with a high emotional charge, is only a beginning, and there is no guarantee that this love, biodegradable like any other, will not turn sour and again reduce the black hero to a 'sale nègre' [dirty nigger]. If for its romanticism alone, *Un homme pareil aux autres* largely escapes the shadow of Othello, the reference to him as the epitome of jealousy being merely made in passing as an almost inevitable courtesy to a more illustrious black predecessor in love with a white woman. It is as if Maran had been prompted by Camus's *Le Mythe de Sisyphe* of 1942 to think that 'il faut imaginer Othello heureux' [you have to imagine Othello happy]. But the hope seems pious: we are not necessarily persuaded that the future is all roses, especially as both the precedent of Shakespeare's play and the *dénouements* of the majority of the other works we are investigating here leave little room for optimism.

Although not published until 1953, Jean Malonga's *Cœur d'Aryenne* is, no doubt with intentional ironic symbolism, dated 14 July 1948 at the end. Set in the author's native Congo, it has a dramatic beginning: Solange, a ten-year-old white girl, carried away in a flood on the Likouala river and threatened by a cayman, is saved by the heroic efforts of a local boy, Mambéké. It is in fact a proleptic analogue of the tragic ending. Marie-Rose, Solange's mother, is scolded by her brutish, depraved, racist husband, Roch Morax, a white trader in the isolated village of Mossaka, for allowing Solange out of her sight. Yet he has, so to speak, fostered interracial contacts by fathering several mixed-race children. 'Roch Morax, qui s'est frotté à la femme noire, ne peut plus s'en passer et s'en détacher' [Roch Morax, having tasted black flesh, can no longer do without it or keep away from it]. He has sex with black girls as young as ten, and Mambéké's sister aged eleven is made pregnant by him.

What is sauce for the gander is clearly not, in his mind, sauce for the goose. Morax represents an improbable absolute of racial intolerance and abuse. His attitude is clearly exacerbated by the colour of his daughter's rescuer, who becomes her best childhood friend. Their friendship blossoms into love in which, because of Mambéké's deference, Solange invariably takes the initiative.

A sense of real exchange emerges in the children's friendship: when Solange offers lessons in French and the catechism, Mambéké in return teaches her to swim, fish and paddle a canoe. Communing with Solange, aged fourteen, after her mother's early death, Mambéké, aged sixteen, engages in self-examination:

> il faut qu'il s'entraîne sérieusement à savoir se contrôler, diriger ses impulsions, discipliner avec sévérité ses impulsions spontanées et mettre un frein à son impétuosité innée. Oubliait-il donc qu'il se trouvait en face d'une personne blanche, d'une jeune fille du camp aryen, camp impénétrable, rendu encore plus inaccessible par le rideau racial? Ne lui avait-on pas déjà assez dit?

> [he must make a serious effort to control and channel his impulses, severely discipline his spontaneous impulsions and rein in his natural impetuousness. Was he forgetting that he was with a white person, a girl from the impenetrable Aryan camp, made even more inaccessible by the racial curtain? Had he not been told that time and again?]

Solange 'lui sourit de tout son cœur, de tout son petit cœur peut-être prêt malgré le barrage épidermique à s'ouvrir pour lui' [smiled at him with all her heart, with all her little heart, ready perhaps despite the epidermic barricade to open itself to him.]

Those naive notions of 'le rideau racial' [the racial curtain] and 'le barrage épidermique' [the epidermic barricade] are entirely learned concepts on both sides. The problem is that, even in the mouths of children, they reinforce the lack of subtlety evident in the book, whose good intentions are worn on its metaphorical sleeve. Indeed, following an innocent embrace, the author's laboured comment reveals his ignorance of a long tradition, but in a real sense every relationship is pioneering:

> nous croyons sincèrement devoir nous incliner bien bas devant ces jeunes précurseurs, ces maçons hardis et courageux d'un édifice indispensable à la famille humaine, à la société de demain dans un monde plus sensible [...]. Tant pis! si c'est une utopie.

> [we sincerely believe that we must bow low before these young precursors, these bold and valiant builders of an edifice which is indispensible for humanity, for tomorrow's society in a more sensitive world [...]. Too bad if it's a utopia.]

When Malonga refers to them as 'nos deux révolutionnaires' [our two revolutionaries], Stendhal's tongue-in-cheek precedent, referring insistently to the floundering Fabrice at Waterloo as 'notre héros' [our hero], seems sadly missing.

Solange proudly asserts:

> Je l'ai tué, moi, ton sale complexe [d'infériorité], ce serpent visqueux, ce garrot qui t'entourait la gorge, t'empêchait de parler, de m'ouvrir ton cœur. Tu me demandes si je sais ce qui me reste à faire? Eh bien! oui, je le sais. Je vais devenir tout simplement ta femme devant Dieu. Je viens de tuer en moi l'Aryenne en même temps que j'écrasais ton complexe. Maintenant je t'offre mon cœur d'Aryenne. [...] Allons! cher époux, viens maintenant embrasser [...] l'Aryenne inaccessible.

> [I have killed it, your wretched [inferiority] complex, that slimy snake, that noose around your neck which stopped you speaking and opening your heart to me. You ask me if I know what I'm to do next? Of course I do! I shall simply become your wife before God. I have killed the Aryan in me at the same time as I crushed your complex. Now I offer you my Aryan heart. [...] Come here, my husband, and kiss your inaccessible Aryan.]

The orphaned youngsters in town are taken under her wing by a school inspector's wife, who foresees l'impossibilité d'une union légitime entre ses deux protégés [...] à cause des préjugés de l'époque non encore faite à l'idée du mariage des couleurs.

[the impossibility of a legitimate union between her two wards because of the prejudices of an age not yet ready to embrace the idea of a mixed-race marriage.]

Writing fifty years later of Europeans in the Congo at the same period, Henri Lopes confirms that for them a *Blanche/Noir* relationship was unthinkable.[218] It is, as we have seen, a prejudice embodied in Morax. Without his wife to help him at the trading-post, he summons Solange to return and then, when she becomes ill (in fact pregnant unbeknown to him), appoints a young White, Linard, as an assistant, and likes him enough to propose marrying him to his daughter. Meanwhile, Mambéké, after training in Europe, takes up a post as head of a new school in Mossaka, while Morax and Linard conveniently go off hunting elephants for three months. Solange has a son, Bienvenu, in their absence, and Morax, on his discovery of the father's identity, grabs a pistol which goes off accidentally in his struggle with mother and child, and kills him. Solange thinks she is guilty of murder, flees towards the river and drowns herself. Mambéké symbolically strips off and heads towards the river, but his sister arrives with Bienvenu and Alexis (her own child by Morax) in time to persuade him to live so as to look after the children and the school.

The literary inadequacies of good intentions show all too clearly in such a novel. With Blacks consolidating new-found skills and clamouring increasingly for political independence, the coming years will show those powers being put to better use.

CHAPTER 6
STRUGGLES FOR INDEPENDENCE

'Une pointe d'étrangeté donne du piment à l'amour.'
[A touch of strangeness give love extra spice.]
Geneviève Billy[219]

EMANCIPATION from insidious prejudice is harder than throwing off the physical shackles of slavery. The decade before 1960, the year in which so many French colonies were granted their independence, shows considerable variety of response to a relationship which is as important affectively as it is symbolic politically. We need to recognise in addition that an ethic of confrontation has unfortunate effects on literary models which tend in turn to be confrontational and produce what might be called 'banana westerns'. Any systematic reversal by black writers of the age-old symbolism associating black with evil and white with innocence produces merely a new set of cardboard-cut-out goodies and baddies. Despite the facile attractions of such a formula, the 1950s see the appearance of novels by Africans and Europeans alike looking for ways ahead in the evolving situation of more or less enforced respect.

Those of mixed race who 'come out'—sometimes in retrospect: witness the recent recognition of the importance of the African component in Pushkin and Dumas, for example—may no longer have to apologise for living or writing, but it does not exempt them from compensating for the contempt in which they were often held by Whites, by despising Blacks in their turn. The eponymous heroine of the Senegalese Abdoulaye Sadji's *Nini, mulâtresse du Sénégal* (1947), from an intermediate group seen in the preface as 'l'être physiquement et moralement hybride' [physically and morally hybrid beings], is unabashed about declaring:

130

Je ne suis peut-être pas une Blanche, mais je ne me marierai
jamais avec un nègre, serait-il président de la République.

[I may not be a white woman, but I shall never marry a Negro,
were he the President of the Republic.]

No doubt such attitudes were adopted in real life and are
therefore plausible in literature, but it is important to
remember that the economy of a novel puts pressure on
character portrayal. Nini, despite her very modest background and position, 'semble écraser d'un dédain universel
toutes les personnes qu'elle rencontre' [seems to crush
everyone she meets with universal disdain].

Florian is the mixed-race, mixed-up Martinican hero of
Frenchman Maurice Bedel's schematic and sentimental *Le
Mariage des couleurs* (1951). Fascinated by hybridity—a
concept which will enjoy special favour among postcolonial
critics—he pursues the concept through higher studies in
the natural sciences, and botanical hybrids are a recurrent
point of reference in the novel.[220] From France, where he
first meets Jasmine, the unsophisticated daughter of a wine-
grower bent on improving strains of grape by cross-
pollination, he turns to the Ivory Coast in search of his
roots (and of epiphytes, those in-between plants *par
excellence*), only to discover that 'going native' is not the
solution. In the end, with his love for Jasmine reluctantly
acknowledged, we are given rose-tinted promises for their
future together.

The Black in Robert Sabatier's *Alain et le Nègre* (1953),
seen from a French perspective and in a French setting,
appears far less anguished, more ordinary and three-
dimensional. Moral absolutes of both a sexual and a racial
nature are set aside, helped by the fact that we watch from
the child's point of view—such as Calixthe Beyala will use
in *Le Petit Prince de Belleville* and its sequel *Maman a un
amant*[221]—the relationship develop between Vincent, Alain
and the latter's mother, who runs a bar-cum-grocery-store.
Gentle but penetrating observation ousts didacticism.
Vincent's colour is significant only insofar as it marks him
out as a stranger in Alain's world, one whom he gradually

gets to know and appreciate as a human being, without any grand claims being made on his behalf. The only established paradigm to which it might be considered to conform, set as it is in the 1930s, is that of Blacks consorting with lower-class white women. But Vincent is precisely not an intellectual, whereas at that time, apart from largely illiterate sailors and *Tirailleurs*, it was by definition the most intelligent students who travelled from the colonies to France to pursue their studies and thereby set a long-lasting agenda whereby intellectuals and intellectual preoccupations loomed large in their writings.

Yet Vincent is no fool:

> Jamais il n'avait envié la blancheur. Il la jugeait larvaire et tout homme blanc lui paraissait un être inaccompli. [...] Il rêva à la jeune fille qui l'aurait aimée pour lui, rien que pour lui, et non pour ses facultés physiques, pour sa puissance à "faire l'amour". Car ce "lui" existait.

> [Never had he envied whiteness. He thought it larval, and every white man an unfinished being. [...] He dreamed of a girl who would love him for himself, just for himself, and not for his physical prowess, for his power to 'make love'. For this 'him' existed.]

From the point of view of the mentality represented, this is well ahead of its time, moving towards a straightforward descriptive recognition of difference while simultaneously acknowledging a shared humanity, neither better nor worse than any other, and equally available for analysis and development.

Dated 1953 at the end, *Climbié*, by the Ivory Coast writer Bernard Dadié, contains a brief but telling episode referring to a marriage between a Frenchwoman and a *Tirailleur sénégalais* who has returned with her to his native Guinea:

> C'est à Conakry. Un sergent indigène débarque avec une Européenne. Une femme vraiment jolie. Lorsqu'elle passait, chacun s'arrêtait pour la regarder. Des Européens, par jalousie, arrivèrent à faire coffrer son mari. Mon colon! Ah, mais il fallait entendre la dame parler lors de l'audience. Elle disait:

"Messieurs! cela peut vous paraître étrange, à vous autres, que nous épousions des Nègres. Pour nous cela n'a rien d'insolite. Durant cette guerre, dans notre région, ils nous ont aidés à vivre à une époque où l'on se demandait à tout instant ce que sera demain. Nous n'avions nous autres ni boys, ni vivres à discrétion. Il vous est loisible de faire du racisme. En France, nous connaissons ce mot parce qu'il est dans le dictionnaire. Il n'est pas dans nos actes, dans nos faits, dans nos pensées. Il n'existe pas. Je vous demande donc de libérer mon mari."

Ah! Ils ont eu chaud, ce jour-là, les juges de Conakry. Ils avaient de ces têtes Mon colon!

[It was at Conakry. A native sergeant disembarked with a European woman. When she went by, everyone stopped to look at her. Some Europeans, out of jealousy, managed to have her husband shopped. Man! Oh but you should have heard the woman talk at the hearing. She said: 'Gentlemen, it may seem strange to you that we should marry Negroes. For us, there is nothing unusual about it. During the war, in our region, they have helped us to live through a period when we were wondering at every moment what tomorrow would bring. None of us over there had servants or provisions aplenty. You may wish to indulge in racism. In France, we know the word because it's in the dictionary. But it doesn't exist in our actions, in our deeds, or in our thoughts. It simply doesn't exist. So I ask you to free my husband.'

Oh! The Conakry judges were hot under the collar that day, I can tell you. You should have seen their heads man!]

It is clearly wishful thinking on the loyal wife's part that racism did not—does not—exist in France, but the view is often expressed. It remained and remains a fiction fostered by the legal equality guaranteed by the Republic to its citizens. But even that theoretical framework was better than the situation in many another country and as such could be used to suggest France's higher moral ground.

Writers both black and white continue more often than not to provide a tragic or negative ending to *Blanche/Noir* relationships. Even in a European setting after the war, as Schipper-De Leeuw suggests,

le romancier ne croit pas, ou pas encore, à la réalisation durable de l'amour entre l'homme noir et la femme blanche, c'est pourquoi il fait intervenir un destin défavorable pour y mettre fin.

[the novelist does not believe, or does not yet believe in a lasting flowering of love between a black man and a white woman, and therefore introduces some unfavourable fate to put an end to it.][222]

That was already true in the pre-war *Mirages de Paris*, and it remains true of *Blanche/Noir* relationships in Sembène Ousmane's first novel *Le Docker noir* (1956).[223] As is so often the case in this post-war writing, the web of characters includes biracial couples as part of the social texture. Here Andrée Lazare, expecting a child by Paul Sonko, is pressurised by her prim mother into an abortion and dies as a consequence. Of the principal character, Diaw Falla, a witness is asked: '[Diaw] vous paraît-il un obsédé sexuel?', the answer being: 'Chez les Noirs, c'est une chose naturelle et surtout quand il s'agit d'une femme blanche' ['Does [Diaw] appear obsessed with sex to you?' 'With Blacks, it's completely natural, and especially where white women are concerned.'] Yet this caricature is part of the distorted case for the prosecution against him: when he is imprisoned and cannot see his child, his partner Catherine takes to prostitution so as to survive and preserve their relationship as best she can.

Two short stories by Olympe Bhêly-Quenum, not published until 1968 but written in the 1950s, might be taken as a significant diptych. In one, 'Aventure africaine', the couple is *Blanc/Noire*; in the other, which shares the title of the collection, 'Liaison d'un été', it is *Blanche/Noir*. The outcome in the former is happy; in the latter, tragic, suggesting that it still has to be seen as the more difficult one to realise fruitfully. We shall return to these texts when setting them in the context of Bhêly-Quenum's essentially optimistic vision of Black/White relations, developed in novels produced over the following four decades.

Sembene focuses centrally on a *Blanche/Noir* couple in his second novel, *Ô pays, mon beau peuple!* (1957). Shifting his setting from France to his native Senegal, the tragic end is exclusively the result of European racism. Oumar Faye, a larger-than-life hero who puts his talents and political vision at the service of his countrymen, has been to Europe as a *Tirailleur sénégalais*, married Isabelle and returned

134

with her. In this instance, his father-in-law shows admirable percipience: 'Ce n'est pas la race qui fait l'homme, ni la couleur de sa peau' [It isn't the race that makes a man, nor the colour of his skin]. Indifference to entirely superficial characteristics is reiterated elsewhere, emerging as a new criterion of the utmost importance in our investigations: 'Le fait d'être marié avec une *minnediérou brancou* (femme blanche) n'élève ni n'amoindrit personne' [The fact of being married to a *minnedierou brancou* (white woman) neither enhances nor diminishes anyone]. This point represents an important escape from the mesh of presupposition and prejudice in which such a simple human truth had become entangled. Yet, given subsequent writings as well as subsequent transracial socio-political quarrels, it still seems to represent an unattainable ideal.

Oumar Faye's character and his experiences in Europe combine to make him evenhandedly 'colour-blind', but other people's perceptions are different. The exploitative and racist Whites, as Faye himself observes, 'ne tolèrent pas qu'un nègre s'accouple avec une blanche, c'est bafouer leurs lois' [can't bear a Negro marrying a white woman: it flies in the face of their laws]. Such, however, is the sum total of the overt commentary on the issue in the novel: in all other respects the question is represented through the actions and interplay of characters.

The distinction made between colour and character which we have noted in respect of Othello has its exact mirror-image in Iago's recognition of his carefully masked diabolical nature:

> When devils will their blackest sins put on,
> They do suggest at first with heavenly shows,
> As I do now.   (II, iii, 340–42)

Precisely the same double pattern of reversals occurs in Oumar Faye and the Whites installed in his country. Furthermore, in both contexts, each takes the longest of spoons to sup with the other. Outlining his plot against Desdemona, Iago extends the metaphor by threatening to 'turn her virtue into pitch' (II, iii, 349). This too has its parallel in Sembene's novel in the besmirching of Isabelle's character by the Whites.

Unlike Othello, however, Oumar ignores such taunts and taints. No shadow is cast on his marital bliss: his attention is therefore free to focus exclusively on socio-political action beyond the domestic sphere (which Sembene analyses more sceptically in other works), and his unassailable bond with Isabelle takes on political force because of the security and self-confidence it affords him. So the very unity of the couple represents a threat to both of the social power-blocks: in direct ratio to the conservatism of those they confront, Isabelle is suspect to the Blacks no less than Oumar is anathema to the Whites. In colonial times, such a couple would have been a maverick phenomenon: here their synergy, however idealised, is a political threat. Oumar—and through him Sembene—builds his base for black solidarity on his domestic solidity, challenging white superiority from the firm platform of his marriage. This is sexual politics with a difference, particularly as Oumar and Isabelle fulfil entirely traditional roles within their marriage.

Faye is given heroic stature through a series of what might be called defensive attacks. The equivalent to Othello's Cyprus wars is Faye's single-handed struggle against oppression, his fisticuffs with Raoul in the opening sequence, in defence of poor deck-passengers taking shelter from a sudden storm, being a proleptic analogue of the more generalised struggles against white exploitation to come, firstly in further physical violence as a protest against the plight of the women made to carry huge loads at the docks, then in his non-violent endeavour to create a local cooperative to reduce dependence on the Whites.

His violence will be returned with interest when literally unseen hands bring about his bloody death. No single Iago emerges from the shadows to accept blame, yet the Whites who are responsible for his death are goaded to action by a socio-political intolerance which is primarily encapsulated in a sexually orientated objection to the very coexistence of black man and white woman. Iago's taunts to

Brabantio—who, in Emilia's view (V, ii, 207–09) was to die of grief at what he considered the mismatch—that 'an old black ram/Is tupping your white ewe' (I, i, 89–90) and that 'your daughter and the Moor are now making the beast with two backs' (I, i, 117–18), masking his own repressed and diverted desires, have an equivalent in the sexual banter and fantasies of the Whites, becoming violently explicit in Jacques's attempted rape of Isabelle, watched by the drooling Raoul. It, in turn, is a prelude to the violence meted out to Oumar, and ironically it is Isabelle herself who forewarns of its coming in another projected multiplication of individuals:

> —Vous aimeriez bien le voir se mettre dans un mauvais cas? Ce jour-là, il faudra que vous ayez un motif valable. Mais je vous donne un conseil: venez plus nombreux!

> ['Would you like to see him in a mess? That day, you'd better have a valid motive. But I warn you: there'd better be more of you!']

Her advice will be all too well followed.

In *Ô pays, mon beau peuple!*, it is the antagonism of social groups, with their representative types, that forms the backcloth and impinges on the principal characters. Oumar and Othello, given mighty stature as men of action, fall mightily but by different means, and again the shift is from the individual to the collective. Eldred Jones argues that 'in the end Othello emerges, not as another manifestation of a type, but as a distinct individual who typified by his fall, not the weaknesses of Moors, but the weaknesses of human nature'.[224] True though this may be, it must also be said that his downfall is not separable from his colour, since it is the visible source of the general prejudice which, distilled into venom, leads Iago to act as he does. But Oumar is self-consciously a symbol.

Instead of the murder of Desdemona by Othello followed by his suicide, we have Oumar's murder by persons unknown. Othello's jealousy, manufactured by the machiavellian Iago, is transposed to self-induced group jealousy bred by racial intolerance out of sexual frustration.

The Whites in *Ô pays, mon beau peuple!*, to whom the 'demi-devil' Iago's manipulative skills are transferred, cloak their lustful desires with words of contempt, but whereas the Shakespearean tragedy depends on a final catharsis, Sembene's ideal social vision grows almost literally out of Oumar's grave: 'Ce n'était pas la tombe qui était sa demeure, c'était le cœur de tous les hommes et de toutes les femmes' [The grave was not where he lay, but in the hearts of every man and woman]. In the social sphere, the authority and seniority of Papa Gomis augur well for the future of the cooperative. At the individual level, the clear expectation is that Isabelle's child will be born a male and embody the best of both worlds, taking up Faye's noble mantle. But in several ways, mirroring Sembene's social(ist) interests, there is a shift from focus on the individual to concentration on the collective, the individual either being stereotypical, as in the case of the hero, Oumar Faye, a variant on the noble savage, or less than fully rounded, and so no less stereotyped, as with Isabelle, Rokhaya, Raoul and others.

The marriage of two cultures embodied by Oumar and his French wife is further adumbrated in the relationship between Isabelle and her mother-in-law, Rokhaya. It is in stark contrast to the antagonism felt and expressed between Mireille and her mother-in-law, Yaye Khady, in *Un chant écarlate*, that we shall investigate in the next chapter.

The European and African perspectives on the cusp of granting/achieving (some black nationalists would say winning) independence are naturally quite different from one another and the prism of the *couple domino* treated from each is particularly instructive. *Ô pays, mon beau peuple!* has established its credentials as an important novel.[225] *La Fête des sacrifices*, by Christine Garnier (1959) seems to have sunk without trace, but is particularly interesting for present purposes, full of social comment about the mixed-race marriage between Thierno and Irène.

A parallel is established between traditional, 'primitive' festivities in Belgium and Senegal, equally incomprehensible to outsiders. In Dakar, Thierno is a specialist in African masks and has his fellow-Wolof Awa as a partner. On a trip to Belgium, he meets Irène: it is love at first sight. She abandons everything, including the favour of her father, and, somewhat in a dream, takes the ship for Dakar and marries Thierno. Thereupon, all white acquaintances (with the exception of one, Marc) fall away, and the black ones fraternise with Thierno but effectively exclude Irène. Complications ensue. Irène is left with Marc during Ramadan; Thierno uses this time to have sex with Awa, whereas Irène is faithful to him, but there is privacy for neither pair, which leads to squabbles and fights, the fiercest and most clearly symbolic of which involves masks being hurled. The climax comes when, fifty days after the end of Ramadan, what is locally known as *Tabaski* and more generally in the Islamic world as *'Id-al-Kebir*, 'la fête des sacrifices' of the title, is celebrated, and sheep are killed in commemoration of Abraham's sacrifice. Awa takes freedom of action to the point where she uses a sacrificial knife to stab the husband of whom she is the fourth wife; and Thierno and Irène split up, unable to bear the pressure.

In the course of the novel, a number of observations by different characters or the author herself represent standard viewpoints on biracial relationships as a stigma. 'Mon ami Khardjatou dit que faire l'amour avec un Blanc, c'est manger un plat sans sel' [My friend Khardjatou says that making love to a white person is like eating a dish with no salt]. Awa declares to Thierno:

> Fou, en vérité, tu l'es, pour donner raison aux colonialistes qui clament: "Ces nègres ne veulent plus de Blancs en Afrique mais ils n'ont cependant qu'une idée en tête: épouser une Blanche!"

> [Crazy, you're really crazy to agree with the colonialists who shout: 'The Negroes don't want Whites in Africa any longer, yet they've only one idea in their heads: to marry a white woman!']

Thierno anticipates accurately both the reaction of his parents to Irène's arrival as his wife and the eventual outcome:

Ma mère, j'en suis certain, l'accueillera avec affection, mais elle ne pourra prononcer que ce seul mot: bienvenue; elle ne parle que le ouolof. Mon père, lui, refusera tout net de voir ma femme. Il a toujours montré grand mépris pour les soldats, pour les étudiants qui revenaient avec une Infidèle: "Ce n'est pas la couleur de la peau, explique-t-il, c'est la religion! Epouse qui tu veux, Noire ou Blanche, mais épouse une musulmane!" [...] Il y aura les Blancs, aussi! Ils nous recevront parfois, mais sans chaleur, sans amitié sincère. Un couple "domino" comme on dit ici. Serons-nous condamnés à la solitude?

[My mother, I'm certain, will welcome you affectionately, but she will be able to pronounce only one word: welcome; she only speaks Wolof. As for my father, he'll refuse flatly to see my wife. He has always been scornful of soldiers and students coming back with an Infidel: 'It's not the colour of their skin,' he explains, 'it's their religion! Marry who you want, Black or White, but marry a Muslim!' [...] There will be the Whites too! They will invite us sometimes, but coldly, with no real friendliness. A *couple domino* as they say here. Will we be condemned to total isolation?]

As to Irène's father's reaction, it reveals a specifically racial intolerance: 'Tu t'obstines dans ta folie, tu vas vraiment épouser ce nègre?' [You persist in your madness; are you really going to marry this Negro?] But youthful idealism pays no heed: Irène believes that

Thierno et elle sauraient abattre les barrières de la couleur, de la religion, de la race. Unis, ils deviendraient un trait d'union entre ces Blancs, ces Noirs, ces Maures. Pourquoi pas?

[Thierno and she would break down the barriers of colour, religion and race. Together, they would become a hyphen between these Whites, these Blacks, these Moors. Why not?]

A hint of Fanon's psychology is suggested in passing:

N'était-ce pas, presque inconsciemment, chez Thierno, une revanche au passé de ses frères noirs, si longtemps asservis? Dans l'amour même, ce regard de triomphe qu'il avait parfois...

[Was there not, almost unconsciously, in Thierno, a sense of revenge for his black brothers, so long enslaved? In making love, the look of triumph that he sometimes wore...]

The concept of revenge is given a broader sweep by local leaders hinting retaliation for the evils of colonisation. With such outside pressures, one understands Irène's self-deceptive reply when asked whether she is happy: 'Etre deux, deux seulement, refuser de voir les autres, de se mêler à eux, n'est-ce pas cela, le bonheur?' [Being two, just two, refusing to see other people and mingle with them, isn't that happiness?] Rejection leads to increasingly negative introspection:

> Les Blancs me rejettent, pensait-elle. Trouverai-je ma place dans cette Afrique qui a hérité de tous nos poisons?... L'Afrique que je pressentais fraternelle, c'était celle des fêtes de la pluie, des circoncisions, c'était celle des tam-tam, des gris-gris et des masques... Cette Afrique-ci, qui ne rêve qu'usines, tracteurs, gratte-ciel, cette Afrique haletant dans sa course et qui, avidement, désespérément, veut se bâtir à notre image, saurai-je la comprendre?... M'acceptera-t-elle?

> [Whites reject me, she thought. Shall I find a place for myself in this Africa which has inherited all our poisons?... Africa for me was fraternal, full of rain-festivals, circumcision rites, tom-toms, amulets and masks... This Africa, which dreams of nothing but factories, tractors and skyscrapers, this Africa dashing breathlessly forward and avidly, desperately wanting to make itself in our image, shall I ever understand it?... Will it ever accept me?]

Small wonder that the marriage goes awry. Confronting Thierno, Irène, herself a victim of racial prejudice, uses its distortions in turn to victimise him. The alienation is total and contagious: 'Irène a dressé entre elle et l'Europe l'opaque écran d'une peau noire au grain serré...' [Irène has erected between herself and Europe the opaque screen of a fine-grained black skin...]. At a picnic with other *Blanche/ Noir* couples, she formulates questions in her mind in her search for a community, but never gives them voice:

> Dites-moi, qu'a répondu votre père quand vous lui avez annoncé que vous épousiez un Noir?... Les Blancs d'ici vous invitent-ils à leurs fêtes?... De quel œil vous regarde-t-on quand vous passez dans la rue au bras de votre mari?... Ne regrettez-vous rien?... Etes-vous heureuses?...

141

[Tell me, what did your father say when you told him you were going to marry a black man?... Do the Whites here invite you to their parties?... How do people look at you when they pass you in the street arm in arm with your husband?... Do you have any regrets?... Are you happy?...]

Attempts at reconciliation prove fruitless. In defending himself against her reproaches, Thierno lays himself open to more:

— Tu oses me parler ainsi parce que je suis Noir.

Elle hausse les épaules. Toujours ces complexes de race, de couleur qui les obsèdent tous!

— Ce n'est pas le Noir que j'ai épousé, dit-elle avec lassitude, c'est l'homme. Un homme que je voulais, que je croyais fort, exceptionnel, tout à moi.

— Je n'ai jamais cessé d'être à toi. Et puis, écoute, assez de ces mots inutiles! Viens contre moi. Viens que je te prenne...

— Oh! toi, tu t'imagines qu'on rattrape tout avec un "coup de lit"!... Eh bien non, pas aujourd'hui!

— Viens, je te dis! insiste Thierno avec rage.

— Non.

['You dare to speak to me like that because I'm black.'

She shrugs. Always those race and colour complexes which they are all obsessed with!

'I didn't marry a Black,' she said wearily, 'I married a man. A man I wanted, one I thought strong, outstanding, just for me.'

'I've never stopped being yours. Oh listen! Enough of these useless words. Come and hug me. Let me take you...'

'Oh, you! You imagine every problem can be solved by a "bit of bed"!... Well, no, not today!'

'Come here, I tell you', Thierno insisted, his blood boiling.

'No.']

This refusal is a prelude to their temporary separation, which in turn exacerbates their violent reunion (including violent sex). First insults, then masks are hurled on what is referred to as 'la nuit des masques' [the night of the masks]. In their traditional function these are a 'projection de l'instinct' [expression of instinct] or 'rêves fixés' [fixed dreams] and, by extension, we see them as such for the symbolic role they play in the book.

Symbolic too, as the title of the novel suggests, is the purification rite, followed by ritual slaughter of sheep, of ʿId-al-Kebir. It is the occasion of a review of the couple's difficulties:

> [...] elle a compris que la Tabaski marquerait pour elle la fin d'un impossible amour.
>
> — Nous avons essayé de toutes nos forces de nous comprendre, n'est-ce pas? dit Thierno, avec une tendresse douloureuse. Nous nous sommes aimés avec passion. Nous n'avons pas cessé de nous aimer. Et pourtant, jour après jour, nous nous sommes l'un l'autre détruits. Est-ce ta peau blanche, est-ce ma peau noire? Qui pourrait le dire?... Est-ce le pays où tu n'as cessé de te sentir étrangère? Le climat qui t'a épuisée? Ma famille dont tu as honte? Notre dialecte que tu n'as pu apprendre, mes habitudes de pensée, ma religion?... Dakar?... Sans doute n'avons-nous pas trouvé ici le cadre indispensable, ces supports faits de subtibilités [sic], d'impondérables, qui seuls maintiennent, enrichissent et renouvellent l'amour. Dans ton désarroi, tu t'es un instant tournée vers Marc. Moi, auprès d'Awa, j'ai tenté de retrouver une Afrique dont, malgré toi, par ta seule présence, tu m'avais éloigné. Et vois, vois où nous en sommes aujourd'hui!
>
> — Oh! je sais bien, murmure-t-elle, tu as raison! Nous avons voulu l'absolu, l'exceptionnel, et nous voici ramenés à la pauvre mesure des hommes.

> [[...] she understood that Tabaski would mark for her the end of an impossible love-affair.
>
> 'We have made a huge effort to understand one another, haven't we?' said Thierno, sadly and tenderly. 'We have loved one another passionately. We have never stopped loving one another. And yet, day after day, we have destroyed one another. Is it your white skin, is it my black skin? Who can tell?... Is it the country, where you never stopped feeling a foreigner? The climate which exhausted you? My family, that you're ashamed of? Our language that you never managed to learn, the way I think, my religion?... Dakar?... Perhaps we never found the indispensable framework, those supporting factors made up of subtibilities [sic] and imponderables which alone are able to maintain, enrich and renew love. In your confusion, you turned to Marc for a moment. As for me, I tried to rediscover with Awa an Africa from which, in spite of yourself, by your very presence, you had distanced me. And look, just look where we are today!'

143

'Oh! I know,' she murmured, 'you're right! We wanted the absolute, the exceptional, and we've been brought down to the meagre measure of men.']

She is disappointed because her expectations were unreal. Half-consciously, she is aware of fundamental humanity being more important than skin-colour.

Seized by some 'ardeur mystique' [mystic ardour], Thierno's plan is to go off into the bush to rediscover Africa's ancient secrets. The book's final image is of Irène handing Thierno the keys to her Mercedes which she will not be taking back to Belgium with her: 'Maintenant, c'est à toi de conduire' [Now you're in the driving-seat]. This is clearly a symbolic handing over of Africa's future to the Africans on the eve of independence.

Il faudra attendre l'indépendance pour que tout change vraiment et qu'on voie à leur tour les Africains séduisant en masse leurs anciennes colonisatrices ou plutôt leurs filles. Revanche des temps modernes, les années soixante marquent un tournant dans l'évolution des femmes. Elles acquièrent une nouvelle liberté, veulent être salariées, voyager, créer, explorer à leur tour d'autres possibilités que celles de la famille traditionnelle. Attirées par les grands espaces, l'horizon nouveau, le visage étranger de l'ami, elles n'hésitent plus à partir, à s'unir à un Noir, à mettre au monde des enfants de couleur.

[You have to wait for independence for everything really to change and for a lot of Africans in their turn to start courting their former female colonists or rather their daughters. The 1960s, the revenge of modern times, mark a turning-point in women's development. They acquire a new freedom, want to earn a living, travel, create, explore in their turn possibilities other than those of the traditional family. Attracted by wide-open spaces, a new horizon, or the face of a foreign friend, they no longer hesitate to leave, to marry a Black, and to give birth to mixed-race children.][226]

Not only, of course, was (is) women's liberation longer coming to Africa, but literature also bides its time before reflecting such a social revolution which, while it had its champions, also had its detractors as well as many slow to adapt to its implications.

With his usual corrosive humour, Ferdinand Oyono plays on the stereotypes relating to *Blanche/Noir* couples in his 1960 novel, *Chemin d'Europe*. The subject forms a telling episode (chapters III–VII) in Aki Barnabas's unreal ambition to earn millions and go to Europe. One of his successive jobs is as tutor to the cocky, know-all eight-year-old daughter of the Gruchets. He has erotic fantasies about Madame Gruchet as part of his unlimited capacity for self-delusion. The writing is correspondingly tongue-in-cheek, its irony directed against both real and literary models of self-deception by Blacks: the road to Europe is a long, stony and winding one which proves never to reach its destination.

Aki's mother gets wind of his infatuation:

> — Cette femme! dit-elle [sa mère] d'une voix vibrant de rage impuissante.
> Nous nous isolâmes dans une minute de silence: elle tourmentée, se demandant comment me guérir maintenant de cette folie que redoutait son infaillible instinct maternel depuis longtemps alerté: l'amour d'une femme blanche, chose qui, pour elle, dépassait les limites de la raison et menaçait de perdre son fils, et moi, furieux de cette brutale entrée en matière, furieux d'être incapable de cacher mes sentiments, cherchant l'astuce, une montagne d'astuce propre à contrebalancer sa prescience indiscrète.
> — Fou! fou à lier! fit-elle à part soi. Les femmes, mais prends-en une au quartier! A quoi bon se compliquer encore la vie... Une femme blanche! Te rends-tu au moins compte? Et mariée, en plus!... Et tu sais... son mari... est de ces blancs qui vous tireraient un coup de fusil pour rien...

> ['That woman!', his mother said, her voice quivering with impotent rage.
> We isolated ourselves in a minute's silence. She was tormented, wondering how to cure me of this madness which her infallible maternal instinct, long since alerted, dreaded: love for a white woman, something which for her was totally unreasonable and threatened to ruin me. As for me, I was furious a t the matter being brought up, furious at my inability to hide my

feelings, searching for some clever way out, a mountain of tricks capable of counterbalancing her indiscreet premonition.

'He's stark raving mad!', she said to herself. 'Take a local woman! What's the point of complicating your life? A white woman! What are you thinking of? And married into the bargain!... And you know... her husband is one of those Whites who would shoot you on sight...']

M. Gruchet, as racist as Roch Morax in *Cœur d'Aryenne*, also leaves a trail of biracial bastards in the negro quarter. In addition, however, he leaves something which shows the shift to an ironic register, 'ses pyjamas de soie en train de sécher' [his silk pyjamas hanging out to dry].

None of this stops Aki fantasising about his leaving Cameroon for France with M. Gruchet's blessing:

> Mme Gruchet demanderait le divorce, son mari, bien qu'il fût Falstaff et Méphisto à la fois, ne pourrait l'empêcher d'être heureuse: rien n'arrête une femme à la recherche de son bonheur et contre le cœur il n'y a point de justice devant laquelle on puisse recourir.

> [Madame Gruchet would ask for a divorce; her husband, despite being Falstaff and Mephistopheles in one, could not prevent her being happy: nothing stops a woman in search of her happiness, and against the heart there is no court to which recourse is possible.]

Then follows the admission: 'rien de positif ne s'était réellement passé' [nothing positive had actually happened]. Nevertheless:

> Elle m'attirait, m'excitait avec tout le romantisme de la femme blanche interdite, et ma nature inquiète, enthousiaste et passionnée, avait fait de ce sentiment quelque chose qui dépassait toutes les limites, tant je ne cessais de la recréer dans le feu de mon désir en lui devinant une ardeur qu'exagérait ma sensualité africaine.

> [She attracted and excited me with all the romanticism of the forbidden white woman, and my anxious, enthusiastic and passionate nature had turned this feeling into something which exceeded all limits, so often did I reshape it in the forge of my

desire, imagining in it a passion which my African sensuality exaggerated.]

The splendidly overblown sentiments and rhetoric are punctured in ways reminiscent of Stendhal. The narrator's fidelity is such that he is constantly at Madame Gruchet's side, whether taking breakfast, writing a letter, picking flowers, having a shower or... pulling the chain. Yet it dawns on him that he is, in Ralph Ellison's sense, an 'invisible man', not even being seen, as Fanon had it, to be classified as black: 'Alors une âpre évidence se fit jour en moi: elle ne m'avait pas vu, elle ne me voyait pas' [Then something blindingly, bitterly obvious struck me: she had not seen me, she did not see me]. Even so, his wishful thinking propels him to imagine deeply frustrated love on her part,

> qu'elle en souffrait, qu'elle pleurait sur son oreiller la nuit, se faisant violence pour taire son grand amour que, paradoxalement, j'estimais proportionnel à son indifférence.

> [that she was suffering from it, crying on her pillow at night, forcing herself to stifle in silence a grand passion which, paradoxically, I assumed was in direct proportion to her indifference.]

A delectable passage, again in the Stendhal manner whereby a character completely misreads a situation, has Madame Gruchet, in a highly emotional state, tripping up three or four steps and ending up pressed against Aki's chest:

> Que faire? Renverser cette femme, et en finir tout de suite, j'aurais dû le faire depuis un moment—ou l'écraser contre le mur, la prendre debout avant que ne réapparût quelque importun? [...] Quant à Mme Gruchet, elle pleurait, continuait à pleurer, son corps écrasé contre le mien, dans cette même posture de petite fille désespérée s'accrochant à n'importe qui et à n'importe quoi. [...]
> — [...] Ma fille a 40 de fièvre!
> Ah! ce n'était que ça, moi qui croyais... [...] "Trop imaginatif", pensai-je en la suivant.

[What should I do? Up-end this woman and have done with it, as I should have done long since—or press her against the wall and take her standing up before someone unwelcome happens by? [...] As for Madame Gruchet, she was crying and continued to cry, her body pressed against mine, in the attitude of a desperate little girl clinging to anyone and anything. [...]
'My daughter has a temperature of 40!'
Ah! that's all it was; I thought... [...] 'Too much imagination', I thought to myself as I followed her.]

Irony is clearly an appropriate way to spike the stereotypes and cut both parties down to size. It is none the less significant that the Black's quest for self-improvement should here include an association with a white woman as a compulsory stage on his journey. Aki's failure to achieve his goals can be seen as a signal, at the onset of national independence, that they are misguided, pandering as they do to outmoded assumptions of white superiority.

The 1960s continue to show the proliferation that we have observed in the 1950s.[227] The author's standpoint determines his or her approach as more or less conservative, and in general it is French rather than African writers who fall into the former category. There is a marked shift towards an evocation of Africans in France as proletarians rather than as intellectuals.[228] Indeed, Ake Loba's *Kocoumba, l'étudiant noir*, of 1960, signals that shift, the title masking the hero's work in a factory to finance his studies. Francis Fouet makes the general point that black African novelists of this period are discreet in their presentation of love, concentrating rather on their socio-political struggle:

> on est frappé par le peu d'importance relative du thème de l'amour. [...] Premièrement, le concept occidental de l'amour n'existe guère en Afrique [...] et d'une manière générale n'occupe pas dans les civilisations africaines une place aussi envahissante que dans la nôtre. En second lieu, la grande majorité des romanciers sont contemporains du réveil de l'Afrique et de la lutte pour l'indépendance: la littérature africaine est avant tout une littérature engagée.

148

[one is struck by the relative unimportance of the theme of love. [...] Firstly, the western concept of love hardly exists in Africa [...] and in a general way does not occupy in African civilisations the all-pervasive one it does in ours. Secondly, the vast majority of novelists are contemporaries of the political awakening of Africa and its struggle for independence: African literature is primarily a committed one.][229]

Thérèse Kuoh-Moukoury makes the general point that

> le puritanisme nègre en amour n'est d'ailleurs pas une réaction de honte face à l'acte charnel, mais une attitude de respect vis-à-vis de soi-même, du partenaire et de l'amour.

> [the Black's puritanism in love is not a reaction of shame at the carnal act but an attitude of respect towards himself, his partner and love.][230]

Kocoumba, from the Congo like his creator, is an innocent abroad; his fellow-Africans are more than once shown as sharks, using him as much as anybody else. Durandeau in particular, judged at the outset to be a fop, turns out to be worse than that: dishonest in misappropriating money destined for Kocoumba and an unscrupulous philanderer in his use of a succession of white girl-friends and mistresses. Jane and he meet Kocoumba on his arrival in Paris in her red sports car. Françoise, pregnant by him, is dumped unceremoniously. Alice, Lucienne and Agnès are exploited by him in their turn.

Kocoumba is the only one of the group to stick to his studies despite desperate poverty. His relations with women are made all the more difficult because he sees himself as tarred with the same brush as his fellow-Africans. In the rue Saint-Denis, a street renowned for its prostitutes, he looks for a girl, but in vain because of his conscience:

> Devant chaque fille qu'il croisait il avait envie de se mettre à genoux pour lui dire que lui au moins il était franc, sincère, honnête, qu'il avait besoin d'être aimé, d'aimer, que son cœur ne recélait nulle hypocrisie, qu'il n'était pas un Durandeau. S'il avait pu, il aurait ouvert son cœur pour le montrer à toutes les passantes. Plus il se lamentait en silence, plus les filles

149

rencontrées s'enveloppaient de beauté angélique. Ses yeux les convoitaient avec détresse. Mais chaque regard féminin restait sans réponse. Elles ne comprenaient donc pas quel besoin, loin de son pays, de tout ce qu'il avait aimé, quel ardent besoin il avait d'être aimé, ne fût-ce qu'un peu...

[Before every girl in his path he wanted to throw himself to his knees and protest his candour, his sincerity, his honesty, that he needed to be loved and to love, that his heart hid no hypocrisy, that he was no Durandeau. If he could, he would have opened his heart to show it to every passing girl. The more he moped, the more the girls he came across were sheathed in angelic beauty. His eyes yearned for them in his distress. But each woman's gaze went unanswered. They did not understand what a need, far from his homeland and from everything he loved, what a burning need he had to be loved, if only a little...]

The link between Blacks and the proletariat is implicitly criticised in the way Kocoumba is treated at the factory. It is there, however, that he is introduced to Denise, a feisty communist activist.

Tout à coup, il [Kocoumba] pense qu'elle pourrait être son amie. Elle n'est pas belle, mais c'est une femme dont la sensibilité se cache sous une franchise brutale.

[Suddenly, he thought she could be his friend. She was not beautiful, but a woman whose sensitivity hid behind her gruff straightforwardness.]

A light kiss on her forehead releases her tears and with them an admission that she has suffered from growing up without her parents. 'Il s'attachait à elle sans le savoir, et elle l'aimait plus qu'elle ne l'avait supposé' [He became attached to her without realising it, and she loved him more than she had imagined]. But she is killed in a railway accident, and Kocoumba is left to realise how deeply he had become attached to her.

In such a narrative, social pressures based on racial assumptions furnish the psychological grounds for the individual relationship, but do not determine it absolutely. The same is true of the celebrated 1967 novel by Claire Etcherelli, *Élise ou la vraie vie*.[231] Charles Nokan, on the other hand, depicts in *Le Soleil noir point* (1962; written 1959) a dream-like, disjointed narrative in which the importance of skin-colour stimulates a fleeting passion between the Ivoirian, Tanou, and Sarah, his Parisian landlady's daughter. She spies on him as he undresses; he sees her as the forbidden fruit, 'une autre voie de l'amour' [another way for love]. Returning to find her in his bedroom one day, they enjoy 'des douceurs infinies' [infinite delights], but these are specifically heightened by the joining of different coloured skins: 'La différence de leur peau créait chez tous deux un état psychique qui intensifiait leur bonheur' [The difference of their skin produced in both of them a mental state which made their happiness more intense]. The truth emerges when an accident makes Tanou impotent: Sarah sleeps with one of his friends, showing that her fascination with a black skin is greater than her commitment to Tanou as a person.

That cannot be said of the friendship between Alain Cambier and Charlotte, prominent in the first part of Bertène Juminer's first novel *Les Bâtards* (1961). He is a Guyanan studying medicine in Paris, and we learn of his intimate attachment at the outset. By the end of the section, however, 'Un couperet allait tomber sur la tranche d'existence que Charlotte avait partagée avec lui' [A guillotine was about to fall on the slice of life that Charlotte had shared with him]. It effectively cuts her out of the last two parts of the novel, recounting Cambier's medical work in Guyana. The very ordinariness of their relationship, its biodegradability as it were—'Entre elle et lui, la vie avait fait sa besogne' [Between her and him, life had done its business]—is a mark of increased sophistication and self-confidence. There is no over-dramatisation when another *Blanche/Noir* couple in the book discuss his unannounced arrival at her parents' house:

— Pourquoi n'as-tu pas précisé à tes parents qui j'étais?
— Qui tu étais?
— Oui: un homme de couleur.
— Je n'en voyais pas l'utilité.
— Ça aurait facilité les choses.

151

— Facilité quoi? Si tu devais parler de moi aux tiens, tu
préciserais que je suis blanche?
— Ce n'est pas pareil: tu es métropolitaine.

['Why didn't you specify to your parents who I was?'
'Who you were?'
'Yes: coloured.'
'I didn't see the point.'
'It would have made things easier.'
'Made what easier? If you had to speak about me to your
family, would you specify that I was white?'
'It's not the same: you're French.']

The novel is undoubtedly autobiographical, but its main
purpose is to explore West Indian identity as a form of
bastardy, metaphorically rejected, as Césaire observes in his
preface, both by the European father and by the African
mother. While a texture of mixed-race relationships is
woven, it is simply part of that broader search for identity.

The second part of Juminer's 1963 novel, *Au seuil d'un
nouveau cri*, explores *Blanche/Noir* relationships to
emphasise the universality of love. In *La Revanche de
Bozambo* (1968), however, Juminer will make some
sweeping distinctions between *Blanche/Noir* relations in
Europe and those in the U.S.A., but because he is specifically
playing on archetypes and reversing them to satirical
purpose, he is manifestly not a dupe to them. Up-ending his
topsy-turvy world, we understand that white racists in the
States, happy to lynch Blacks, are none the less fascinated by
black woman. White women in Europe are seen as having
the self-confidence to disdain Whites in favour of Blacks. In
the United States, by contrast, they are perceived as being as
racist as their menfolk. Intent on maintaining their
supremacy over both Black and White, they are said to use
'un atroce impérialisme vulvaire' [a dreadful vulvar
imperialism] over the latter so as to have them work out
their frustration on the former.[232]

CHAPTER 7
THE FREEDOM TO CHOOSE

'Nous ne serons pas les premiers à réaliser un mariage mixte
mais tous ceux qui l'ont fait ont connu cette rupture
et moi je ne suis pas prêt à la subir ni à te l'imposer.'
[We shan't be the first to have a mixed marriage,
but all those who have are familiar with this split,
and I'm not prepared either to undergo it or to impose it on you.]
Abdoul Doukouré[233]

TO FIND STEREOTYPES persisting beyond Independence, one has only to turn to Guy des Cars's *Sang d'Afrique* (1963), as populist and popular as the historical tales from the same period set on American slave plantations and signed Kyle Onstott.[234] Its basis is identical to an archetypal case-history, recorded by Augustin Barbara, in which two students, one black one white, gradually break down the race-barrier and become close.[235] Yolande Hervieu and Jacques Yero marry clandestinely and go to live in Oubangui-Chari. Yolande's father is a military ex-colonial racist of the old school, hostile and unbending even when Yero becomes 'Premier Ministre et Président du Conseil de la République centrafricaine' [Prime Minister and Head of Government in the Central African Republic]. Referring to Jacques as 'Président-Poète' [Poet-President], Des Cars clearly had Senghor in mind, so much so that Yero, whose poetic gift and nature prove highly seductive to Yolande, consistently quotes Senghor's poetry as his own, without acknowledgement.[236] The contempt for a black poet implicit in such plagiarism is consistent with the formulaic manner and the stock attitudes adopted to everything and everybody—not only African—throughout the novel. The fact that doubt about Jacques's honesty undermines the very basis of the character and plot seems never to have entered the author's mind.

Jacques is said to have '[d]es appétits de mâle primitif qui n'a plus qu'un désir: se repaître de blondeur lumineuse...' [the appetites of a primitive male with only one desire: to feed on luminous blondness]. As for Yolande, 'l'héritière des Hervieu commençait même à ressentir une étrange volupté à s'afficher avec un Noir' [the Hervieu heiress even began to feel a strange voluptuousness to be seen in public with a Black]. When Col. Hervieu learns of their marriage, he expostulates:

> — Ma fille aimant un Noir! Mais qu'ai-je donc fait au ciel pour qu'il me réserve une telle humiliation?
> D'une voix douce, presque résignée, Mme Hervieu répondit:
> — Étienne, le ciel ne permet pas que l'on méprise les autres. Tous les hommes sont frères...

> ['My daughter in love with a Black! What in heaven's name have I done to deserve such a humiliation?'
> Her voice quiet and resigned, Madame Hervieu replied:
> 'Étienne, heaven doesn't allow us to be contemptuous of other people. All men are brothers...']

The French bishop in Africa equally falls into stereotypical platitudes:

> Pour toutes nos populations de l'Oubangui, ce mariage va prendre l'aspect d'un symbole: ne sera-t-il pas la preuve éclatante que notre religion ne fait aucune discrimination raciale et cherche même à encourager ces mariages, qui ne peuvent que contribuer au rapprochement des peuples? [...] N'était-ce pas là une preuve éclatante que l'esprit de ségrégation n'avait plus cours et que la haine des races était un sentiment révolu? Pour les générations futures et pour tous ceux qui imiteraient leur exemple, Jacques et Yolande symboliseraient désormais l'harmonie par l'amour.

> [For all our Oubangui peoples, this marriage will take on the appearance of a symbol: will it not be the shining proof that our religion makes no discrimination between races and even seeks to encourage these marriages, which can only help bring peoples together? [...] Was it not a shining proof that segregation was over and done with and that racial hatred was a thing of the past? For future generations and all those who would follow their example,

Jacques and Yolande would be the symbol of harmony through love.]

A sceptical friend compares stock white responses to the couple in France and Africa:

> Là-bas, un couple tel que le vôtre peut, tout au plus, exciter la curiosité ou soulever l'ironie. Ici, il risque de déchaîner la haine...

> [There, a couple such as you can at most excite curiosity or prompt irony. Here, it threatens to unleash hatred.]

Urban Blacks are more tolerant according to this wholesale psychology: .

> à chaque fois qu'un Noir croisait le couple de la femme blonde et de celui qui la tenait tendrement par le bras, un large sourire éclairait le visage du passant. Mais il n'en était pas de même lorsqu'ils rencontraient un Blanc, ou surtout une femme blanche. L'homme blanc regardait le couple avec une réelle expression de mépris ou préférait détourner la tête comme si la vision de ces amoureux était répugnante. La femme blanche, elle, ne cachait pas son sentiment de totale réprobation et, pour peu qu'elle fût accompagnée d'une amie, elle n'hésitait pas à faire à haute voix des remarques désobligeantes.

> [each time a Black went by the couple of the blond woman and the man holding her tenderly by the arm, a broad smile lit up his face. But it was quite different when a white man crossed their path, and even more a white woman. The white man looked at them with utter scorn in his expression, or preferred to avert his gaze as if the sight of these lovers was repugnant to him. As for the white woman, she did not hide her feeling of absolute reproof and, if she were accompanied by a lady friend, did not hesitate to make disobliging remarks out loud.]

By contrast, attitudes in outlying villages would be far less tolerant:

> S'il paraît flatteur pour un Noir qui habite une ville complètement européanisée comme Dakar d'avoir une épouse blanche, il n'en est pas de même au centre de l'Afrique: c'est le pire des affronts! N'oubliez pas non plus que le matriarcat y est solidement implanté dans chaque village, chez la moindre peuplade... Vous aurez pour ennemies toutes les femmes noires! Ce

155

seront elles qui monteront les hommes contre vous et contre votre
mari… Pour elles, vous êtes à la fois une insulte et un défi!

[If it looks flattering for a Black who lives in a completely
Europeanised town such as Dakar to have a white wife, it's not
the same at all in the heart of Africa: it's the worst insult! Don't
forget that the matriarchy is solidly entrenched in every village,
in the smallest tribal group… You'll have every black woman as
an enemy! It's they who will stir the men up against you and your
husband… For those women, you are both an insult and a
challenge!]

On their wedding night, Yolande has the decidedly
suspect impression

que ce n'était pas le corps et la volonté d'un seul homme qui la
prenaient, mais toute l'Afrique avec sa chaleur animale, avec son
rythme et son mystère…

[that it wasn't the body and will of a single man which were
taking her, but the whole of Africa, with its animal heat, its
rhythm and its mystery.]

When the couple goes to live up-country, the author
indulges in the kind of excessive anthropological detail that,
as we have seen, unbalances so much earlier colonial
fiction. Whereas Demaison, however, had at least made his
own field observations, Des Cars is beholden to a single
book by Vergiat and parades page after page of borrowed
folklore.[237] Spice is added to the plot by Yolande witnessing
a clitoridectomy, the related songs being translated at length
when she has recovered from the experience, but many of
the traditional poems are present as gratuitous emphasis on
the 'primitive' nature of African society. It is scarcely
surprising that Jacques should finally assert his authority
through a series of melodramatic confrontations with the
forces of evil which beset him.

A similar set of attitudes, minus the plagiarism but with
double standards no less firmly in place, appears in Georges
Conchon's L'État sauvage (1964), sufficiently popular to be
made into a film. A European obsessed with the fear of a
Black getting too close to a white woman has no com-

punction in responding to his desire to approach a black woman, but it is the woman in both cases who becomes the forbidden person according to the social rules of each group. How refreshingly different to read in Cheik Dia's *Avant Liberté I* of the same year a bright echo, as it were, of the rain's biblical impartiality (Matthew 5. 45): 'Bien sûr il est Noir et moi Blanche, et après? Ça n'empêche pas le soleil de briller et de briller pour tous' [Of course he's black and I'm white: so what? That doesn't stop the sun shining, and shining on everybody].

In other respects this text is disappointingly stereotyped. The *Blanche/Noir* episode in Dia's piece is brief, but counterbalanced by other relationships, whether biracial or not. When Jean Nehmann opens his door to a black student seeking lodgings, it triggers off the recollections which fill the rest of the novella. He had been a business employee, working firstly in Dakar as an accountant and then up-country. It is Martha, who joins his business as a secretary, who recounts to him her affair with Doudou, acknowledging that she had idealised him and taken the initiative. On the beach on the island of Gorée,

> je rencontrais souvent Doudou, généralement seul. Il est grand, bien cambré, avec sa peau d'ébène qui faisait un contraste frappant avec sa petite serviette blanche qu'il aimait jeter sur l'épaule. [...] Moi qui n'avais jamais vu que des monstres noirs au cinéma ou dans les revues, cet homme, un véritable Dieu terrestre me fascinait. [...] C'est moi qui fis les premiers pas pour devenir sa copine de plage, et ensuite la grande amoureuse.

> [I often met Doudou, generally alone. He is tall, nicely shaped, with his ebony skin which made a fine contrast with the little white towel which he liked to throw over his shoulder. [...] I had only ever seen black monsters in the cinema or magazines, and this man, a veritable God on earth, fascinated me. [...] It was I who took the first steps to become his beach pal, and then the great lover.]

Such stereotypical idolisation is followed by familiar social pressures which lead to their separation and to marriage, on either side, to members of their own race. Martha's unconventionality is not strong enough to 'abattre cette muraille de la peau' [break down this wall of skin] so as to reveal 'une viande, méprisable, et le même sang rouge...' [contemptible meat, and the same red blood...].[238]

Opportunites for a black man to meet a white woman in France or elsewhere multiplied at and after the time of Independence, and this is reflected in the fiction. Almost every novel written by a black African seemed to contain an obligatory *couple domino*, if only as a passing episode among minor characters. The long shadow of European domination continued to be present even in the most independent-minded of books such as those published during the watershed year of 1968: Ahmadou Kourouma's *Les Soleils des indépendances*, Yambo Ouologuem's *Le Devoir de violence* and Bertène Juminer's *La Revanche de Bozambo* bear witness in their very different ways to the limits of independence. Increasingly, however, even if confrontation persisted in many instances, it came to be recognised that the confrontational mode, whatever its value for constructing a narrative, was inappropriate to the new circumstances.

Just as the phenomenon of political independence took time to be assimilated and its implications absorbed, and the twin problems of neocolonialism and corruption to be recognised and at least partially dealt with, so the new status of formerly colonised peoples involved a significant psychological adjustment. We therefore have, in addition to the inevitable perpetuators of outmoded stereotypes, writers who show that love between two individuals can abstract itself from prejudice and rise above its sweeping positions, whether thoughtlessly hostile or no less thoughtlessly favourable, to establish an essentially irenic mode in which genuine cultural differences can be explored.[239] Chamfort's celebrated maxim that 'l'amour, tel qu'il existe dans la société, n'est que l'échange de deux fantaisies et le contact de deux épidermes' [love, such as it exists in society, is only the exchange of two fancies and the contact of two skins], for all its cynicism, mentions no skin-colour.

Denis Oussou-Essui's *La Souche calcinée*, of 1973, like *Kocoumba, l'étudiant noir,* brings a secondary-school boy to

France only to strand him without money and force him to take menial work. It echoes the social realism of the earlier novel. Kongo Lagou lives in penury at Caen with his 'cousin' (a vague relative, in the usual African sense of the term) who has shacked up with a local waitress. Kongo himself, in Paris, goes with a prostitute who takes the initiative, but as in so many of the writings of this period, such relationships are just part of the background web, the main focus lying elsewhere. This is very clearly the case in Amadou Hampaté Bâ's *L'Etrange Destin de Wangrin* (1973), where, late in the book, Madame Terreau (aka Madame Blanche-Blanche) becomes Wangrin's mistress. Rife with fantasy, Jean-Louis Baghio'o's *Le Flamboyant à fleurs bleues*, also of 1973, traces generations of mixed-race couplings, most of them incidentally *Blanche-Noir*, in Guadeloupe. Pubescent black twins experience their first seminal climax with heavily feminised white phenomena (a beach of white sand and a dolphin imagined as a white girl) before full sexual initiation by their pale-skinned *chabine* mother.

A short story by Abdou Anta Ka, 'La Terrasse', the last of four in the collection entitled *Mal* (1975) seems to announce a new manner of exploring African cultural traditions which, at the end of the decade, is more fully developed in Olympe Bhêly-Quenum's *L'Initié*. Martine, a white wife in Dakar, learns of traditional Africa from her raggedy brother-in-law whom she ends up by idolising. She learns to adapt and so to avoid turning her husband, Amadou Sarr, into an alienated 'Nègre blanc' [white Black].

On a public bench, on a terrace overlooking the sea at Dakar, the narrator meets a beggar, Lamine, who proves to embody the traditional wisdom of Africa. Lamine is seeking his brother, the lawyer Amadou Sarr, married to Martine, 'la petite française [*sic*] quelconque, avec un boy, une bonne, un chauffeur' [your average little Frenchwoman, with a house-boy, a maid and a chauffeur]. The narrator leads him to their house, where Lamine finds Martine, childless, desperate to have one, and keen to consult the local *marabouts*. Their encounter is recounted retrospectively by each in turn. Lamine expostulates:

Je vis la femme de mon frère. Une blanche! Amadou avait osé épouser une blanche! J'étais dans un tel état d'irritation, d'exaspération. Elle s'avançait sur moi. Alors je fermai les yeux pour ne pas voir sa blancheur et lui tournai le dos. Comment auraient réagi mon père et ma mère? Mon père l'aurait maudit.

[I saw my brother's wife. A white woman! Amadou had dared to marry a white woman! I was in such a state of irritation and exasperation. She came towards me. I closed my eyes so as not to see her whiteness, and turned my back. How would my father and mother have reacted? My father would have cursed him.

This is followed by Martine's account of the same meeting. Lamine insists on 'l'eau de l'hospitalité' [the water of hospitality] being offered by her on her knees. She is found in that apparently compromising position, in some distress, by her husband: his indignation leads him to call the police. She is mesmerised by Lamine and cannot sleep, so Amadou agrees to have him freed and brought to the house, where he stays several months. Martine is completely subjugated by him and listens endlessly to his tales of traditional Africa. Their exchange on the subject is instructive:

— Ton mari en sait autant que moi.
Ce à quoi Martine répondit:
— Il ne le dit pas avec autant de conviction.
— C'est peut-être ta faute, fit Lamine.
— Comment ma faute? réagit Martine
— Les africaines [sic] qui épousent des blancs finissent par ressembler à leurs maris. Pourquoi toi tu ne cherches pas à ressembler à une africaine?
— Je n'en ai jamais ressenti le besoin, répliqua Martine en rougissant.
— Alors c'est la faute à mon frère?
— Comment ça?
— C'est lui qui cherche à te ressembler.
Enervée, Martine dit:
— Je ne sais pas.
Puis elle ajouta en trébuchant sur les mots:
— C'est un mal de ressembler, de ressembler à un français [sic]?
— Peut-être pas. Seulement, c'est un mal de ne pas ressembler à son père.

['Your husband knows as much as I do about it.'

To which Martine replied: 'He doesn't tell it with such conviction.'

'Perhaps that's your fault,' Lamine said.

'What do you mean, my fault?', Martine replied.

'African women who marry white men end up looking like their husbands. Why don't you try and look like an African?'

'I never felt the need to,' Martine answered with a blush.

'So it's my brother's fault?'

'What do you mean?'

'It's he who's trying to look like you.'

Irritated, Martine said: 'I don't know.' Then she added, stumbling on her words: 'Is it wrong to be like... like a Frenchman?'

'Perhaps not. Only, it's wrong not to be like your father.']

Martine learns her lesson and becomes notably gentler, especially in her treatment of the servants. She has learned respect for Africa. Only with such reconciliation can she 'donner des enfants à ce pays... Qu'est-ce qu'ils seraient devenus sans ce respect?' [give this country some children. What would have become of them without this respect?]. Through her, her husband is also transformed. As the blurb indicates, this is a story 'promettant le salut par la recomposition de soi dans l'authenticité humaine retrouvée' [promising salvation through the reintegration of self in rediscovered human authenticity].

A similar search for the elusive phenomenon of authenticity also lies at the heart of Abdoul Doukouré's *Le Déboussolé* (1978). One of the episodes in Kaydot's search for identity and a sense of purpose is spent with the Parisian, Sylvie, and they consider marrying, but Kaydot has serious doubts:

Il y aura aussi nos enfants qui ne seront acceptés ni par les Blancs ni par les Noirs, de vrais bâtards et, plus important, il y a toute l a renégation dont l'un d'entre nous sera l'objet. [...] Non, il y a trop de choses à sacrifier. [...] Nous ne serons pas les premiers à réaliser un mariage mixte mais tous ceux qui l'ont fait ont connu cette rupture et moi je ne suis pas prêt à la subir ni à te l'imposer.

[There'll also be our children, who won't be accepted by either Whites or Blacks, genuine bastards, and, even more important, a l l the disowning which each one of us will suffer. [...] We shan't be the first to have a mixed marriage, but all those who have are familiar with this split, and I'm not prepared either to undergo i t or to impose it on you.]

A twist is given to the usual scenarios in Cheikh Aliou Ndao's short story 'Le Nègre et la dame blanche', in *Le Marabout de la sécheresse* (1979). The framing narrative presents a reunion between the anonymous 'Nègre' and 'Dame blanche'. Within that frame is a flashback to their protracted affair in a mountain chalet, when the white woman was separated from her husband, Jacques. It transpires that the Black has in effect served to reunite them, and a bittersweet flavour is produced when the Black is confronted by Jacques who thanks him for bringing them together again.

We have noted already how Olympe Bhêly-Quenum, in his collection of short stories, *Liaison d'un été* (1968), included a matter-of-fact account of a successful *Blanc/Noire* relationship. The *Blanche/Noir* one in the title story which closes the collection is set in a resort in Normandy and revolves around the close friendship between Cofi, a Ghanaian student, and Christa, an English girl staying with her family, the improbably named Gemcleaners, at the same guesthouse for a summer holiday. Cofi's ability to translate for the visitors puts him in a privileged position, and he finds Christa's auburn hair and tinkling laughter irresistible. Although the relationship blossoms discreetly, it comes to a sudden and tragic end when Christa is drowned. The tale nevertheless gives Bhêly-Quenum the opportunity to present his essentially optimistic vision of race relations.

Shedding both his reticence about mixing with Whites and the inferiority complex generated by his African upbringing, Cofi befriends Christa and they find themselves by chance side by modest side, hand in demure hand, watching the film of *The Invisible Man*:[240]

162

Christa était contente... heureuse. Il y avait longtemps qu'elle souhaitait en finir avec les préjugés ancestraux conformément auxquels les Gemcleaner ne devaient avoir le moindre rapport avec les *coloured men* que Mrs Gemcleaner appelait irrémédiablement *niggers*, parce que le mot *negro* lui semblait vraiment trop gentil. [...] A Londres, Christa n'aurait pu avoir l'occasion qui, en France, s'offrait à elle d'aider un rêve dont la réalisation, déjà, lui paraissait vouée au néant: avoir une aventure avec un Noir, aller au-delà de l'interdit, advienne que pourra!

[Christa was pleased... happy. She had long wanted to be rid of the ancestral prejudices according to which the Gemcleaners should have nothing whatever to do with the 'coloured men' that Mrs Gemcleaner invariably referred to as 'niggers' because the word 'negro' seemed to her too nice a word. [...] In London, Christa would not have had the opportunity, as she did now in France, to help promote a dream whose realisation already seemed doomed to failure: to have an affair with a Black and break the taboo, come what may!]

Cofi, somewhat nonplussed by the increasing intensity of Christa's clasp at the cinema, finds her waiting for him when, a couple of nights later, he returns late from a dance. They go into his room for coffee and a snack; much to Cofi's embarrassment, Christa tearfully negotiates the inevitable clinch. It all remains highly proper, unlike the scene of Sarah's advances to Tanou in Nokan's *Le Soleil noir point* which we have already noticed. Bhêly-Quenum picks his way delicately through the young couple's unequal emotions.

Christa is resolutely anti-racist,

Car pour moi, un homme est un homme; on peut le mépriser pour n'importe quel motif, mais non parce qu'il est un homme de couleur.

[For me, a man is a man; you can despise him for whatever reason you like, but not because he's coloured.]

She further declares that she held this view long before meeting Cofi and that it has often been a bone of contention between her parents and herself. This means, however, that she uses her friendship with Cofi as a challenge to parental authority: she needs to assert her independence and Cofi is the almost arbitrary occasion of it.

The inevitable showdown occurs when Christa angrily stands her ground against the Gemcleaners' stereotypical racism. Cofi overhears sufficient of the exchange—'Il y avait du barouf, en effet, et le mot *nigger* revenait sans cesse' [There was a row, indeed, and the word 'nigger' kept cropping up]—to persuade us to eavesdrop:

> — C'est un homme, un vrai gentleman et je l'aime! cria Christa.
> — Tu es folle, ma petite! hurla sa mère.
> — C'est-à-dire anti-raciste et anti-stupidité?
> — Mais, mon Dieu, qu'est-ce que tu trouves chez ce négro?
> — La gentillesse, l'amour!... Ah! l'amour tel que je le cherchais depuis très longtemps!
> — Sans blague, ma petite Christa!... Et à quoi tendent ces mariages mixtes si ce n'est seulement à vulgariser des sortes d'accouplements comme chez les bêtes, entre races pures et races impures. De sorte que les enfants qui en naissent ne savent ni à quel sang, ni à quel culte ils appartiennent, moitié blancs, moitié négrillons, ils ne sont pas même d'accord avec eux-mêmes! déclara M. Gemcleaner.
>
> C'était le comble. Christa éclata en sanglots; Cofi était comme saisi de vertige.

> ['He's a man, a real gentleman, and I love him,' Christa shouted.
> 'You're out of your mind,' her mother flung back at her.
> 'You mean anti-racist and anti-stupidity?'
> 'But, my God, what do you see in this negro?'
> 'Kindness, love... the love that I've been looking so long for.'
> 'You don't say, Christa!... And what do these mixed marriages lead to if it isn't just to people coupling like beasts all over the place, mixing pure and impure races? So that the children don't know what race or what religion they belong to, half white and half black, they can't even agree with themselves!' declared Mr Gemcleaner.
>
> That was the limit. Christa burst out sobbing; and Cofi felt sort of giddy all of a sudden.]

The family leaves precipitately for Deauville. Christa sends cards and finally a few lines of farewell tantamount to a suicide note. Cofi's landlady draws his attention to a newspaper report of a drowning at Deauville, and when he confirms that it is Christa he gives way to the sobbing that ends the story.

Bhêly-Quenum has stated:

> écrire la vie d'une Blanche qui aura vécu avec un Noir ou d'une Africaine et d'un Européen ne m'intéresse pas. Trop de poncifs à ce sujet.

> [writing the story of a white woman who has lived with a Black or of an African woman with a European man doesn't interest me. There are too many stereotypes in that area.][241]

Clearly, he wants to direct our attention to the imaginative stimulus of his writing rather than to relationships which, from being taboo, have become something of a totem. Yet his very return to the motif, firstly in the short stories we have recalled and then in two further novels, *L'Initié* (1979) and the as yet unpublished *C'était à Tigony* suggests that he sees in it at least a fascinating nexus for the exploration of other issues. If race is not a problem, why does it figure so insistently? Bhêly-Quenum's persistently positive and sometimes central representation of mixed-race marriages or intimate relationships contrasts starkly with that of the out-and-out racists (often but not exclusively European) who bring pressures to bear on the couple. So however one might approve in human terms of an enlightened, liberal attitude, one cannot but regret, from a literary point of view, that the devil continues to have the best tunes. The intensity of racist passion felt by the Gemcleaner couple is scarcely matched by the youngsters' tentativeness and discretion.

The longer form of the novel and the writer's growing experience conspire to help Bhêly-Quenum avoid well-intentioned simplicities. *L'Initié* enacts, rather than merely postulates, a successful *Blanche/Noir* marriage. It becomes the most natural thing in the world simply because it is a given. The questions with which the novel deals lie elsewhere, notably in the exploration of the validity and nature of seemingly irrational forces welling up from powerful African traditions, in which good and evil are as central as in western moral philosophies.

Apart from a substantial prologue set in France, *L'Initié* is set in Djên'Kêdjê, a pseudonymous West African country, the initiate of its title being Kofi-Marc Tingo, whom we see first as an articulate medical student and then as a doctor practising in his native country. He meets his wife-to-be, Corinne Le Ferlier, a devout Roman Catholic, when he consoles her for failing an examination and, as so often occurs in this literature, their relationship becomes, in T.S. Eliot's term, an 'objective correlative' for interracial relations in general. While the author's view remains rosy, he is no dupe to naive idealism: 'épouser un nègre, ça ne doit pas être la découverte d'un Eldorado' [marrying a negro is not like discovering an Eldorado].

Some of the intense student discussions relate political positions to personal relations, with different speakers at a rally coming to different conclusions. One declares:

> Vos pays dépendront de la Métropole [...] tant que vous, les Nègres, vous vous obstinerez à nous imiter, nous les Blancs, et à épouser nos filles au lieu de vous apparier avec celles de votre race.

> [Your countries will depend on metropolitan France [...] as long as you Blacks insist on copying us Whites and on marrying our daughters rather than pairing off with women of your own race.]

Implicitly denouncing the *non sequitur* in such an argument, and doubtless as hostile to slavish imitation as he is to mindless endogamy, Bhêly-Quenum presents another point of view to end the prologue:

> moi je ne dissimule pas ma préférence: elle est pour les Nègres qui se marient franchement avec la femme—noire, blanche ou jaune— qui leur plaît [...]. J'ajoute que ce n'est pas parce qu'un Africain a épousé une Européenne ou une Asiatique qu'il perd ses racines nègres et ne peut plus être utile à son pays.

> [I do not hide my preference: it goes to Blacks who marry the woman—black, white or yellow—they love. What is more, it is not because an African has married a European or an Asian woman

that he loses his negro roots and his capacity to be useful to his country.]

Implicitly, Marc Tingo embodies this latter position, which he illustrates during the rest of the novel.

Part of its texture involves comment on changing African attitudes to Whites. Evoking the formerly exclusive European sector of the town where Marc has settled with Corinne, now fully qualified in tropical medicine, the author reflects on the infiltration of the 'quartier européen' [European quarter] by the emerging Black bourgeoisie:

> il y avait des Africains, fonctionnaires du cadre européen, qui s'étaient mis à construire des pavillons dans ce quartier, à courtiser des femmes blanches qui ne les méprisaient point...
> Alors le mur qu'on croyait avoir élevé entre la communauté noire et la communauté blanche s'effrita progressivement, sans violence ni heurts.

> [there were African civil servants working with the European administration who had begun to construct detached houses in the area and to pay court to white women who made no objections...
> Then the wall that was thought to have been built between the black and white communities gradually crumbled, with neither violence nor confrontation.]

The resultant *couples domino*, among which, willy-nilly, Marc and Corinne find themselves, are emblematic of that lowering of barriers and raising of levels of understanding.

Inevitably, market women make assumptions, chosen by the author precisely because they represent universally the archetype of prejudice masquerading as popular wisdom:

> "Rien que d'avoir épousé une yovo [une Blanche] prouve que tu es riche"; "Tu ne vas tout de même pas marchander, toi qui a épousé une Blanche!"

> ['The mere fact of marrying a white woman proves you're rich!' 'You're not going to haggle, are you, you who've married a white woman!']

Such banter is an integral part of barter, and good humour remains the order of the day. It is quite different from the vicious and deep-rooted prejudice evinced by a group of bar-propping Frenchmen still trailing their colonialist mentality. When Marc, for good medical reasons, advises them to encourage one of their number, Jacques Vacher, to reduce his alcohol intake, the reactions are unanimous:

> — Quel emmerdeur! grogna Robert.
> — On le croirait entré dans l'Armée du Salut! dit Bourtel.
> — Sale rat des loges, ajouta Vacher.
> — Je me demande comment il arrive à s'entendre avec sa bonne femme, tout Franc-Maçon qu'il est et elle, bigote comme on n'en voit qu'en enfer, dit Barrel.

> ['What a pain in the butt!', Robert grumbled.
> 'You'd think he'd joined the Salvation Army!' said Bourtel.
> 'Filthy mason,' Vacher added.
> 'I wonder how he manages to get along with his wife, what with him a freemason and her such a bigot as you'd only come across in hell,' said Barrel.]

It is almost inevitable that Marc's intellectual and moral qualities which so irritate this group should be housed in a handsome body, the description of which is held over until he has his first direct confrontation with a far more formidable rival in the person of Djessou, who embodies the evil abuse of fetishism. It is impossible not to recall the idealised portraits of noble Blacks from Oroonoko on, even to the 'lèvres à peine lippues' [not very fleshy lips], and so to observe in passing the irony of a black writer echoing, however mutedly, a stereotype established by Whites. Marc's inner qualities are of a piece with his handsome appearance. Indifferent to gossip and intent on using his gifts to positive effect, Marc is presented as worthy of the novel's title:

> Authentique enfant du pays et initié, dans le sens absolu du terme à Djên'Kêdjê, c'est-à-dire en homme qui ne pense jamais à la mort, il utilisait avec conviction les forces dont Atchê lui avait transmis les secrets; et comme il s'agissait de forces essentiellement constructives, il s'en servait ou pour édifier, ou pour construire, ou bien pour maintenir debout ce qui avait été créé en lui insufflant la vie.

[A genuine child of his country and an initiate, in the absolute sense of that word in Djên'Kêdjê, that is to say a man who never thinks of death, he used the forces whose secrets Atchê had transmitted to him with conviction; and as it meant essentially constructive forces, he used them either to construct or to maintain in place that which had been created when life was breathed into him.]

Djessou is represented by contrast as using 'ses puissances sur toutes les forces occultes' [his power over occult forces] to gain power over superstitious and fearful people, including some returned with a degree of European sophistication or even with a white wife. It is stressed that reason alone cannot explain everything and that an acceptance of the existence of the irrrational is an important factor in coming to terms with life in Africa. When Bhêly-Quenum writes:

en Afrique, deux et deux ne font pas quatre nécessairement, mais [...] il y a toujours, implexe à cette addition, quelque unité en deça ou au-delà du résultat admis dans le monde des Blancs,

[in Africa, two and two do not necessarily make four, but there is always, involved in this addition, some unit below or above the result admitted by Whites,]

he is clearly on the side of imaginative writers like Dostoievsky and Césaire who have recognised that reason, represented by arithmetic, is not everything.[242] In truth, it would be difficult to find anywhere a rational thinker who did not acknowledge the existence of an imaginative capacity in human beings neither bounded nor explicable by reason alone.

Chapter X of L'Initié brings the question of interracial relations to the fore while suggesting that it is individual imaginative capacities which determine the degree to which the irrational and otherness are apprehended and understood. If Corinne remains to some extent outside Marc's world, it is in part because he cannot unlock for her the 'porte étroite' [strait gate] leading to full awareness because it would require him to make her face some unpalatable truths of colonial history. Some of his unease is expressed, however, in a measure of pomposity assigned to the language used:

> Que Corinne, parfois, ne le comprît pas et qu'il pût y avoir des moments d'asymbolie entre eux lui était assez pénible; mais il n'y pouvait rien; les secrets des civilisations africaines ridiculisées, étouffées dans leurs germes, s'étaient concentrés en noms premiers et en d'intelligibles onomatopées réfugiées dans le cœur de rares illettrés, initiés chez qui on découvre la liberté que l'Afrique est en train de perdre: celle qui confère à l'homme total sa supériorité sur l'anarchique syndrome de la civilisation occidentale qui la méprise.
>
> C'était ce dont Marc, une fois encore, venait de prendre conscience: un monde clos dont il ne pouvait pas ouvrir la porte étroite devant Corinne sans quelques explications politiques et historiques préalables et, partant, sans la peiner parce qu'elle était Européenne.

> [That Corinne, sometimes, should fail to understand him and that there should be moments when they were out of kilter with each other was hard for him to bear; but he could do nothing about it; the secrets of ridiculed African civilisations nipped in the bud had been concentrated into primary names and intelligible onomatopœias which had taken refuge in the hearts of rare illiterate people who had been initiated and in whom can be found the freedom that Africa is in the process of losing: the kind of freedom which confers on the complete man his superiority over the anarchic syndrome of contemptuous western civilisation.
>
> That was what Marc had once again just become aware of: a closed world whose strait gate he could not open in front of Corinne without first giving her some political and historical explanations and so in the process hurting her feelings because she was European.]

The barrier between them stems from 'la naïveté de l'exotisme facile et trop littéraire dont Corinne gardait le souvenir' [the naivety of the facile and over-literary exoticism which still filled Corinne's mind], and Marc is fortunate in being more perspicacious regarding this feature in his wife than Charles Bovary had been.

> Hormis les premières semaines de leur amitié, bien avant qu'il se fût agi de fiançailles entre eux, les problèmes de différence raciale, de blancheur ou de noirceur de peau, voire d'autres que

l'on dit inhérents aux europoïdes, ne s'étaient jamais posés à leur conscience d'amoureux...

[Apart from the very first weeks of their friendship, long before they had thought of getting engaged, problems of racial difference, of black or white skin, or even of other things said to be inherent in Europoids, had never occurred to their lovers' minds.]

Yet there remain areas of Marc's awareness which Corinne will never penetrate, and these relate specifically to his initiation, thanks to his uncle's ancestral powers, into the mysteries of the 'noms premiers' [primary names] of occult forces which underlie appearances. Those 'forces obscures' [dark forces], which lent the book its originally projected title, give Marc the rationally improbable potential to 'anéantir une foule, terrasser une panthère, rendre des hommes difformes ou les métamorphoser en cochon' [annihilate a crowd, bring a panther down, make people misshapen or transform them into pigs]. Manifestly, in the author's eyes as well as those of his hero, the easy-going mixed-race society which strolls along the beach or dances the night away is lightweight, even contemptible, compared with the profound importance of an episode recalled in the intervening pages: Marc's initiation by Atchê into the Ogboni ritual society.[243]

Marc eventually triumphs over Djessou in spectacular fashion by summoning the powers with which he has been entrusted. On the final page of the novel, he confides in Corinne:

J'ai désiré avec ardeur [...] que tu voies un jour, de tes propres yeux, la force des choses simples qui me font aimer et craindre à la fois mon pays.

[I wanted with all my heart [...] for you to see for yourself one day the force of those simple things which make me both love and fear my country.]

By the same token, however, she becomes aware of an unbridgeable gap between them:

171

Cette façon de Marc de s'écarter d'elle, de la tenir hors de cause afin de se considérer comme l'unique responsable de la mort de Djessou peina Corinne. Elle se sentit seule et frustrée; elle ferma les yeux. La voiture roulait vite, et Corinne avait l'invincible impression d'être précipitée dans un abîme dont elle n'atteignait pas le fond [...].

[That way Marc had of detaching himself from her, of not involving her so as to consider himself the only person responsible for Djessou's death hurt Corinne. She felt alone and frustrated; she closed her eyes. The car sped along, and Corinne had the irresistible impression of being hurled into an abyss whose bottom she never reached...]

The completion of this last sentence closes the novel on a contrasting note of self-assurance, even of self-satisfaction, supported by the image of the dawn of a new day:

tandis que Marc, décontracté, maître de lui-même et singulièrement tranquille, conduisait, les mains mollement posées sur le volant, le regard fixé sur la route encore mouillée, mais faiblement scintillante des premiers rayons du soleil. (p.250)

[whereas Marc, relaxed, totally self-controlled and extraordinarily calm, drove on, his hands limp on the steering-wheel, his gaze fixed on the road still wet from the rain, but glinting slightly in the first rays of the sun.]

Even if Corinne's education is unfinished, the basis for its continuation and ultimate completion is set. Skin-colour is not an issue in the book but a given, and while primary racism occurs sporadically around the *couple domino*, it is at a much deeper level that the novel makes its cultural exploration. The ending of imperialism conspires with increased African self-confidence to powerful effect in both author and black protagonist. Because of their shared personal and professional experiences, Marc and Corinne are not left on a naively optimistic threshold at the end, as is the case with Veneuse and Andrée in *Un homme pareil aux autres*, since their solidarity as a couple has been tested, their harmony and solidity proven, and their optimism at facing the future together well grounded.

CHAPTER 8
LIBERTY AND LICENCE

'Si vous voulez un aperçu de la guerre nucléaire,
mettez un Nègre et une Blanche dans un lit.'
[If you want a taste of nuclear war,
put a black man and a white woman in bed together.]
Dany Laferrière[244]

THE 1980s, which, as we have seen, allowed continuing exploration of social and political issues through the focalising *Blanche/Noir* couple, also saw the revival of *libertinage*. While few new permutations were left to be imagined after those revealed with such gusto in the late eighteenth century, the theme is given a new twist in the form of *géolibertinage*, implying an endless romp which takes the whole world as its bedroom. In giving a rather special gloss to the concept of globalisation, it raises the question of the compatibility of pluralism and integration, in this case both cultural, psychological and aesthetic. As a new generation seizes the opportunities and confronts the problems of political independence, so the literary ground shifts, reducing the antagonistic potential of biracial pairings. The pressures on the couple, jointly and severally, may continue to include both the overt and the insidious, reflecting social realities, but another, often neglected, factor needs bearing in mind: the requirements of psychological verisimilitude and of efficient, individuated narrative.

The master/slave or coloniser/colonised relations of earlier periods were superseded by the personal and political liberation so long desired. But freedom proved double-edged: not only did the outside forces of neocolonialism impose limits, but its ostensible boundlessness also needed circumscribing from within. The self-confidence already apparent in some writings from the 1950s and 1960s—in Mongo Beti, Bhêly-Quenum and Sembene for example—might have been expected to spread exponentially through the ranks of emerging writers. What we find in many, indeed most, cases is rather a continuing search for and assertion of social and cultural identity in relation to the former coloniser. In this regard, therefore, exploring the representation of mixed-race couples still provides a critical litmus-test for judging attitudes.

One might expect all writers treating the *couple domino* in recent years to be so steeped in Fanon, whose early death in 1961 served to add an almost mythical dimension to his massive influence, that they are unable to escape his interpretation of *Blanche/Noir* relations as an intimate form of revenge by the latter alone for centuries of exploitation, whereas the former might also feel aggrieved. Only rarely in fact, as we shall see, is that interpretation (extended and adapted to circumstances in the United States by Eldridge Cleaver in his *Soul on Ice* of 1967) made to dominate the psyche of a black protagonist, as if writers sought to avoid Fanon's shadow as much as they did the even longer one cast by Othello. Seen perhaps as creatively unfruitful, an ironic use is more often than not made of it. Such sophistication is also apparent in the readiness of writers to avoid many of the traditional, stereotypical re- sponses to the *Blanche/Noir* couple by probing more deeply into the social and political pressures brought to bear upon them. While, in some cases which we shall examine, therefore, the *couple domino* is a significant datum of the narrative, its importance is outweighed by broader socio- political considerations, not to mention sexual fantasies.

As we noted earlier, location is crucial in mixed-race marriages: it is relatively easy for such a couple to cope in a modern European city, where cosmopolitanism conspires with anonymity to foster the principle of 'live and let live'. The social traditions and expectations in West Africa, even in its urban jungles, create circumstances in which the European wife finds adaptation far more difficult, especially where, as is usually the case, she does not speak the local language(s). Entrenched attitudes on both sides tend to set her apart. One may deplore those attitudes, but their force cannot be denied: for centuries, superior fire-power reinforced the Eurocentric assumption of all other brands of superiority, and even the most liberal-minded White still lapses occasionally into a loaded use of terms—'civilisation', 'culture' etc.—which prolong that assumption.

The 1980s are acknowledged in the western world as years of unabashed sexual diversity, and this is reflected in the promiscuousness evidenced in many of the novels of that decade and the next. While René Depestre's characters explore straight sex with a variety of multinational partners enjoying what he terms 'géolibertinage', several others cheerfully present in addition homosexual relationships and group sex, along with a generous apparatus of fetishes and perversions. The healthy scepticism appropriate with regard to *fin-de-siècle* recycling is nevertheless compelled to recognise a disturbing proliferation of pornographic fantasies towards the end of the eighteenth, nineteenth and twentieth centuries. The last two decades have renewed the earlier tradition of unbridled variety (late nineteenth-century mixed-race relations being dominated rather by the *Blanc/Noire* pairing), sometimes forgetting that too much spice jades the palate just as too much salt causes dropsy.

Before investigating works of *géolibertinage*, however, we turn to a significant novel by Mariama Bâ. *Un chant écarlate* (1981) focuses no less centrally but far more pessimistically than *L'Initié* on the fortunes of a *Blanche/Noir* couple in West Africa. This posthumously published second novel recounts the love of two young people of essentially noble lineage, Ousmane being a scion of traditional Muslim stock in Senegal and Mireille being born into a minor French aristocratic family. His father, a former *Tirailleur sénégalais*, is a highly respected and senior member of the Islamic community, of modest means and with a single wife, whereas hers is in the diplomatic corps, professionally veiling, as appearances require, his profound contempt for

Blacks. For half the novel, we follow the sentimental education of their children through a series of ordeals which their love survives. Those ordeals include Mireille's immediate dismissal to France when a lovingly inscribed photograph of Ousmane is discovered. Each completes the studies necessary to become a secondary-school teacher, thereby gaining financial independence.

'Beauty and the Beast' is the nickname given Mireille and Ousmane by their French neighbour, and it is repeated particularly on occasions when this racist busybody hears or senses discord between the pair. Prominent too by implication in the novel's final chapter is the myth of Medea when Mireille, driven to frenzy by Ousmane's infidelity and her mother-in-law's ostracism of her, kills her child.[245] The very choice of Mireille's family name, de La Vallée, may hark ironically back to the author of *Le Nègre comme il y a peu de blancs* mentioned above in respect of *Un homme pareil aux autres*. And there is much to be said on another occasion about the Freudian id of M. de La Vallée's reiterated reference to Ousmane as 'ça' [that/id], an appellation to which the unhinged Mireille herself resorts late in the book.[246] It is not that Ousmane is exempt of Othello-like jealous potential, indeed 'les affres de la jalousie le torturaient' [he was tortured by pangs of jealousy] as a youngster, rather that Mireille, utterly devoted to him, gives him no cause. In an entirely plausible development, it is she who becomes jealous because of his return to the childhood friend, Ouleymatou, who had once inspired jealousy in him.

The overt discussion of interracial marriages is vigorously pursued. At an early stage, Mireille states her belief in 'l'amour sans patrie' [love without a country] and Ousmane asks himself the rhetorical question: 'Était-il un partenaire possible pour Mireille? Pourrait-il assumer telle mutation?' [Was he a possible partner for Mireille? Could he undergo such a transformation?]. Both of them have to engage in strategic warfare (the words 'combat' and 'lutte' [struggle] recur) against their milieu, embodied in particular in one of their parents, Ousmane's mother Yaye Khady and

Mireille's father Jean de La Vallée. Opposition strengthens their resolve but, in making them more absolute in their determination, leads to a degree of over-reaction which contains the seeds of disaster.

In a *style indirect libre* which allows third-person detachment from himself,[247] Ousmane reflects before opening the first letter received from Mireille after their enforced separation:

> Il pressentait une lutte âpre dont Mireille était l'enjeu. Les parents de son amie avaient pour armes des arguments solides. Si Mireille se ralliait à leurs désirs, il serait vaincu. Fétu de paille tordu, il serait relégué dans la déception dont il avait connu les prémisses [*sic*, for 'prémices'] avec Ouleymatou.
>
> Et si Mireille le choisissait, à la place de la richesse et de la facilité?
>
> Et si Mireille choisissait le Nègre, fils d'un invalide de guerre et d'une ménagère analphabète?

> [He had a premonition about a bitter struggle of which Mireille was the object. His friend's parents had solid arguments as weapons. If Mireille rallied to their ideas, he would be defeated. Like a twisted wisp of straw, he would be relegated to the disappointment which he had begun to know with Ouleymatou.
>
> What if Mireille chose him instead of wealth and simplicity?
>
> What if Mireille chose the Negro, the son of a disabled ex-serviceman and an illiterate housewife?]

Having read the letter, Ousmane finds himself torn between love and duty, each of which agonisingly, as in Corneille's classic dramas, contains elements of the other:

> La lettre l'orientait vers le "sérieux". Son contenu l'entraînait vers les déchirements entre les choix inconciliables. Ousmane retrouvait la situation "cornélienne": "D'un côté, mon cœur épris d'une Blanche... de l'autre, «ma société». Entre les deux, ma raison oscillante, comme le fléau d'une balance qui ne peut trouver un point d'équilibre entre deux plateaux aux contenus également chers".

> [The letter guided him towards 'serious' things. Its contents led him towards the rift between irreconcilable choices. Ousmane

recognised the 'Cornelian' situation: 'On the one hand, my heart in love with a white woman... on the other, "my society". Between the two, my reason see-sawing like a balance-beam on scales unable to find a point of equilibrium between two pans containing things equally dear to me.']

A litany of his love for his *quartier*, punctuated by the anaphora 'Renier Usine Niara Talli?' [Renounce Niara Talli Factory?], occupies the next two pages and the perceived 'treachery' of stepping outside his race is forcefully encapsulated not only by the term *'guena het'*, glossed in a footnote as 'Traître à sa patrie (littéralement: sortir de sa race)' [Traitor to one's country (literally: stepping outside one's race)], but also by the protestations of his friends which, given the outcome of the novel and various other signs, seem to echo the author's reservations:

> "Ah! Non et non! Le règne des couples mixtes est révolu. Ce genre de mariage se défendait dans le système colonial où les Nègres intéressés tiraient promotion et profit de leur union avec une Blanche. On doit choisir sa femme chez soi. Ces Blancs sont des racistes. Leur humanisme d'hier n'était que leurre, une arme d'exploitation honteuse pour endormir nos consciences [...]." [...]
> "Au-delà de vos sens, quelles sources de communion aurez-vous toi et ta «toubab»? On ne bâtit pas l'avenir sur «des passés sans liens». Tant de ménages mixtes sont broyés par l'incompréhension. L'Afrique sait être jalouse jusqu'à la cruauté, méfie-toi."

> ['No, no and no! The era of mixed-race couples is over. That type of marriage was justified in the colonial system when the Negroes involved reaped promotion and benefit from their union with a white woman. You should choose your wife at home. These Whites are racists. Their humanism of yesteryear was a lure, a weapon of shameful exploitation to dull our awareness.' [...] 'Beyond your senses, what will you have in common with your white woman? You don't build the future on a past without bridges. So many biracial households are destroyed by incomprehension. Africa can be jealous to the point of cruelty: watch out.']

The same reservations are repeated by some of Ousmane's friends in Mireille's presence after her marriage:

Les traditionalistes du groupe s'acharnaient à démolir le mariage mixte:
"Une femme ne peut être qu'une femme, grande ou petite, noire ou blanche. Pourquoi dès lors la prendre ailleurs que chez soi? Le mariage est déjà un problème épineux. Pourquoi se créer d'autres difficultés?"

[The traditionalists in the group did everything to destroy mixed marriages:
'A woman can only be a woman, tall or short, black or white. So why take one from somewhere other than at home? Marriage is already a thorny problem. Why create more difficulties for yourself?'

Ousmane's high-handed *machismo,* revealed in its full ugliness only after his marriage, is anticipated by his insistence on Mireille's becoming a Muslim as a sign of her submission:

avant tout engagement, il criera son attachement à sa condition de Nègre. Il exigera de Mireille, comme préalable, sa conversion à l'Islam. Élevé dans la voie d'"Allah", musulman convaincu et pratiquant dans le sillage d'un père ancien "talibé", Ousmane ne concevait pas de mariage en dehors de la mosquée.

[before any commitment, he will shout his attachment to his condition as a Negro. He will demand of Mireille, as a prerequisite, her conversion to Islam. Brought up in the way of Allah, a convinced Muslim following in the wake of a former student of the Koran, Ousmane could not conceive of marriage outside the mosque.]

Only later does a distasteful mixture of special pleading and bad faith emerge to vie with the no less specious argument that transracial marriages were justified in colonial times but not in independent Africa: the following passage is particularly significant in this respect:

Des couples mixtes existeront toujours: hommes blancs nantis de femmes noires; hommes noirs, souvent honnêtes dans leur engagement, mariés à des Blanches.
Ousmane fréquentait des couples mixtes. Certains de ses camarades, plus anciens que lui dans la vie conjugale, n'approuvaient pas son mariage, malgré leur propre option.

— À l'époque coloniale, par égoïsme, paresse, faiblesse ou opportunisme, selon leurs termes, nous avions choisi cette voie. Mais toi! Avec la renaissance de notre pays et la percée de l a femme noire! Toi, c'est l'espoir des Négresses.

[...] L'homme était "blanchi" en profondeur, impitoyablement détaché de ses origines. "Piètres pantins!" grondait Ousmane. Du Nègre ils n'avaient que la peau.

[Mixed couples will always exist: white men consorting with black women; black men, often honest in their commitment, married to white women.

Ousmane frequented mixed couples. Some of his comrades, married before he was, did not approve of his marriage, despite their own option.

'In colonial times, out of egoism, laziness, weakness or opportunism, in their terms, we had chosen this way. But you! With the rebirth of our country and the advancement of our womenfolk! You are the hope of our black women.'

[...] The man was 'whitewashed' in depth, pitilessly separated from his origins. 'Paltry puppets!', Ousmane grumbled. The only Negro thing about them was their skin.]

At this juncture, Ousmane seems to accept that where the black husband remains dominant, 'ce genre de métissage enrichit l'Afrique' [this kind of miscegenation enriches Africa]. Yet his ground shifts, and arguments good in another context are found to bolster bad ones in his attempt to legitimise his renewal of ties with Ouleymatou:

— Il y a la force des habitudes, poursuivit-il, la force des croyances dont on ne peut se départir sans être déraciné. Le poids du passé reste déterminant. Je me cherche en vain en Mireille. Elle ne répond pas à mes aspirations.

['There's the force of habit', he continued, 'the force of beliefs which you can't give up without being uprooted. The weight of the past remains decisive. I look in vain for myself in Mireille. She doesn't correspond to my aspirations.']

As he reiterates later, 'souvent quand un Noir épouse une Blanche, sa patrie le perd' [often when a Black marries a white woman, his country loses him]. Mireille's submissiveness proves inadequate to prevent his infidelity, which he justifies as a profounder fidelity to Africa, since 'Ouleymatou se confondait dans son esprit avec l'Afrique' [Ouley-matou coincided in his mind with Africa]. Provoked beyond reason, Mireille does more than shout 'Sale Nègre!' [Dirty Nigger!] at Ousmane. Faced with a dead son and a wife out of her mind, he realises in a flash that it is he who is mad and that it is his madness which has sparked Mireille's:

> La vérité, brutalement, se révélait à son esprit: Mireille était devenue folle. L'immobilité froide de son fils était éloquente! Une œuvre de démente! [...] En Ousmane, un déclic tardif de la raison issu de la peur. Une clarté humaine se frayait encore une voie dans la densité des ombres. Un dégoût nauséeux de lui-même le submergea. Fou à lier, il avait contaminé Mireille. La folie seule expliquait son aveuglement et ses actes. Au-delà de certaines limites, l'engagement est déraison, s'il piétine des zones où fleurissent la pitié et la charité. [...] D'une femme jeune et belle, intelligente et gourmande de tendresse, pleine à craquer d'amour et de qualités, il avait pétri inconsciemment une furie.

> [The truth was brutally revealed to him: Mireille had gone mad. The cold immobility of his son spoke volumes! The work of a madwoman! [...] In Ousmane, there was a belated realisation born of fear. Some human clarity still shone through the thick shadows. He was sick with disgust at himself. Stark raving mad, he had contaminated Mireille. Madness alone explained his blindness and his actions. Beyond certain limits, commitment is not reasonable, if it tramples underfoot zones of pity and charity. [...] Out of a beautiful young woman, intelligent and hungry for tenderness, full to the brim with love and positive qualities, he had unconsciously fashioned a fury.]

The relationship explored in *Un homme pareil aux autres* is explicitly condemned by several characters in *Un chant écarlate* as one justified only by colonial circumstances. The thrust of the narrative in the latter novel furthermore suggests the author's implicit agreement with this position, aligning herself with a desire for self-sufficiency redolent of the early years of political independence. The failure of socialism to change conditions in Africa led to a revival of traditionalism. Even if Bâ allows herself to end the novel on a seemingly open-ended question, the fact that that question, *'Lane-la?'*, repeated no less than eighteen times in the keening at Ousmane's hospital bedside, is put in Wolof seems to reinforce traditional hostility to exogamy.[248] The idealised white female, so long a model, is now rejected. Mireille is disposed of briskly and efficiently in both real and literary terms: 'Maîtrisée par les pompiers sans difficulté. [...] L'Ambassade de France prévenue a pris le cas en mains' [Overpowered without difficulty by the paramedics. [...] The French Embassy, duly advised, has taken the case in hand].

A particularly revealing contrast with the principal couple is provided by a minor but singularly happy *Blanche/Noir* pair, Pierrette and Lamine. Whereas Ousmane is steeped in the ideas propounded by Negritude, Lamine is denounced for abandoning his race and allowing himself to be assimilated into all things European. Pierrette's parents are supportive and she ignores her in-laws; Lamine is not tortured by ideology and gives up his faith and its practices without turning a hair. Their happiness clearly comes, however, at what the author considers an unacceptable price. The torment and tragedy of the main couple are the inevitable birth-pangs of independence.

The critique of Negritude which Sembene presents in his 1981 novel *Le Dernier de l'empire*, is of a far more savage and satirical variety. One episode focuses on the emblematically absent black president's choice of a white wife: Léon Mignane is a thinly veiled caricature of Senghor, a 'Nègre blanc' [white Black] perceived as a neocolonial stooge alienated from his roots. The idea that 'pour l'orgueil et la fierté nationale, le couple présidentiel doit être originaire du pays' [for the sake of personal and national pride, the presidential couple should be from the country itself] lends private feelings a political dimension: in this case the *Blanche/Noir* couple attracts the author's carefully orchestrated condemnation.[249]

Two relevant books by Mongo Beti were published in the early 1980s. *Les Deux Mères de Guillaume Ismaël Dzewatama, futur camionneur* (1982) and its sequel *La Revanche*

de Guillaume Ismaël Dzewatama (1984), somewhat like other post-Independence novels by Mongo Beti, continue to fight old battles. In contrast to Bâ's novel, the focus is political rather than sociological. Their presentation of the *Blanche/Noir* relationship is none the less both substantial and novel.

In the first volume, we meet the Guillaume of the title, the son of Jean-François and Agathe, Blacks married according to local custom. Jean-François goes to study law in France, however, where he meets and marries Marie-Pierre, judged by Agathe on her photograph as 'cette horrible femme qui a une peau et des cheveux d'albinos' [that horrible woman with the skin and hair of an albino]. Marie-Pierre joins Jean-François when he has accepted the prominent but sensitive post of Procureur de la République [State Prosecutor] with the one-party government. Marie-Pierre is kept in the dark both about the true nature of the government and Jean-François's work for it—he is, for example, blackmailed into signing death warrants under the threat of losing his post, house, status etc.—and about Agathe's and Jean-François's true relationship to Guillaume—she is told that he is the son of Jean-François's sister who died in childbirth.

The novel is much more concerned with shady politics than with the mixed-race question, which is categorised either as incommensurable ('l'Afrique n'est pas la France' [Africa is not France] is a repeated comment used with increasing irony) or as no problem at all (Marie-Pierre is largely free of prejudice, and acts as a loving mother to Guillaume: 'c'était véritablement sa deuxième mère' [she really was his second mother]). When Marie-Pierre is told of Guillaume's 'two mothers', she realises her naivety. The volume ends with Jean-François, involved in the preparation of an unsuccessful *coup d'État*, arrested and put in prison.

· *La Revanche de Guillaume Ismaël Dzewatama* finds Marie-Pierre alone after Jean-François's imprisonment, and totally uncertain as to his fate. It opens on a dialogue between her and the chairman of the 'Association des

Epouses étrangères des Disparus' [Association for Foreign Wives of the Disappeared], the solicitor Michèle Mabaya-Caillebaut, who seeks to use Marie-Pierre as spokesperson in France to publicise the abuses of the regime and so stop aid (which is being siphoned off for personal profit). In her vulnerable state, she is open to being used by others to their own ends. But there is also a preparedness to fantasise about her social role, as when she is talked into imagining herself as 'rédemptrice blanche des déshérités africains' [a white redemptress of disinherited Africans], a 'Madone blanche des descamisados noirs!' [white Madonna for black ragamuffins] equivalent to Eva Perón.

The vicious regime does not spare her, but Whites are even more directly vindictive. She is interrogated and sexually attacked by them, held in utter contempt for being a 'pute à nègres' [nigger-whore]. The situation prompts her to accept Mabaya-Caillebaut's mission, which gives us an opportunity to see French racism through Mongo Beti's eyes:

> Longtemps maintenu par le mépris et les préjugés dans l'inconsistance vaporeuse de l'ectoplasme, l'immigré de couleur, facile à pourchasser parce que seul repérable dans la foule, n'avait commencé à émerger à l'existence officielle que pour devenir la bête noire constamment en butte aux rigueurs de l'administration, à l'hostilité de l'homme de la rue si docile aux injonctions tacites des classes dirigeantes.

> [Long held by contempt and prejudice in the hazy insubstantiality of ectoplasm, the coloured immigrant, easy to chase because he stands out in a crowd, had begun to emerge into official existence only to become the constantly harrassed *bête noire* of the administration, and subjected to the hostility of the man in the street who soaked up the unspoken injunctions of the ruling classes.]

Denunciation of well-intentioned bodies, including Amnesty International, and of commercial multinationals is part of the author's broad sweep. He shows several instances of the usually hidden machinations, including the forces which, despite the courage shown by Marie-Pierre, disrupt the meeting she addresses on behalf of the association. Woven into the narrative are examples of petty or violent racism which regrettably reinforce the paradigms of prejudice: corruption blocks the way forward. A technical feature of the writing even reinforces the effect: the reader is advised more than once of good or bad news to come in a calculated refusal of suspense.

❧

There are already signs of *géolibertinage* in Bhêly-Quenum's short stories, published in 1998 under the title *La Naissance d'Abikou*, but written up to forty-five years earlier. Several of the tales contain mixed-race relationships in various venues. Thus in 'Madame Vénihale' (written winter 1958–59), Irène is attracted to Kouglo and, as a frustrated widow, allows him some intimacies. The principal *Blanche/Noir* couplings occur, however, in 'La Conférence de Berlin' (undated), where Alihonou Aniko-kou and Milena meet during a scientific conference at Berlin, and in 'Sacrifice au soleil de midi' (written spring 1965), with its fierce indictment of small-town racism, in which Kwamé Guidoglo has sex successively with Ursula Pénisset and Madame Paniel. Elsewhere there are hetero-sexual relations between Blacks and between Whites, and even one lesbian approach (by Faith at Oxford on Irène, the narrator in 'Madame Vénihale', before her marriage). Once again, Bhêly-Quenum shows himself to be a precursor. In a world of increasing ease of travel, *géolibertinage* is a seam which contains ore yet to be exploited.

The proliferation of sexual partners is both more apparent and more central in Depestre's first collection of short stories, *Alléluia pour une femme-jardin* (1981). Predominantly straight sex is the *raison d'être* of the different narrators' lives and of the stories. The variety stems from the range of provenance of the partners rather than from the type of sex involved. In 'Mémoires de géolibertinage', for example, Olivier Vermont, a Black from the West Indies, launches on *géolibertinage* when he is at the Cité Universitaire in Paris, selecting at random 'noires,

185

blondes, jaunes, rousses, brunes, mulâtres' [black, blonde, yellow, auburn, brunette, mulatto women]. 'L'Enchantement d'une heure de pluie' is set in Rio de Janeiro and its narrator, a 'fils de la Caraïbe' [son of the Caribbean], is a kind of sex-sandwich between Ilona Kossuth (Hungarian) and Margareta (French of Swedish lineage), 'l'une aussi belle que l'autre' [each one as pretty as the other].

A more political note is struck with 'Noces à Tiscornia'. Jean-Paul Eginhard and his wife Evelyn ('*de parents d'origine hongroise de Transylvanie*' [of Hungarian parentage from Transylvania]) arrive in Cuba only to be arrested for being a *couple domino,* or in the words of the immigration police report: '*un couple mixte: en effet, le* señor *Eginhard est mulâtre et la* señora *une femme blanche du meilleur type caucasien*' [a mixed couple: señor Eginhard is a mulatto and the *señora* a white woman of the best Caucasian type]. While held in Tiscornia prison, Soledad Cortès García, who has arrived to meet a man whom she has married by correspondence and who has not met her at the port, is also admitted, and told:

> Dans ce pavillon-ci, vous avez comme voisins seulement un couple: l'homme est mulâtre et sa femme est aussi blanche que vous, et je dois dire aussi décente et belle. Mais dans notre République le couple mixte n'a pas sa place; c'est pourquoi on le renvoie d'où il vient.
>
> [In this wing, you have just one couple as neighbours: the man is a mulatto and his wife is as white as you and, I must say, as decent and beautiful. But in our Republic the mixed couple has no place; that's why we send them back where they come from.]

In an episode reminiscent of others in Depestre's writing, Jean-Paul deflowers her joyously before she is collected by her husband.

'Un retour à Jacmel' has Dr Hervé Braget, a Haitian returnee, break his Hippocratic oath more than once. He miraculously makes Sister Nathalie des Anges pregnant at the convent clinic as he tends her in the presence of other nuns, so she is sent back to Europe.

186

Depestre continues in a similar vein, multiplying colour combinations in a further collection of short stories, *Éros dans un train chinois* (1990). 'Il était une fois une jeune fille yougoslave et un étudiant haïtien [...]' [Once upon a time there was a Yugoslavian girl and a Haitian student], in 'La Jupe', is a typical tongue-in-cheek approach allowing a new application of the fairy-tale formula. In 'Noël au Mont d'arbois', another Haitian, Jacques Agoué, born in Jacmel as was René Depestre himself (but this is not the place to speculate on the precise autobiographical nature of the writing), enjoys the company of the film actress Vanessa Hopwood, from Memphis, Tennessee. 'L'Œillet ensorcelé' presents Vincent Lozeroy and a series of Haitian girls with various propensities and pleasures. The narrator enjoys relations with women from China, Haiti, Brazil and Japan. In the case of 'Coq gaulois et vin de palme' a Senegalese, Dr Sem Masséna, at whom a Negro homosexual also makes a determined pass, takes advantage of the wife of a Brazilian bookshop owner, but is shot dead by the husband for his pains.

A vignette in Abasse Ndione's *La Vie en spirale* (1984), narrated by a drug-pusher, indicates the sexually suggestive force of the mixed-race pairing when a pornographic booklet is thrust into his girl-friend's hands. It feeds (on) the stock fantasies. All its twenty-nine photographs feature a naked couple, a shameless redhead and 'un éphèbe noir ébène [...] le sexe gros comme une cuisse de nouveau-né, dressé, l'angle pénien très aigu' [an ebony-black young man, his sex the size of a new-born baby's thigh erect at a steep angle].[250]

Ken Bugul presents with apparent relish an even greater variety of sexual encounters, including what she calls 'l'amour en groupe, le brassage des races' [group love and racial mixtures]. Her first novel, *Le Baobab fou* (1984), sets a hotchpotch of sexual partners, free love, group sex and so forth in the swinging seventies in Brussels. Ken Bugul the narrator (the pseudonym means 'Nobody wants me' in Wolof) has affairs with Louis (followed by an abortion), Jean Wermer, Souleymane, an unspecified young Frenchman, and an equally anonymous girl, while earlier lesbian gropings are mentioned. Jean Wermer, having divorced a wife now living with a Tutsi, discovers his own homosexual propensities and sets up with François, to which Ken Bugul is added in a *ménage à trois* which breaks up because of François sleeping with her, before he goes into partnership with a Senegalese. If this appears sadly unedifying, it must be remembered that it represents an extraordinary feminist assertion of independence for the Senegalese author whose real name is Mariétou Mbaye. The significance of the double liberation involved for one both black and female in a deeply traditional, patriarchal society emerging from French rule should not be underestimated. She is fully aware of 'les désastres de l'aliénation' [the disasters of alienation] and uses the gestures of immorality to make a moral point.

The particular case of Léonora, an Italian cleaning-woman who has also had an abortion, going out with an African, allows the author to comment on *Blanche/Noir* relations:

> Elle sortait avec un étudiant africain, mais cela ne marchait pas. D'après tout ce qu'elle m'en dit, je constatai que son étudiant rejoignait le clan de tous ces étudiants étrangers qui cherchaient à sortir avec une Blanche pour être peinards et aussi pour obéir au mythe de l'hypersexualité de l'homme noir. De plus, la femme blanche restait le fantasme refoulé du colonisé agressé par ses attitudes provocatrices. La femme toubab habituée aux préludes interminables, trouve souvent dans le Noir, un surexcité, un refoulé qui lui fait l'amour avec violence. Frustration sur culpabilité. [...]
>
> Léonora refusait d'appartenir à cette catégorie de Blanches qui sortaient avec les étrangers pour l'originalité et le sexe, les "Blanches à Nègres".

> [She was going out with an African student, but it wasn't working. From what she said to me, I recognised that her student joined the club of all those foreign students trying to go out with a white woman so as to have an easy time but also to obey the myth of the black man's hypersexuality. What's more, the white woman was still the repressed fantasy of the colonised man under attack from her provocative attitudes. The white woman, used to endless foreplay, often finds in black men someone overexcited and

188

repressed who makes love violently. Frustration on top of a guilt complex. [...]

Léonora refused to belong to that category of white women who went out with foreigners for the sake of originality and sex, the 'Negro-lovers'.]

In her next novel, *Cendres et braises* (1994), Ken Bugul concentrates on a *Blanc/Noire* couple, Y. and Marie Ndiaga Mbaye, but there is a passing mention of 'une jeune bretonne [*sic*] irlandaise [...] tombée dans les bras de certains Africains' [a young Irish Breton who has fallen into the arms of certain Africans]. She clearly continues to see, as she remarks in *Le Baobab fou*, the profound interactive forces at work in the *couple domino* as 'un enchevêtrement d'histoire et de métahistoire' [a tangle of history and meta-history].

Dany Laferrière's riposte in *Comment faire l'amour avec un nègre sans se fatiguer* (1985, subsequently made into a film) is 'L'HISTOIRE NOUS SERT D'APHRODISIAQUE' [HISTORY SERVES AS AN APHRODISIAC]. Reminiscent of Nerciat's *Le Diable au corps* and not a little influenced by Chester Himes, James Baldwin and Henry Miller, this is the most rumbustious and iconoclastic novel of the period and seems to encapsulate and propound Fanon's revenge theory (most directly in the second chapter) but does so in such a way as to show both its limitations and its joylessness.

It can scarcely be said that the novel has a plot: everything revolves around the sexual escapades of the eponymous Black, and the reader, while appreciating the unbridled wit, makes up for his seeming lack of exhaustion. The author, a Haitian settled in Canada, is reflected in his larger-than-life hero and chooses a style replete (in the original edition but not in subsequent reprints) with the extensive capitalisation of words which also partakes of the comic strip. Everything about the book will offend the delicate reader. It nevertheless remains hilarious testimony to a self-confidence all too frequently absent from earlier fiction in French by Blacks. Judge by this foretaste:

> Dans les années 70, l'Amérique était encore bandée sur le Rouge. Les étudiantes blanches faisaient leur B.A. sexuelle quasiment dans les réserves indiennes. [...] À chaque hurlement entendu la nuit dans les dortoirs, on pouvait deviner, suivant la modulation, qu'un Huron, un Iroquois ou un Cheyenne venait d'ensemencer une jeune Blanche de son foutre rouge.

> [In the 70s, Redskins were what made America horny. White sophomoresses went on to do their B.A. in Sexual Studies on Indian reservations. [...] With each yelp heard at night in the dormitories, you could guess, according to its modulation, whether a Huron, an Iroquois or a Cheyenne had just released his red sperm into a young white girl.]

Now the turn of the Black has arrived with a vengeance:

> BAISER NÈGRE, C'EST BAISER AUTREMENT. L'Amérique aime baiser AUTREMENT. LA VENGEANCE NÈGRE ET LA MAUVAISE CONSCIENCE BLANCHE AU LIT, ÇA FAIT UNE DE CES NUITS! En tout cas, il a fallu tirer des dortoirs nègres les filles aux joues roses et aux cheveux blonds. [...] LA HAINE DANS L'ACTE SEXUEL EST PLUS EFFICACE QUE L'AMOUR. C'est fini tout ça. La dernière guerre livrée en Amérique. À côté de cette guerre des sexes colorés, celle de Corée fut une escarmouche. Et la guerre du Viêt-nam, une plaisanterie sans incidence sur le cours de la civilisation judéo-chrétienne. Si vous voulez un aperçu de la guerre nucléaire, mettez un Nègre et une Blanche dans un lit. Mais aujourd'hui, c'est fini. Nous avons frôlé la DESTRUCTION TOTALE sans le savoir. LE NÈGRE ÉTAIT LA DERNIÈRE BOMBE SEXUELLE CAPABLE DE FAIRE SAUTER LA PLANÈTE. Et il est mort. Entre le cuisses d'une BLANCHE.

> [SCREWING BLACK IS SCREWING DIFFERENT. America likes screwing different. Black revenge and white guilty conscience in bed, what a night that makes! Anyway, girls with pink cheeks and blond hair had to be dragged out of black dormitories. [...]HATE IN THE SEX ACT IS MORE EFFECTIVE THAN LOVE. All that's over and done with. The last American war. Compared with that war of coloured sex, the Korean war was a mere skirmish. And the one in Vietnam a joke with no effect on the course of Judeo-Christian civilisation. If you want a taste of nuclear war, put a black man and a white woman in bed together.

190

But today it's all over. We have come close to TOTAL
DESTRUCTION without realising it. THE NEGRO WAS THE
LAST SEXUAL BOMB CAPABLE OF BLOWING UP THE
PLANET. And he's dead. Between the thighs of a WHITE
WOMAN.]

The macho narrator takes full advantage of the fascination he exerts over the range of young women he meets. If
he philosophises, it is almost exclusively on the subject of
mixed-race sexual relations, reaffirming the traditional
pecking order:

C'est que dans l'échelle des valeurs occidentales, la Blanche
est inférieure au Blanc et supérieure au Nègre. C'est pourquoi elle
n'est capable de prendre véritablement son pied qu'avec le Nègre.
Ce n'est pas sorcier, avec lui elle peut aller jusqu'au bout. Il n'y a
de véritable relation sexuelle qu'inégale. LA BLANCHE DOIT
FAIRE JOUIR LE BLANC, ET LE NÈGRE, LA BLANCHE. D'où le
mythe du Nègre grand baiseur. Bon baiseur, oui. Mais pas avec la
Négresse. C'est à la Négresse de faire jouir le Nègre.

[On the scale of western values, the white woman comes
below the white man and above the Black. That's why she can
only really have it off with a Black. There's nothing magic about
it: with him she can go the whole way. Every sexual relationship
is an unequal one. THE WHITE WOMAN MUST MAKE THE
WHITE MAN COME, AND THE BLACK, THE WHITE
WOMAN. Hence the myth of the potent Black. Yes he is. But not
with a black woman. It's up to the black woman to make the black
man come.]

The narrator proceeds to expound his obsessive viewpoint:

Je pense que le couple Nègre/Blanche est pire qu'une bombe. Le
Nègre baisant la Négresse ne vaut peut-être pas la corde qui doit
le pendre, mais avec la Blanche, il y a de fortes chances qu'il se
passe quelque chose. Pourquoi? Parce que la sexualité est avant
tout affaire de phantasmes et le phantasme accouplant le Nègre
avec la Blanche est l'un des plus explosifs qui soit.

[I think that the black man/white woman couple is worse
than a bomb. The Black screwing a Negress isn't worth the rope to
hang him with perhaps, but with a white woman, there's every
chance that something will happen. Why? Because sexuality is
first and foremost a matter of fantasies, and the fantasy coupling

191

the Black with a white woman is one of the most explosive that exists.]

In this game of sexual power-politics, Laferrière observes a nice distinction in the matter of assimilation: for him the modern young Black is

un urbain et un occidental. Mais cela, il ne l'admettra devant aucune Blanche pour tout l'ivoire du monde. Devant le Blanc, il veut passer pour un Occidental, mais devant la Blanche, l'Afrique doit lui servir, en quelque sorte, de SEXE SURNUMÉRAIRE.

[urban and western. But he'll never admit that to any white woman for all the ivory in the world. With a white man, he wants to pass for a westerner, but with a white woman, Africa must serve as a sort of SUPERNUMERARY SEX.]

Ultimately therefore, in this self-mocking, jaundiced fantasy which plays so heavily on the stereotype of the underdog wreaking revenge with his most powerful and secret weapon, the conclusion is unsurprising: 'Vous savez, dans une rencontre entre un Noir et une Blanche, ce qui prédomine, c'est le mensonge' [You know, when a black man meets a white woman, what is uppermost is mendacity].

A quite different love-affair threads its way through the tale: that of the narrator with his precious typewriter. Writing of Lewis Nkosi's *Mating Birds* (1986), in which a *Blanche/Noir* relationship is established in the dangerous South Africa of apartheid, the authors of *The Empire Writes Back* make the excellent point that

the 'book' and the 'pen' are the keys to power, for 'knowledge' in the South African context means 'writing' and hence the control over communication. But in *Mating Birds* the outcome is ambiguous, Ndi is 'a real devil', since the pen and the phallus become interchangeable symbols which have deep and obvious significance in this reverse metaphor of cultural rape.[251]

Mutatis mutandis, this clearly applies to Laferrière's novel. It is also true of the first Polynesian novel by a woman, Chantal Spitz's *L'Île des rêves écrasées* (1991), which takes as its subject the exploration, through a *Blanche/Noir* relationship, of the status of language and literature in the double mythical perspective of Tahiti in European eyes and vice versa. One cannot help but recall not just Diderot's *Supplément au Voyage de Bougainville* but also Victor Segalen's *Les Immémoriaux* of 1907, particularly in view of his seminal reflections on otherness in his *Essai sur l'exotisme.*

Pius Ngandu Nkashama's *Vie et mœurs d'un primitif en Essonne quatre-vingt-onze* (1987) passingly explores the possibility of a *Blanche/Noir* relationship in spite of the paralysing heritage of colonial assumptions. The narrator realises the significance of managing, free of the impotence determined by history and therefore of any inferiority complex, to view his colleague Pascale as an individual.[252]

To return, however, to the motif of sexual variety, we find Diana Mordasini's *Le Botillon perdu* (1990) set in Paris, Senegal and London against the background of apartheid South Africa. It follows the fortunes of various biracial couples. As a black transsexual settled in Switzerland, the author not surprisingly explores sexual and racial variety. The main *Blanche/Noir* pairing is Bakary, a member of the diplomatic corps, and his wife Muriel, who separate but continue to respect each other and to see their child. Unbeknown to each until after they marry, both are involved in clandestine anti-apartheid activities. *Blanc/Noire* pairings end in one case unhappily (Van Hoeck leaves his wife Diary just as he leaves the racist South African ranks, is tortured and killed by the regime), and in another happily (Werner and Esther live in Germany with their two children). There may be little psychological or emotional probing by the author, but at least Bakary and Muriel persist archetypally neither with loving nor with hating one another. The sexual mixture is further complicated by the overt homosexuality of one character, Raoul, and the seemingly repressed homosexuality of another after he has left his wife who believes he has hankerings after Bakary.

The apartheid regime prompted so many powerful books in English that it is not surprising that Mordasini's novel pales beside them. But it is typical of work of the period in that a mishmash of transracial sex is part of a narrative texture which generally has aims other than titillation, whether social or political, and whether earnest or satirical.

Laurence Gavron's *Marabouts d'ficelle* (2000) likewise domesticates an extraordinary, though very different, proposition. The narrator, Madeleine, a free-thinking divorced Jewess happily remarried to the charming, easy-going Étienne Tourneur, embarks on a further marriage, this time before a *marabout*, to Malick Ndoye, a Senegalese long since settled in Paris with his Senegalese wife, Sidonie, to whom he had promised monogamy. Polygamy and polyandry are thus presented in parallel in a provocative and witty fable exploring the limits not of sexual variety—straight heterosexuality is the only item on the menu—but of sexual fidelity. Madeleine believes that she can be faithful to two men simultaneously while at the same time persuading both them and Sidonie to accept the situation just as she does, with total equanimity.

Speaking to Malick, she presents the unusual as entirely plausible as well as desirable:

> — [...] Même si je t'ai épousé, même si je fais l'amour avec toi, je ne suis pas infidèle.
> — Tu l'aimes moins, forcément.
> Là, je suis carrément choquée.
> — Mais pas du tout, au contraire. Plus je t'aime, plus j'aime Étienne!

> ['Even if I have married you, even if I make love to you, I am not unfaithful.'
> 'You love him less, inevitably.'
> That frankly shocks me.
> 'Not in the least; on the contrary. The more I love you, the more I love Étienne!']

Whatever the outcome of her initiative—and it is Madeleine who, like so many other white women we have

194

observed in *Blanche/Noir* relationships, consistently takes the initiative—it puts to the test some standard assumptions. About polygamy, most obviously, or its western equivalent in which a husband routinely takes a mistress, whereas the converse, polyandry or a wife taking a lover, sends shock-waves through societies still dominated by masculinist thinking. About the very possibility of defying conventional morality while remaining within the society concerned. About received notions of identity and the systems of belief which shore it up, challenged by the delights of free-wheeling rootlessness.

The experiment is engagingly presented in this accomplished first novel with its playful title (omit 'Mara' and you are left with 'bouts d[e] ficelle' [bits of string]). Madeleine's logic is impeccable; and the author rises to the challenge, when the heroine and her new husband return to Paris from a 'honeymoon' in Senegal, of having the four parties concerned meet despite both Étienne and Sidonie reacting hostilely in the first place both to their partners' actions and, by extension, to each other. The fact that Malick finally leaves with Sidonie, and Madeleine with Étienne, may appear to conclude that the experiment has failed, but a delicious ambiguity is suggested by a simultaneous backward glance shared by Madeleine and Malick. Will Orpheus lose his Eurydice? Will convention win the day? We are left to surmise the future of the relationships between the foursome, but the very unconventionality of the circumstances draws attention away from questions of colour to questions of love. This thrust brings us full circle after a quarter of a millennium during which a preoccupation with colour, linked to race and so to racism, had usurped the place of normal human relations. In its own way, like *Le Botillon perdu*, *Marabout d'ficelles* moves towards the key proposition that a *couple domino* can enjoy an ordinary love, with neither more nor less chance of success or failure than any other, one where there is, as Maryse Condé remarks in a different context, 'Rien à signaler. Des accouplements ordinaires' [Nothing worth mentioning. Just ordinary couplings].[253]

It is Condé indeed who marks the key shift from an emphasis on racial opposition to the value of cultural variety. The pivotal role in her work is held by *Traversée de la mangrove* (1989), set in Guadeloupe. Structured along the lines of *As I Lay Dying*, and under Faulkner's influence of concentration on the socio-cultural rather than the racial, Condé registers that shift in Man Sonson's reaction to her son's marriage to a European. The old woman has lived through a time of slavery and racial confrontation and has difficulty coming to terms with the idea of harmony replacing the entrenched enmity between Blacks and Whites. But at least her son's attitude makes her—and us—think. Her very reference to Africa and tentative rejection of its use as a yardstick echoes the ground-bass of Negritude and reflects Condé's dissatisfaction with the confrontational postulates and impact of that movement, divisive in an unexpectedly damaging way between Blacks in Africa and those in the diaspora when they discover how divergent their cultures have been.

> — […] Les Blancs nous ont mis en esclavage. Les Blancs nous ont mis des fers aux pieds. Et tu épouses une femme blanche!
> Il a ri:
> — Maman, tout ça, l'esclavage, les fers aux pieds, c'est de l'histoire ancienne. Il faut vivre avec son temps.
> Peut-être qu'il a raison. Peut-être qu'il faut déraciner de nos têtes l'herbe de Guinée et le chiendent des vieilles rancœurs. Peut-être qu'il faut apprendre de nouveaux battements à nos cœurs. Peut-être que ces mots-là, noirs, blancs, ne signifient plus grand-chose!

> ['Whites put us in slavery. Whites put shackles on our feet. And you're marrying a white woman!'
> He laughed: 'Mum, all that—slavery, shackles—is ancient history. You have to move with the times.'
> Perhaps he's right. Perhaps we have to pull up out of our heads all that Guinea-weed and scutch-grass of old resentments. Perhaps we have to teach our hearts new ways to beat. Perhaps those words black and white don't mean much any longer!][254]

From being a betrayal, a *Blanche/Noir* marriage can at last be seen as a refusal to kowtow to a racist agenda.

CHAPTER 9
FULL CIRCLE

'Non! ce n'est pas un problème de Blanc à Noir, de race à race.
Le problème se situe maintenant entre nous.'
[No! it's not a problem between Black and White, race and race.
The problem now is between ourselves.]
Denis Oussou -Essui[255]

WRITING IN 1986, Geneviève Billy noted that 'Un mariage mixte en France aujourd'hui a donc à peu près les mêmes chances de réussite qu'un autre' [A mixed-race marriage in France today therefore has about the same chances of success as any other].[256] A year later, in *Le Défi*, Michèle Assamoua, another white Frenchwoman, writes:

> Les couples mixtes, en Europe, n'ont guère d'autres problèmes que ceux posés par le racisme de certains Européens, mais de retour en Afrique, tout est différent...
>
> [Mixed couples in Europe have no problems other than those posed by the racism of some Europeans, but back in Africa, everything is different...]

She presents five cases of *Blanche/Noir* couples in the Ivory Coast, and since four of the five end in defeat we may reasonably infer that she was less optimistic. Both women, it seems, were married to Africans and write from personal experience: Billy lives in the south-west of France and Assamoua in West Africa. But whether in reality or in fiction, the success or otherwise of a mixed-race marriage is not determined by statistics even if it may become an item in statistical reports.

Billy's *Le Couple mixte* pursues the touching personal account of the author's marriage presented in her 1981 *La Piste de la soif.* With abundant quotation from the affecting

197

correspondence it generated, she records case-histories which, however partial, contribute to the overall picture. A more balanced and reliable one is provided by Augustin Barbara's academic study, first published in 1985 under the title *Mariages sans frontières* and later as *Les Couples mixtes*. Even the earlier sociological work by Thérèse Kuoh-Moukoury, *Les Couples dominos*, in the very exhaustiveness of its analysis of the various permutations available, is inevitably less personal and more objective than Billy's writings.

A play dating from 1985, Luc Blin Niamkey's *La Femme blanche de Monsieur Aka*, encapsulates the shock-waves felt throughout an Ivoirian community when a native son return from a decade in France with a white wife. The material ambitions of Aka's father come in for the greatest condemnation, but the tendency of local girls to lose touch with tradition and ape white manners to the point of using lightening agents to whiten their skin is also condemned. Ultimately Monique, Aka's white wife, though never seen on stage, is greeted warmly by the community, the more so because she is pregnant.

Assamoua's *Le Défi* has an intermediate generic status. It is not the novel announced on the cover (but not on the title-page), but a series of five *reportages*-cum-short-stories, each presenting the particular circumstances of a *Blanche/Noir* couple living in or near Abidjan. It is clear from the heartfelt preface that the white author clearly has first-hand experience of the pressures of such couples surviving in the alien, often hostile climate of Ivoirian society. Four cases end unhappily to an extent (but none tragically), the fifth and last happily. No allusion, overt or covert, is made to Fanon's revenge theory. Instead, there is a massive investment in presenting the problems from the white woman's point of view (each story bears the female protagonist's name as its title), while portrayal of the black viewpoint is much more sketchy. Recurrent features are the imposition of the African family; the unreal, favoured world of *coopérants* [French-government-sponsored workers]; the difficulty for white women of coming to terms with the squalor, noise and gregariousness of local society, exacerbated by limited finances. Despite the problems, an optimistic stance is adopted, even if this seems to fly in the face of the hard evidence. Love, when it survives, conquers all.

The author seems to imagine, however, that she is writing in a vacuum, and her tone assumes an almost missionary fervour:

> Il existe peu de livres traitant du problème des couples mixtes. Sujet tabou? Ignorance? L'Afrique est désormais à cinq heures de vol de Paris. Africains et Blancs se côtoient journellement en Europe comme en Afrique et il me semble qu'il serait temps d'exorcicer [*sic*] quelques vieux préjugés en tentant de faire mieux comprendre les difficultés auxquelles sont confrontés ces couples.
>
> Beaucoup de livres écrits sur ce sujet ne révèlent rien, faussant le problème ou ne le posant même pas, faute de documentation sérieuse...
>
> Puisse ce recueil ne pas sembler trop pessimiste—il l'est sans doute un peu—car mon intention première est d'informer des véritables problèmes et non de décourager d'éventuels candidats à un mariage mixte, afin qu'ils connaissent mieux les difficultés qui les attendent, qu'ils soient plus à même de les surmonter le moment venu.
>
> [...] épouser un Africain, c'est un peu lancer un défi à la société, à ses préjugés et à ses coutumes.

> [Few books exist which treat the problem of mixed-race couples. A taboo subject? Ignorance? Africa is now only five hours' flying time away from Paris. Africans and Whites rub shoulders in Europe as in Africa and it seems to me that it is time to exorcise some of the old prejudices by trying to get people to understand the difficulties confronted by these couples.
>
> Many books written on this topic reveal nothing, distort the problem or do not even pose it, for lack of serious documentation...
>
> May this collection not appear too pessimistic—it undoubtedly is to an extent—because my prime intention is to inform people about the real problems and not to discourage possible candidates for a mixed marriage, so that they are more fully aware of the difficulties awaiting them and better equipped to overcome them when the time comes.
>
> [...] marrying an African is a bit like throwing a gauntlet down to society, its prejudices and its customs.]

She goes on to suggest that

> Les quelques cas exposés ici n'ont rien d'exceptionnel, ils sont même en dessous [sic] de la vérité. Un couple mixte heureux, ça existe, mais ce couple se met en marge de la société comme tous ceux qui se refusent à suivre les sentiers battus [...].

[The few cases presented here are not exceptional, in fact they fall rather short of the truth. Such a thing as a happy mixed couple does exist, but it lives on the margins of society like all those who refuse to follow well-trodden paths.]

The case of 'Christine' emphasises the practical problems of everyday life for a modest couple—she is a nurse and Kouamé Amany an electrician—first in the Paris suburbs and then in West Africa. Thrown out of the family home by her violently racist father, they are faced by the usual lies of prospective landladies. Africans drop in for meals unannounced, stretching their already meagre budget. After a while they marry and in due course have a son, two daughters arriving later. There are instances of petty racist hassle in Paris: Christine is insulted at her hospital; Kouamé is always singled out for his papers to be checked.

They decide to adjourn to the Ivory Coast and start by settling in a village compound. The practical difficulties are emphasised: the experience of communal family life, the heat, the mosquitoes. But Christine learns Baoulé in a valiant effort at integration. She notes wryly the identically unequal sharing of tasks between men and women in the two continents. As the rainy season brings extra problems, Abidjan beckons, both for work (which they find) and lodging. Despite their very modest income, they are happy enough. The point is made here and elsewhere that the huge difference of income and therefore of status between *coopérants* and white wives of Ivoirians creates real problems for the latter. Another telling juxtaposition is made between the extreme courtesy of Africans (a passer-by stops to change a wheel after a puncture) and the expectation of free meals, lodging and monetary gifts on the part of any family member who drops in... and stays indefinitely. Kouamé, like Ousmane in *Un chant écarlate* but to less tragic effect, is constantly torn between tradition and a multiplicity of invasive pals on the one hand and loyalty to his wife on the other.

Three years pass, and an Ivoirian friend established in France offers Kouamé a job in the provinces. They decide that they would rather face occasional racism than penury and exhaustion.

In the second story, the eponymous Janine is a maniac for cleanliness, and even before settling in Abidjan the bond of her childless marriage to Karim Kanté is beginning to break. Mariam, his nine-year-old niece, is left in their care, but can do nothing right in Janine's eyes. Their home is too immaculate: Karim, made to feel a stranger in his own house, prefers the company of lively friends. He suffers taunts about his virility and her sterility, and Janine, with wealth and social pretensions, refuses all things African.

At a reception, Karim meets Fanta. Their affair drives a wedge between the married couple: he finds alibis for not coming home at the usual time, promotion within government ranks (to ministerial level) providing the excuse. Black magic proves stronger than white magic, but Janine comes to hear of Karim's infidelity. Hostile confrontations ensue, but also reconciliations and wiles, and a daughter is born to them. Janine visits a *féticheur* [fetish priest]. Fanta has a son by Karim, and Janine tracks her down. There is a violent showdown with Karim and divorce proceedings are instituted. Janine is consoled after her depression by her white psychotherapist, Geoffroy, and after some two years together, they marry, persuaded that their love will be enough for their own child and the biracial daughter from Janine's first marriage to face the racist taunts.

'Nicole' opens with a description of the squalor and noise of the area where she and François live on the breadline with their two children, Isabelle and Frédéric. François's sister descends on them, unannounced as ever, expects hospitality, and walks off with part of Nicole's trousseau. François doesn't stand up to her or for Nicole, and they drift apart. A further demand for money comes from François's brother and this time Nicole speaks her mind. This, so out of keeping with African patriarchal traditions, is distorted when reported back, and a family council pronounces judgement against her. Again François does not defend her, so she gives him a piece of her mind, the last thing to do in the context. She returns exasperated to her native Alsace with the children, much loved by her parents.

Two years pass. François has a better job, is offered a local wife, but still loves Nicole and remains faithful. When he has a chance to join her for a while, he does so, and she is persuaded to try again, returning to a better area and more especially to a husband who seems to have learnt his lesson and is now more prepared to stand up for her. There is qualified optimism at the end.

In the fourth tale, left almost entirely alone with her three children, Annie comes gradually to learn of her husband Lucien's infidelity. Again the discrepancy of circumstances between *coopérants* and others is underlined. All the family income goes towards setting up house with a local wife in a village. Humiliated, Annie decides to leave the country secretly with the children, gives up her job, and sneaks away to the airport. Lucien learns of her plan and has them stopped. Annie goes into hiding with the children, but is tracked down. The husband has all the rights in Ivoirian law, over both wife and children, so Annie abandons the idea of a lawsuit. She returns home, but refuses to make up to Lucien, and, when he is out of the country, finally escapes via Liberia, but not without considerable nostalgia for the Ivory Coast.

The final tale shows Diane, a determined young lady, married to her school-friend Serge Amany and living in Abidjan. He has a post as a secondary-school official with a house that goes with the job. She looks for employment but in the process discovers her ambivalent status, being treated as neither French nor Ivoirian. Hypocrisy is all around them:

Du néocolonialisme, oui, un colonialisme pudique qui dit Noir au lieu de Nègre—et encore pas toujours—qui s'incline bien bas

devant les ministres ou les PDG africains et qui est au fond plus
méprisable que l'ancien, étant plus hypocrite.

[Neocolonialism, yes, a demure colonialism which says Black
instead of Negro—though it sometimes forgets—which bows low
before African ministers and company directors and which is
basically more contemptible than the old form, because it's more
hypocritical.]

Other opportunities are taken to denounce gaps between
preaching and practice, and old chestnuts are occasionally
given an airing. But if this story ends happily, it is in part
because Assamoua accepts what Mariama Bâ, in presenting
the minor case of Pierrette and Lamine in *Un chant écarlate*,
had rejected, namely the virtues of assimilation (shorthand
for the adoption of a white mindset by Blacks).

Diane overhears a conversation between Serge and a
tempter trying to lead him into corruption: he emerges
angelic, absolutely incorruptible and lovingly faithful to his
wife. But at work Serge is blamed for being too 'Europeanised', and his case for promotion is set aside: 'autant choisir
l'un d'entre nous, un Africain authentique' [better choose
one of us, a genuine African]. Serge faces a further corruption test when a new *lycée* is being built: if he hijacks large
sums for the ministry, he could do very well out of it
himself. He is disgusted, and he now represents a threat
since he knows too much and could talk out of turn. Set up
by a crooked accountant who cooks the books, Serge is
arrested, imprisoned, and his bank account blocked. And
because Diane too is incorruptible, he suffers all the more.
He resigns his post and goes into private business after
various refusals of employment, nobody wanting to be seen
to take on someone disliked by the authorities. Thanks to
Serge's efforts, they move to a better house and area, have
two children and live, apparently, happily ever after. At
least their optimism has been fully tested.

Manifestly not the novel it proclaims itself to be, *Le Défi*
has rather a lightly fictionalised quasi-sociological status. As
such its focus on the problems encountered by *Blanche/
Noir* couples living in Africa is highly informative, and if I
have dwelt on each case it is because of this (and the

difficulty of obtaining the book) rather than because of its literary qualities.

The last decade has seen some major cases, to which we shall return, alongside a continuation of permutations on established attitudes more often than not relegated to passing references or minor characters. Aboubacry Moussa Lam, for example, touches more than once on the question in *La Fièvre de la terre*, set in Paris (1990), and disapproval emerges as the consensus determined by the author:

> Certaines [Françaises] même veulent tout simplement goûter au Nègre pour voir si sa puissance sexuelle légendaire est un mythe ou une réalité alors que d'autres cherchent en revanche à assouvir un appétit sexuel insatiable. Rares sont celles qui abordent le Noir avec sincérité et sans arrière-pensée.

> [Some Frenchwomen simply want to have a taste of Blacks to see if their legendary sexual power is a myth or for real, while others are looking to satisfy their insatiable sexual appetite. Rare are those who meet Blacks sincerely, with no ulterior motive.]

However well the main character, Sammba Jah, gets on with Marie Duval, we infer that a *Blanche/Noir* love relationship is to be avoided: 'Merci pour avoir préféré l'amitié à l'amour' [Thank you for preferring friendship to love].[257] Around this time, Sembene shows himself more feisty and cynical in commenting in an interview:

> Moi je dis toujours que si j'étais une femme, je n'épouserais jamais un Africain. Il faut épouser un homme, et non pas un infirme mental.

> [I always say that if I were a woman, I'd never marry an African. You should marry a man, not a head case.][258]

In *La Dette coloniale* (1995), by Maguy Kabamba, a Zairean living in Canada, discussion of *Blanche/Noir* marriages is rather a fleeting episode. 'Combien en avez-vous vu qui vieillissent ensemble?' [How many have you seen growing old together?] asks one character disenchantedly. The homodiegetic narrator's sad reply comes: 'Ma foi, je n'ai jamais vu un vieux couple interracial, je veux dire noir et blanc' [You know, I've never seen an old mixed-race couple, I mean black and white]. The blame is focused on social pressures rather than on any intrinsic incapacity. Particular reference is made to likely reactions in an unspecified village in southern France:

> Dans de petits villages pareils, un Noir est un véritable objet de curiosité. Les vieillards et les femmes te regarderont par la fenêtre, les enfants te suivront et n'hésiteront pas à te demander si tu as une queue.

> [In such small villages, a Black is a veritable curiosity. The old men and the women will peek out at you from their windows; the children will follow you around and won't hesitate to ask you if you've got a tail.]

In my experience, one does not have to be black to elicit such responses. Idle curiosity seems a natural response to difference. Only if the ignorance it bespeaks is used to bolster prejudice should its dangers be denounced.

Daniel Biyaoula's novel *L'Impasse*, which won the Grand Prix littéraire de l'Afrique noire in 1997, is particularly important for our purposes. It is a fascinating example of a *Blanche/Noir* couple in a working-class context presented as part of a complex investigation into 'l'être-dans-le-monde du Nègre' [the being-in-the-world of the Negro].[259] His second novel, *Agonies* (1998) pursues this investigation, again through mixed-race couples, but the *Blanche/Noir* relationships there involve only minor characters.

The impasse in which Joseph Gakatuka is cornered is emblematic of his almost psychotic inability to come to terms with the reality of his skin-colour, symbolically particularly dark, and its social implications in the no less symbolically named provincial French town of Poury (cf. *pourri* [rotten]). Equally, he is out of place in his native

Brazzaville and among Blacks who seem uniformly to indulge in depigmentation. This double exile is represented geographically in the first two sections of the novel, given the titles 'Première Constriction' and 'Deuxième Constriction' which are, retrospectively, all the more telling when the image of the boa-constrictor appears towards the end of the book. The third and final part, entitled 'La Mue' [Sloughing a Skin], signals a change in which Joseph adopts actions and positions which he had previously condemned out of hand.

This reversal is both profound and, literally, skin-deep: what he refers to as the monster within him is what previously had led him to assert his black identity in the face of all those fellow-Africans, especially women (and including his mother) who had, with various whitening agents, sought to alter their skin-colour. His white girl-friend, Sabine, by being, so to speak, colour-blind, had helped him in this self-assertion but is ultimately powerless before Joseph's perception of the mass of prejudice stacked against him. She is perceived in any case as being the whitening agent who will implicitly do genetically for Joseph's progeny what other Blacks are doing chemically with mercury soap and bleach. He is in the end entrapped by his bad faith, encouraged by the, again, symbolically named psychiatrist, Dr Malfoi [Dr Illfaith], who, in the process of helping him out of one impasse, the madness of solipsism, guides him, smiling like the tiger of the limerick, into the far worse one of the supine acceptance of and conformity to the mindlessness of stereotypical racial habits and assumptions.

The shift is registered by the motif of the mirror, familiar to us from 'William der Neger' and *Ourika*, which reflects Joseph's increasing self-acceptance the more he learns the survival strategies of hypocrisy from his psychotherapy. From his comment: 'Je n'aime plus me trouver face à moi-même' [I don't like looking at myself any longer], which is matched by his increasing distaste for being seen, he shifts first to an acceptance of mirrors—'je peux me regarder dans une glace sans me voir, qu'il ne suscite plus rien en moi, mon visage, qu'il ne me désespère plus' [I can look into a mirror without seeing myself, without my face rousing anything in me, without it making me feel desperate]—and finally to the point where he positively seeks mirrors out, 'incapable que je suis de passer devant une glace ou une vitre sans m'y regarder' [incapable as I am of passing in front of a mirror or a window without looking at myself], using them to practise his posturing: 'un mouvement de la main recherché, que j'ai, des heures durant, étudié devant ma glace' [a knowing movement of the hand practised for hours in front of a mirror]. True to Lacan's idea that the mirror-stage 'symbolise la permanence mentale du je en même temps qu'elle préfigure sa destination aliénante' [symbolises the mental permanence of the ego while simultaneously prefiguring its alienating goal], Joseph submits his identity to a crisis which the author sees as stemming from a racist stereotyping which, for the individual to survive, requires submission to its imperatives.[260] Appearances, a key theme in the novel, precisely those superficial values to which Joseph had objected throughout the first two sections, get the better of him in the end.

If the monster occasionally makes itself heard in the final phase, its voice, perceived by the reader as that of a nobler if more difficult truth, is quickly suppressed. Joseph does precisely what had most upset him about other black people around him in the earlier parts of the novel: replace reality by appearances and quite literally, but in a way that cannot help but echo Fanon, put a whitened mask over a black face. The phenomenon of the *nègre blanchi* [white-washed Negro], once restricted to ritual and dance, is here exclusively attributed to those who use bleaching ointments and lotions to effect a more permanent lightening of their skin, particularly on their faces.[261] Against that falsity, Joseph stands his ground all the more firmly thanks to his partner, Sabine, but their love proves inadequate to survive Joseph's obsession.

It starts positively and is sustained until she finally slams the door on him. In the opening scene of the book, Sabine is seeing Joseph off to his native Congo at Roissy airport.

Before anything else is described or anyone else presented, we are introduced, through his eyes, to Blacks dressed up to the nines. The theme of appearances is launched, intimately associated with the motif of looking and being looked at. Counterbalancing his outward gaze, Joseph inspects himself, as it were, but his difference at this stage does not make him feel awkward. It is this self-assurance on the part of the modestly educated worker in a tyre-factory that will crumble in due course. His hypersensitive analysis of the straw men he sees around him contains the as yet unsuspected irony that he will himself become in turn a victim of appearances in all their hollowness.

The way in which the *Blanche/Noir* couple is linked inextricably with the theme of appearances is apparent in this opening scene. The comments about Joseph, pointedly made in his hearing, are intended to hurt: his clothes are the subject of ridicule, but so is the very darkness of his complexion, and so too is his association with a white woman, as if this were some blot on African honour. Part of the sustained attack runs:

> — Hé!... Hé! Voyez-moi celui-là!... Là, en face de moi! qu'il dit. Regardez comme il est habillé! C'est des gens comme ça qui font honte à l'Afrique! [...]
> — Oui, c'est comme tu dis, que dit un autre gars. C'est un vrai bœuf, un cul-terreux, ce type! Les Blancs, quand ils voient des Noirs fringués comme ça, ils pensent tout de suite qu'on est tous pareils! Heureusement que nous sommes là pour sauver l'honneur du continent!

> ['Hoho! Look at him! There, opposite me!', says he. 'Look how he's dressed! That's the sort that put Africa to shame!' [...]
> 'Yes, it's like you say', says another guy. 'A real ox, a redneck, that one! When Whites see Blacks turned out like that, they immediately think we're all the same! A good job we're here to save the honour of the continent!]

Sabine's loyal, open-minded affection helps to sustain Joseph psychologically against such attacks for a considerable time, but the seed of self-doubt is sown and it will grow into an unbalanced obsession ultimately diagnosed as madness. At first, as we have seen, Sabine is a given.

208

Increasingly, during his disenchanted three-week stay in Brazzaville, Joseph thinks of her, defending her against the taunts and ruses of those who want him to marry a local girl. The pressure is direct and has implications which worm their way unanswerably into his mind. They are best measured from a passage which extends over several pages to reveal different angles of attack on his certainties. Samuel, Joseph's eldest brother, is blunt and outspoken, and assumes, in the traditional African manner, that his younger sibling will comply unquestioningly with his recommendation to avoid white woman:

> Il se met à discourir sur les mariages mixtes. Une catastrophe, des unions anormales, contre-nature, qu'il dit. Père et mes oncles enchérissent. [...] Mais il n'est pas besoin de mariages mixtes pour que ça ne marche pas! que je dis. Toi, tu as déjà eu deux femmes! Pourtant c'était pas des Blanches! Et puis j'en connais, moi, des Blancs qui se sont mariés entre eux qui ont divorcé!

> [He embarks on a disquisition about mixed marriages. 'A catastrophe, abnormal unions, against nature,' says he. Father and my uncles raise the stakes. [...] 'But a marriage doesn't have to be mixed not to work!', says I. You've already had two wives, you have! Yet they weren't white! And then I know Whites married among themselves who've divorced!']

Joseph's defence is entirely valid; he would have strengthened his case, however, if he had not just emphasised the negative generality but also been able to quote instances of positive success in biracial marriages. Samuel exploits the weakness in his argument, but Joseph plays his trump: 'c'est pas avec des femmes blanches que je suis! C'est avec Sabine!' [I'm not going with white women, I'm not! I'm with Sabine!]

This last retort, singularising the case against Samuel's invalid generalisation, is surely the strongest argument of all. It does not, however, take account of certain social realities which, apart from vapid protestations, then become the weapons in the family's armoury. Joseph inwardly recognises their force:

En effet je n'imagine pas Sabine se soumettant à Mère, lui obéissant sans se poser de questions comme le feraient mes belles-sœurs, quoique les conflits ne manquent pas non plus dans ce cas. Finalement, je commence à me demander si elle pourrait vivre dans ma famille, Sabine, si elle supporterait. C'est que c'est un vrai problème qu'il a soulevé, Samuel.

[It's true, I can't see Sabine submitting to Mother, obeying her without question like my sisters-in-law do, even though they have their fights. In the end, I start wondering if Sabine could live in my family, if she could put up with it. It's a real problem Samuel's raised, it is.]

This, the basic impasse of the novel's title, is a sufficiently real problem, as we have seen Le Défi stress, for Joseph to return to France so disenchanted with his experience in Brazza that by implication he has to relaunch on a new footing the question of his marrying Sabine. Even the matter of depigmentation, already raised as a problem by Awa Thiam in La Parole des Négresses, makes appearance become part of the substantive issue:

Depuis quelque temps, ça me triture la cervelle cette histoire de décoloration et de défrisage. [...] Et l'équation:

$$x + Africain + Africaine + produits\ cosmétiques$$
$$= décoloration\ de\ la\ peau + défrisage\ des\ cheveux$$

me paraît une évidence. Et je veux le comprendre, moi, cet x. Je veux qu'il m'apparaisse clairement cet x.

[For some time, I've been trying to get my head round this matter of bleaching and hair-straightening. [...] And the equation:

$$x + African\ man + African\ woman + cosmetic\ products$$
$$= bleaching\ of\ the\ skin + straightening\ of\ the\ hair$$

seems self-evident to me. And I want to understand it, I do, this x. I want it to be completely clear to me, this x.]

Sabine is not fully introduced until the beginning of the 'Deuxième Constriction'. The analysis of her relationship with Joseph takes place entirely within this section, although, as we have seen, she is present at his departure for Brazzaville and meets him fleetingly with her (their?) son in the final part, when Joseph is a changed man. His defence of his love for Sabine to his family adds up, however, to an important ingredient in the reader's apprehension of the relationship. The problem as to how Sabine would fit into Congolese society is obviated by Joseph's return to Europe, but we remain aware of that other crack in his armour: the lack of a role-model for a successful mixed-race marriage.

We cannot legitimately argue that he should have looked around rather more: his character, with its limitations, is a given of the novel, and it is in any case entirely consistent and plausible that in his conservative working-class milieu, with its inveterate racism reinforced by the largely mindless menu of the popular French television channels which he watches, he would not be familiar with any such model. It is an authorial decision, one that the reader is therefore bound to accept, that the relationship should not work out. Within the traditional realist manner which Biyaoula adopts (with its special attention to capturing speech-patterns not just in dialogue, with its special tics, disrupted syntax and excessive exclamation marks, but also in the predominant first-person stream of consciousness which largely voices Joseph's narrative), we have rather to ask if the way in which it evolves is appropriately motivated and psychologically reasonable. We can in any case note with approval that the relationship is particularised: in Joseph and Sabine, we are not dealing with cyphers or archetypes but with the representation of plausibly authentic people.

At the same time, we recognise the novel to be an exploration beyond Negritude, caustically dismissed as 'Noiritude' [Blackitude], complete with a reference to the unthinkable 'zèbre sans zébrures' (an echo of Césaire's *Cahier d'un retour au pays natal*, where 'tous les zèbres se secouent à leur manière pour faire tomber leurs zébrures' [all the zebras shake themselves in their own way to get rid of their stripes]), of what Du Bois called 'the souls of black folk'. The legitimacy of such a preoccupation is widely recognised by today's black Francographic writers, who still need to assert their identity while persuading a largely white readership to publish and purchase their products. Essentialism has been replaced by its *cousin de plaisanterie* [joke cousin] the search for identity, but Joseph is haunted, as he acknowledges on the psychiatrist's couch, by the concept of the black soul and what he sees as its betrayal in depigmentation.

A telling exchange between Sabine and Joseph occurs after he has shown a particular sensitivity to what people say about him and so revealed yet again the insecurity which tracks him throughout the novel. Her words are a lesson for us all:

> — Mais enfin, Joseph! [...] Tu n'as qu'à ne pas te penser en Noir! Pense-toi en humain, Joseph! Regarde-moi! Moi, je me vois comme un être humain! Jamais je ne me suis vue en Blanche! Jamais je ne me suis posé une seule question là-dessus! Je suis! C'est tout! [...]
> J'avais trouvé beaucoup de vérité dans les propos de Sabine. Un sacré déclic que ça m'avait fait dans la tête, ses paroles. Pendant des mois, quand elle en eut l'occasion, sans qu'elle le fît exprès, elle les enfonça en moi, ses pensées. Et elle déteignit bien sur moi.

> ['Come off it, Joseph! [...] Just stop thinking of yourself as a Black! Think of yourself as a human being, Joseph! Look at me! I see myself as a human being! I've never lived as a White! I've never asked myself a single question on the subject! I am! That's the end of it!' [...]
> I'd found a lot of truth in what Sabine said. They'd clicked in my head, they had, her words. For months, whenever she had the chance, without doing it on purpose, she stuck them into me, those thoughts. And she rubbed off on me.]

The choice of verb in the last sentence quoted here is pointedly overdetermined, and Sabine's general argument expresses, as Joseph recognises, the utmost good sense.[262] Sustaining the integrity of an intellectual awareness of its aptness alongside the emotional filtering of its implications is less straightforward, however, and indeed proves impossible for Joseph despite his best efforts.

He is increasingly unable to remain detached from taunts about his blackness. Echoing Fanon, Biyaoula has a couple of three- or four-year-old children innocently comment to their mothers on his skin-colour. Joseph acknowledges that he can no longer maintain his previous detachment, and it affects him physiologically as well as psychologically. He is even less able to cope with what he presumes to be the taunts of two fat and vulgar French-women in a restaurant where he is waiting for Sabine to arrive: he is roused to remonstrate, and what had been latent and only potentially offensive becomes overtly so. The two men sitting with the women join in but decline to resort to fisticuffs. Joseph returns to his table seething with rage, his black thoughts leading him, despite anything Sabine can subsequently say or do, to a devastating con-clusion:

> Je me dis que parce qu'elles sont blanches, ces deux grosses, dans leur caboche vide ça leur conférait une supériorité certaine, ce bienfait de Dieu. C'est là que je comprends que le dernier des Blancs, le plus laid, le plus pourri, le plus scélérat, il croira toujours qu'il est mieux que le meilleur des Noirs.

> [I tell myself that because they're white, those two tubs of lard, in their empty noddles they imagine that makes them better, that gift from God. That's when I understand that the worst of the Whites, the ugliest, the most rotten and villainous, will always think, he will, that he's better than the best Black.]

His workmates' taunts ('"Hé! toi noiraud, tu crois que tu vas devenir blanc?" qu'ils ont souvent rugi avec fiel, les hommes blancs, de leur voiture, quand j'étais avec Sabine' ['Hey you, blackie, do you think you'll get white?' they roared venomously, they did, those white men, from their cars, when I was with Sabine]) suggest a causal link between the phenomenon of depigmentation and black men seeking relationships with white women. However impoverished their psychology, it cannot but open another breach in Joseph's defences.

However excellent Sabine's arguments, they gradually have less and less purchase on Joseph's mind. After an anthropological documentary and their different reactions to it, he seeing mainly the exploitation involved while she implicitly applauds the scientific interest, he concludes: 'C'est bien la première fois que le problème de race se pose entre nous' [That's the very first time we've raised the race problem]. Their second difference is even more pointed. It arises from an American film including the rape of a black woman by Whites. Sabine interprets it as representative of the universal suffering of women, since the rape of the Sabine women and beyond one might add, whereas Joseph sees it as a specifically racial attack.[263] The question of race is thus said to cast its shadow between them, and shortly Joseph will state with resignation: 'Entre elle et moi ça va de mal en pis' [Between her and me things are going from bad to worse]. The clearest signal of this widening gulf between them and the impending end of their relationship appears at this point, since it represents something diametrically opposite to everything Sabine stands for: 'Il m'arrive parfois de ne plus la voir comme une femme, mais comme une Blanche' [I sometimes see her not as a woman but as a White].

A subsidiary *Blanche/Noir* relationship in the novel, between Dieudonné, a childhood friend, and Suzanne—itself interrupted by a memorable comic episode when Dieudonné is chased naked from the bed of fair Rosaline into the unwelcoming night air by her Nazi-sympathising husband—comes to an abrupt end when he is stabbed by some white youths and dies in hospital of his wounds. In Joseph's mind, it sharpens the focus on the stark opposition symbolised by the labels black and white. The wave of blame indiscrimately swamps any white friend who seeks to express grief at the senseless killing, and it overwhelms Sabine, unable to cope with Joseph's irremediably black moods. His regret at her departure is expressed by his vain and increasingly desperate attempts to contact her, both directly and through her family. In a blur of migraine, he wrecks his small apartment as he sinks into unconsciousness.

The opening of the final section shows him waking in a psychiatric hospital several months later. His treatment has the effects already mentioned and appears to be analogous to killing by kindness. Daniel Biyaoula's own scientific training as a microbiologist inevitably brought him into contact with sister disciplines and we can fairly suppose that the impossible paradox to which Joseph is led by his treatment is an informed as well as a sceptical comment on the value of the somewhat unorthodox psychiatry practised by Dr Malfoi, whose long exposure to traditional African medicine and its underside, quackery, is emphasised. Joseph throws himself headlong into becoming everything he had previously abhorred. After a long period out of work, Dr Malfoi arranges a job for him at a home for old, incontinent men. It is the most menial and distasteful, clearing out their faeces and cleaning the inmates after they have dirtied themselves or died. Emblematically, he could sink no lower, and his work is clearly intended to provide an ironic contrast with his new appearance, outwardly flashy but inwardly void. Biyaoula catches his disingenuousness with forked irony, striking both Malfoi and his mindlessly faithful patient:

> Mais d'aller le voir régulièrement, ça me laisse de plus en plus avec la sensation qu'il y en moi un trou qui a pris forme et qui grossit et s'agrandit chaque fois un peu plus.

> [But going to see him regularly leaves me more and more with the feeling that there's a hole formed inside me which grows and expands a little more each time.]

He fattens himself by thirty-two kilos to mask this emptiness, look the big man and impress. All his money now goes on clothing and empty parade.

He is so unrecognisable that Sabine, pushing her pram with her son in it, walks straight past him in the street. When he calls out her name and reveals who he is, she cannot contain her surprise or even her mocking laughter at the sea-change in him. After a drink in the dark corner of a café, she walks out of his life for good, refusing his invitation to the dance at the symbolically named 'salle

Denfer' [Hellhole hall] which provides the closing decor of the book.

The dance-hall is reminiscent of the airport hall in the opening scene of the novel. Much is similar, but Joseph (now self-styled 'Jo' for effect) has a very different relationship to what surrounds him. He is now one of the Africans trying to impress, indifferent as to whether the object of his attentions is a whitened black or a buxom white girl. He is and remains essentially alone, with only casual and fleeting partners on the dance-floor or in conversation: leaving the hall for a while, he returns too late to pick up the anticipated date. Yet in this trance, he meets a new character, challengingly introduced on page 319 out of 327, who dominates the closing pages. The story of Justin, otherwise called Tsiwonda, but usually known as 'Le Goudron' [Tarbaby], is clearly intended to bring the book full circle. His nickname, to start with, given him by his mother, not only designates his complexion, as dark as Joseph's, but specifically the latter's own sobriquet which his mother gave him: Kala or 'Le Charbon' [Coalface]. Indeed we are reminded that one of the women at the airport had remarked of Joseph: 'Noir comme il est, il lui faudra des wagons de produits pour qu'il s'éclaircisse un peu! On dirait du goudron!' [Black as he is, he'll need wagon-loads of cream to whiten his skin a bit! He looks like tar!]. Justin is Joseph's *alter ego*, recounting his problems at inordinate length (though the reader is told this and so spared the exhausting details), to the point where Joseph judges him a suitable candidate for Dr Malfoi's therapeutic attention. He is made all the more sinister a *Doppelgänger* by his fate, which is to die in his car as he drives home after the dance considerably the worse for drink. A narrative detail relates his death to the title of the novel and illuminates it indirectly: 'on a trouvé sa voiture écrasée contre le fond d'une impasse' [his car was found crashed against the end wall in a cul-de-sac].

Were it not that his case relates metonymically to Joseph's, reflecting in miniature the essence of the latter's madcap dive into a social, moral and spiritual impasse,

Justin's intrusion would seem ill-timed. As it is, it gathers together several strands of the basic story of Joseph at a literal or metaphorical level and, as we have seen, relates it directly to its beginning. The cyclical element does not preclude the continuation of Joseph's existence, and so satisfies a double aesthetic requirement. Even if it does not present any echo of the interrelated tensions between depigmentation and *Blanche/Noir* relations which occupy so much of the narrative, it rightly focuses on the key theme of being black today, even quite simply being alive today, in a paradoxical world where phenomenal means of communication seem largely devoted to a dialogue of the deaf.

Olympe Bhêly-Quenum's latest and as yet unpublished novel, *C'était à Tigony* is set mainly in a fictional East African country, Wanakawa.[264] It is centred on the international cooperation community and investigates the impact of foreign aid and collaboration between the former colonisers and the formerly colonised. Viewed from different angles as humanitarian charity or unjustified interference, forms of neocolonialism present the backdrop to a professional French couple, Gaëtan, an international civil servant, and Dorcas, a practising and successful geologist, who have radically different outlooks. While he is happy to pursue his philanderings with African women, his liberal-minded wife falls in love with a much younger local man, Ségué n'Di. If this liaison is unacceptable to Gaëtan, to the point where he takes a shot at him and wounds him in the head, it is specifically because the man is black, not because he is younger, a matter he never raises. The couple eventually agrees to a divorce, Dorcas more amicably than her husband. Meanwhile, we are again, as in *L'Initié*, shown the importance of traditional African beliefs, this time inculcated in Ségué n'Di by his grandfather n'Ata. By contrast, the European power-base revolves around the sophisticated society of an international agency and its ostensibly disinterested machinations, in fact imbued with notions of paternalistic superiority and exploitative self-interest.

As with *L'Initié*, the texture of the major problems raised cannot be reduced to the personal relations of a *Blanche/Noir* couple, even if Dorcas and Ségué n'Di represent a nucleus around which the broader issues revolve. Bhêly-Quenum has categorised those broader issues as follows:

> a) la sociologie politique du clan des coopérants en Afrique; b) l'industrialisation de l'Afrique décolonisée avec ou sans le partenariat des Africains qui en ont les moyens financiers; c) l'incompatibilité ou les incompatibilités d'ordre physiologique (cf. les citations d'Aristote, dès l'exergue, et d'Oscar Wilde) et dans la conception des problèmes socio-culturels entre Dorcas et Gaëtan.

> [a) the political sociology of the tribe of aid-workers in Africa; b) the industrialisation of decolonised Africa with or without the partnership of Africans who have the necessary means; c) the incompatibility or incompatibilities between Dorcas and Gaëtan of a physiological order (cf. the quotations from Aristotle, starting with the epigraph, and from Oscar Wilde) and in their conception of socio-cultural problems.][265]

Something atavistic is seemingly suggested when it is revealed that Dorcas was born in West Africa and is therefore better attuned to the mysteries of the continent than her husband, who remains inveterately colonialist in outlook despite the ending of colonialism. A belief in socio-political solidarity leads her to join a protest march, and the simple act of joining hands with a fellow-marcher provides the opportunity for her disenchantment with Gaëtan to be compensated by sympathy and eventually love for Ségué n'Di, whose hand it was. He proves to be immensely talented, but it is only with help from Dorcas that he can, despite his good education, improve on his job as a mere paper-boy and put his talents at the service of his people by winning a competitive exam for work in the geological and geodesic consortium alongside Dorcas. It is as if he honours a contract with his own people, whose sacrifices deserve any benefit they can bring. Gaëtan, self-engrossed and lacking in essential generosity despite qualities which Dorcas is the first to acknowledge, fails entirely to understand such a sense of commitment by his wife and her lover.

If their affair occupies a central position in the novel, it is, as we have seen, by no means its key issue, which grapples in this instance with the harsh realities of contemporary power-politics in Africa. There is virtually no discussion of the question of biracial marriages in general.[266] On the personal plane, however, certain questions remain unresolved at the end of the book. Dorcas is on a business trip to Europe and has taken advantage of it to see her son in Stuttgart and her daughter in Dublin. Her divorce has been confirmed and her children have no reservations about her new relationship. Yet behind her in Wanakawa she has left not only Ségué n'Di convalescing from his head-wound but also evidence amounting to proof positive of Gaëtan's guilt of the shooting, something which has so far been carefully concealed by almost tacit agreement between the three people concerned. While Dorcas may hold a strong hand, therefore, her future with Ségué n'Di is potentially compromised if Gaëtan uses his power to destroy the evidence. Clearly, speculation on what occurs after the novel's last fullstop is idle, but it seems a clear case, as Dr Johnson wrote in respect of second marriages, of the triumph of hope over experience.[267]

Bhêly-Quenum shows himself intent, throughout his work, on persuading us to go beyond skin-deep colour-blindness. Indeed, he takes that colour-blindness for granted. Under his benign guidance, we are not simply initiated by proxy into the mysteries of Africa and encouraged not to impede its development any longer under the false colours of neocolonialism: we are invited to act more humanely and with greater tolerance towards our fellow human beings in general. Can there be a higher moral justification for engaging in the act of writing?

It seems appropriate, however, to finish this review of writing about *Blanche/Noir* relationships in Francographic literature with what is not only one of its most recent avatars but one which is written by a woman and which brings us full circle through a novel in which skin-colour is mentioned no more than it is in the *Histoire de Louis Anniaba*. I refer to Véronique Tadjo's *Champs de bataille et d'amour* (1999). If I had wished for a novel to illustrate my thesis that the focus is now concentrated, as it should be, not on black and white issues, confrontational almost by definition, but on the harmony and vitality of intimate interpersonal relations, I could not have imagined a more apt example.

It could be argued that the novel is too lyrical an evocation, too detached from a fully textured sociological matrix, to provide a convincing case. The couple could well be the one addressed by Ouologuem in his 'Lettre aux couples mixtes':

> C'est par votre amour que l'on dit incongru, affolante nature aux vaines espérances à jamais tenues dans le vent et l'odeur du monde, c'est par vous que l'offrande de commisération et le péché, deviennent l'immortalité même. [...] Vous êtes—romantiques attardés—le temps qui nie le monde. [...] Un soleil singulier en vous se répand, sans commencement ni milieu ni fin, mais avec une puissance infinie, avec une pauvre beauté.

> [It is through your love, said to be incongruous, your frightening nature with its vain hopes for ever held up to face the wind and the smell of the world, it is through you that the offering of commiseration and sin become immortality itself. [...] You are—old-fashioned romantics that you are—the time which denies the world. [...] A special sun shines within you, without beginning, middle or end, but with infinite power, with meagre beauty.][268]

I would suggest that the value of this poetic novel resides precisely in the fact that it does not fall between totem and taboo, but rather lies beyond both. In a series of substantial vignettes entirely rooted in everyday occurrences, with reference even to the impact of the horrors of the civil war in Rwanda, it forms a moving kaleidoscope tracing the shared life of Eloka and Aimée.

While their names can fairly be interpreted as Ivoirian and French, such an interpretation being reinforced by the backdrop of the narrative, which shifts from European to African, and from other paratextual indices such as Tadjo's own dual affiliation and the two places of publication, Paris and Abidjan, their skin-colour is revealed only by the blurb on the back cover, neither written nor sanctioned by the author. The focus is on the nature and difficulty of memory in the process of two people coming together and sharing their lives. Time and again the past is problematised, even abandoned, and the relationship between reality and illusion therefore called into question.

Eloka arrives by bus in an unnamed village and as if in a dream visits a farmstead occupied by a 'fille aux cheveux d'or' [golden-haired girl]—the nearest we get to a colour indication—and her father in his death-throes. Ostensibly motivated by nothing more than the wish to help Aimée to overcome her grief at the death of her father, whose body is promised a simple burial, the couple leaves without further ceremony, travelling by bus, train, ship and lorry to Eloka's unspecified country beyond the desert where they marry. Again no fuss, as the spare writing emphasises: 'ils s'installèrent et se marièrent' [they moved in and got married].

They thereby 'invent a future'. The triad of past, present and future is brought into balance and made available for constructions of the mind. 'Pour éviter l'isolement, il chercha avec Aimée à se faire une nouvelle mémoire' [To avoid isolation, he sought with Aimée to forge a new memory]. Proving Milton's dictum that 'the mind is its own place', Aimée's exile, after years spent growing together with and increasingly like Eloka, 's'était transformé en un lieu habitable' [had been transformed into a habitable place]. The proliferation of everyday social problems detailed by such as Assamoua has no purchase on her: in truth, Eloka's job as a university lecturer, working in a liberal environment, probably affords some protection, but the matter is never brought to the fore in those terms. Only the biodegradable nature of their love gradually modifies the relationship: their very likeness troubles Eloka to the point that he envisages Aimée as his sister rather than as his wife. The very reasons for her love are strangers to her:

Pourquoi s'était-elle éprise de cet homme au point de le suivre jusque chez lui?

"C'est si difficile de se plonger dans un être, se dit-elle, d'essayer de comprendre la logique de ses moments d'aberration, les racines de son amertume. C'est si épuisant d'aimer."

[Why had she fallen in love with this man so much that she had followed him to his home?

'It's so difficult to plunge into someone's being,' she said to herself, 'to try and understand the logic of his moments of aberration, the roots of his bitterness. Loving is so exhausting.]

She views her uprooting as a kind of self-betrayal of which she had been vaguely aware in advance, but her solitude is now a double one and, in her fragile and vulnerable state, the single kind cannot be retrieved. 'Oui, l'amour existait, cela ne faisait aucun doute, mais pas toujours sous la forme désirée' [Yes, love existed, there was no doubt about that, but not always in the form one wanted].

Eloka sees her as a mirror-image of himself; she looks in a mirror and sees only an extra wrinkle. But the mirror assumes other capacities when, later in the book, she imagines taking a step through the looking-glass:

Atteindre le côté caché du miroir qui lui montrerait une réalité aux facettes multiples où mourir n'était pas la fin du monde.

[Reaching the hidden side of the mirror which would show her a multifaceted reality where dying was not the end of the world.]

Love, 'un droit, une évidence' [a right, an obvious fact], remains both a bond and the platform for the mind's marvellous time-machine to do its work: 'Tout était possible: refuser le présent, reconsidérer le passé, bâtir l'avenir' [Everything was possible: to refuse the present, reconsider the past, and build the future].

Nevertheless, fatigue sets in for Aimée; dissatisfaction at all she had not achieved reduces her will to live. Eloka is desperate to understand and to help, but he has his own

agenda and needs to travel, more for intangible psychological reasons than for his work. Habituation brings its self-
contradictions: 'Elle redoutait ses absences, mais elle les
souhaitait aussi' [She dreaded his absences, but she also
longed for them]. Conscious of being unable to control time,
she cannot in consequence manage her loneliness. As for
him,

> partir, pour lui, voulait tout dire. Il en avait besoin pour effacer le
> quotidien des jours par un mouvement perpétuel. Il ne se sentait
> bien nulle part et ne s'arrêtait que lorsqu'il pensait avoir trouvé
> une cause, une raison de se battre.

> [leaving, for him, meant everything. He needed it to erase the
> routine of daily life by perpetual movement. Nowhere did he feel
> good, and he only stopped when he thought he had found a cause,
> a reason for fighting.]

He nevertheless, again out of the very habit of love turned
into an inseparable companionship, finds the idea of returning to an empty house, without Aimée, intolerable: 'il
sentait qu'elle faisait partie de lui-même et qu'elle était
inscrite dans son esprit d'une manière indélébile' [he felt
that she was part of himself and inscribed in his mind in an
indelible way].

When, in their garden, a storm uproots a flame-tree with
its shallow roots, we are led to suppose that it is a reflection,
an objective correlative, of Aimée's exile, unable to put
down roots to hold her in place and time with the necessary
firmness. Another metaphor of transience follows hard on
this one's heels: ephemera infiltrate their bedroom, couple
and die in their hundreds. Everything becomes impossibly
elusive.

> Saisir le vol d'un oiseau. Dessiner la tendresse des premières
> feuilles, garder toujours en mémoire l'essence de la lumière. Tenir
> dans le creux de la main la paix d'un matin.

> [To grasp the flight of a bird. To draw the tenderness of new
> leaves, to keep the memory of light's essence. To hold in the
> hollow of your hand the peace of a morning.]

The understated joins the unstated to underline the impermanence of love and life, and a kind of madness sets in. The couple's legacy is 'un amour deux fois immortel' [a love twice immortal]. It is nourished by the simplest of things: 'Tout était donc là, tapi dans l'ombre des jours ordinaires' [So everything was there, nestling in the shadow of ordinary days].

Eloka shares Aimée's sense of exile, a state of mind rather than a geographical displacement, and they can grow old together, time out of mind, sharing their double loneliness and yet also their companionable inseparability, 'l'essentiel de leur devenir' [the kernel of their becoming].

It has taken over a quarter of a millennium to return to the point where the question of colour, erected as a social, political and ultimately psychological barrier in the lengthy process of white exploitation of Blacks, resumes its proper place in interpersonal relations: a superficial difference which, *pace* Fanon, it is entirely understandable for a child to comment on but not of itself of any consequence. As an index of otherness, however, it remains a manifest and undeniable pointer to a cultural difference to be explored. 'Dieu n'a-t-il pas créé les hommes de couleurs différentes afin de nous obliger à nous étudier?' [Did God not make mankind in different colours so as to make us study one another?][269] Bernard Dadié's pertinent question invites us to acknowledge the simple fact of that difference and, far from using it as an excuse for contempt or exploitation, not to be indifferent to it.

CONCLUSION
BEYOND DIFFERENCE AND INDIFFERENCE

'Je ne dis les autres, sinon pour d'autant plus me dire.'
[I tell of others only to tell more of myself.]
Montaigne, *Essais*, I, 26.

POSTCOLONIAL discourses have accustomed former imperial powers to looking at themselves through the other end of the telescope. Some have chosen to put it to their blind eye. Even with goodwill, however, it is exceptionally difficult to imagine oneself entirely in someone else's skin, yet that it is the effort that must constantly be made if we are to empathise with one or both parties in a *Blanche/Noir* relationship. Todorov has suggested in *Nous et les autres* that 'pour éprouver l'autre, on n'a pas besoin de cesser d'être soi' [to experience the Other, you do not have to stop being yourself]; my feeling is that you cannot help being yourself, however consciously and purposely forgetful or generous you might be.[270]

Insofar as there has been any critical analysis to date of the representation of mixed-race couples in Francographic literature, it has tended to focus on particular periods—mainly from about 1920 to 1980—and, insofar as it has distinguished at all between cases of *Blanc/Noire* and *Blanche/Noir* couples, has concentrated on the former, its dominant presence in the colonialist novel reverberating through subsequent writing. By and large, the vibrant and valuable postcolonial debate has not addressed the question directly, and certainly not from the angle adopted here.

'L'union de l'homme noir et de la femme blanche est restée jusqu'à une date assez récente largement *impensable*' [the union of a black man with a white woman has, until fairly recent times, remained largely *unthinkable*].[271] If the

Blanche/Noir couple has shared the literary shadows with Cinderella before she meets her prince, I hope that it can now emerge to reveal its exceptional interest. Both partners show a degree of emancipation from their native society. The depiction of the couple *qua* couple is a challenge to the existing racial hierarchy, provoking conservative forces to respond and so provide a nucleus of tension for the purposes of engaging narrative and exploring social reactions. It specifically offers the critic a valuable *topos* which, while retaining the piquancy of exoticism for black and white readers alike, provides a dimension favouring analysis of racial attitudes as well as all the narrative potential of any nuclear couple, structurally closed but potentially explosive.

The Guadeloupean writer Daniel Maximin has accurately observed that 'Les lignes de partage des races et des sexes ne coïncident pas' [The dividing lines betwen races and sexes do not coincide].[272] He adds, however, in a way that we can now see as being too close to Fanon not to be unacceptably restrictive, 'Trop d'hommes noirs recherchent la compagnie des Européennes pour se blanchir à leurs yeux ou au contraire pour posséder une victime expiatoire des crimes des colonisateurs' [Too many black men seek the company of European women so as to whiten themselves in their eyes or else to possess a sacrificial victim for the crimes of colonisers]. The simplicity of his conclusion, however, belies the struggle for acceptance which it conceals: 'Il faut faire avec ce que l'on EST' [You have to make do with what you ARE].

In varying ways and to different degrees, in this relationship as in no other, both partners have to step outside the ordinarily accepted parameters of a native culture. That in itself betokens a rare independence of mind. Motivation will of course vary from case to case, but we are likely by definition to find strong-willed characters, and these we have seen in good number. Whatever negative charge may be brought against a white girl or woman for indulging in escapism or erotic fantasy, or reacting to a narrow-minded environment, there is always another side to the coin: the embrace of the Other bespeaks a generous impulse, a sense of adventure, a taste for defiance. Likewise, in a mirror-image of such views, a black man can be charged with sexual fantasies, a wish to escape from deprivation and humiliation, to challenge convention. But positive qualities are similarly present, with mind-enlarging self-improvement tinged on occasion with the still-necessary pedagogic mission to prove that Blacks too are human.

In a recently published conference paper, Ruth Morse recalls that 'the subject which ranges from concubinage to marriage across racial, national, or ethnic boundaries has been problematic in western literature for as long as there has been western literature. Exotic, colonial, and post-colonial literature inherits a range of texts—as well as experience—of interracial sex (or the rejection of it) which no one has yet managed to catalogue or classify.'[273] Her brief study confirms that this tradition concentrates primarily on European men and foreign women. Indeed, she goes so far as to suggest that it is only 'at the end of the twentieth century that the miscegenation plot reverses direction.'[274] The present study, in making its contribution to a largely unexplored area, shows how inaccurate that assumption is.

By choosing a diachronic approach, I have been able to show developments largely parallel to those in interracial relations in general. As slavery and slave-trading brought economic advantages, cultural superiority was increasingly assumed and proclaimed by Europeans. Under threat of vastly greater numbers of Blacks around them, Europeans abroad took that sense of superiority to extremes expressed in violence as well as in intolerant laws. Every possible argument was used to prove the inferiority of Blacks—insofar as they were considered worthy of consideration. Science, the new religion, confirmed those 'proofs' and so provided the basis for the self-satisfaction and arrogance of white racism, the venomous longevity of which, in institutions as in people's minds, is manifest to this day. The massive influx of *Tirailleurs sénégalais* for the First World War, and the even greater numbers arriving from the

Second World War onwards, triggered defensive reactions which sometimes took the form of attack.

Some manifestations of Negritude envisaged a specific overthrow, along racist lines. of the traditional power-base. Senghor moved increasingly, however, towards what he termed 'la civilisation de l'universel' [the civilisation of the universal], a generous if highly idiosyncratic synthesis.[275] From the outset, Césaire extended his sense of Negritude to cover the suffering proletariat of the world. In 1946, under his leadership, residents of the French West Indies were fully incorporated into France as citizens of overseas *départements*. This meant, however, that they found themselves administratively distinct from citizens of what from 1960 would be the newly independent French colonies in Africa. It was the latter category, therefore, that was increasingly excluded, while the former were not always perceived as separate from them. Both groups, especially after the Algerian war, were nevertheless spared the opprobrium reserved for North Africans, partly because of the assumption that they were Christian rather than Muslim. Mankind seems irrestistibly drawn towards the demonisation of some Other. In literature as in life there are fortunately pockets of balance and sanity, however much tinged with idealism and wishful thinking.

Generalisations are necessary for purposes of overview, but they also distort. It is often assumed that the precursors and proponents of Negritude or their outspoken heirs set their faces against interracial marriage. Not only is this not borne out by what they often did in their personal lives but, for example, 'Fanon never claimed that black women should not be romantically involved with white men. He argued that it was pathological to be romantically involved with Whites solely on the basis of their being white.'[276] In the corpus studied, and for the first time since the *Histoire de Louis Anniaba*, the progression from one to the other has begun to appear here and there only in the last couple of decades. In the meantime, the master/slave and coloniser/colonised relationships militated against the more personal option, and that attitude has taken an unconscionable time waning: it has still not disappeared. As Amin Maalouf, in a book expressing a moving plea for tolerance by arguing that we are all products of many cultures, observes of the American cinema,

> toute union, à l'écran, entre un Blanc et une Noire, ou entre une Blanche et un Noir, est quasiment proscrite, parce que l'opinion, nous dit-on, n'est pas à l'aise avec ce genre de métissage. [...] c'est tellement systématique, tellement prévisible, que c'en est exaspérant, et même insultant.

> [any union, on the screen, between a white man and a black woman or between a white woman and a black man is virtually prohibited, because public opinion, we are told, is uneasy about this kind of mixing. [...] it is so systematic, so predictable, that it is exasperating, and even insulting.][277]

The recognition that we are all, in effect, culturally if not biologically mixed unfortunately cannot evacuate the anxieties which we project on to whatsoever or whomsoever we perceive as Other.

Yambo Ouologuem expresses his sympathy for the biracial couple, symbolically alienated from their own cultures and therefore marginalised in a modern society which is largely unsympathetic to them and sometimes overtly hostile:

> Ni nègres tous deux, ni blancs désormais, enfantant une descendance de nègres blancs, vous voilà, ta femme et toi parmi cette masse anonyme des sociétés marginales.

> [Neither both black, nor white from now on, heading a progeny of white Blacks, there you are, your wife and you, in this anonymous mass of marginal societies.][278]

The negative loading of the term 'nègre blanc' [white Black] in current parlance—no longer designating, as it did unambiguously until the late eighteenth century, an albino Black, but one steeped in western culture, modes of thought and style of dress—carries even more contempt in Africa than it does in France.[279]

That sense of cultural betrayal is felt and sometimes expressed keenly by jaundiced observers of a *couple domino*. Each partner is accused, with varying degrees of incomprehension and ferocity, of perversity if not perversion. The couple in turn suffers psychological repercussions from such pressure, and these are often the main reasons for separation: the wedge that European society has traditionally driven between Blacks and Whites is used to sunder partners one from another. On the analogy of Swift's Big-endians and Little-endians, one has only to imagine some lunatic decree that all those with blue eyes should despise, persecute and enslave anyone with brown eyes.[280] This would be no more logical than what Whites have done to Blacks over the centuries, the results of which have been as morally debilitating for Whites as they have been deadly and demeaning for Blacks. Racism is one form of exploitation of the weak by the strong, conveniently colour-coded for exploiters and exploitable to be immediately recognised. When black and white are stood on their heads, as in *Empsaël et Zoraïde* and *La Revanche de Bozambo*, the irony and satire are forceful vehicles for greater tolerance through greater understanding, as it were from the inside, of the Other's sufferings.[281]

Since literature, and specifically the novel, reflects society and uses observation to depict its characters and shape their interactions in a social context, more or less recognisable and realistic, according to its manner and intentions, it is hardly surprising that we should have seen so many books showing polarised attitudes. Such polarisation is the result of a whole raft of myths elaborated over centuries which set Black and White as polar opposites.

Shorthand perpetuates those myths: even Willy Brandt's generous impulse to focus on a North/South divide, stimulating the wealthy former to help the impoverished latter, fosters them. And whether the periphrastic label is 'the under-developed world' or 'the developing world', it assumes criteria determined exclusively by what must then be 'the over-developed world' (like an over-ripe and possibly maggot-ridden cheese) or 'the non-developing world' (stagnating in a slough of self-satisfaction). As C.L.R. James has written, 'The patience and forbearance of the poor are among the strongest bulwarks of the rich.'[282] If the agenda is always written by white standards, even under the guise of a patronising essentialism, without adequate account taken of values established over millennia by other civilisations, Black and White will continue to be symbols for a desperately unequal dialogue.

One way or another, the idea that 'never the twain shall meet' goes beyond being a statement of fact to become an admonitory moral imperative. In a novel, it is supported by the literary imperative for clear delineation, especially of minor characters, to produce memorable vignettes within the overall economy of the writing. The extravagant racism of some of the fathers of white brides we have noted in the course of our investigations can be explained, if not excused, in that way. 'Plus le Blanc est petit, plus sa haine est grande' [The smaller the White, the greater his hatred], as Crouzat has written, echoing Gide.[283] Our awareness that such racial bigots exist ostensibly legitimises their use as representatives of an extreme position against which other positions can be plotted.

Yet the exchanges within literature are only a particular form of those which language affords us in everyday life, so the dangers do not lie exclusively between covers. A sentence by Roland Barthes seems particularly apposite in this context: 'Le langage est une peau: je frotte mon langage contre l'autre' [Language is a skin: I rub my language against someone else].[284] Exchanges within a single language, such as Barthes is envisaging here, are enriched by exchanges between different languages and the cultures they embody and translate. It is not a feature of the present study, which engages only with French, just as the African writers concerned have done through their own education, but they, unlike me, speak one or more indigenous African languages which interact with their French. I regret the limitation, and leave further study along these lines to others with the necessary competence.

It has meant that I have omitted questions of inter-ethnic relationships in favour of the single black/white axis. Such polarisation, and the demonisation it inevitably brings with it, is undoubtedly a historical fact, well recorded in the literature we have studied. But it also serves implicitly to reinforce the very racism it condemns, since it depends on the essentialist assumption that at some time 'races' were pure and can still be used as absolutes against which can be pitted the wish or effort to integrate. Shifting positions *vis-à-vis* taboo and totem have been revealed, and one of the most valuable lessons to be learnt is that neither is a sufficient or satisfactory yardstick: we need to go beyond both totem and taboo.

My work is a call, sometimes explicit and always implicit, for vigilant (if not militant) tolerance on the basis of the respect for otherness. Intolerance must be denounced, but insofar as tolerance implies paternalistic gestures from a self-arrogated position of superiority, it too is ultimately unacceptable, however good an initial position it may be. Oscar Wilde declared that he tolerated everything except intolerance, and this position now seems to be embodied in the German constitution. Paul Claudel's *boutade* sounds almost like a reply: 'La tolérance? Il y a des maisons pour cela!' [Tolerance? There are brothels for that!], and may be less ineptly reactionary than it first appears.

Paul Ricœur, for example, sees clearly the dangers inherent in tolerance by tracing the shift from

> le respect de toutes les différences en un éloge de la différence pour la différence, et finalement en une culture de l'*indifférence*.

> [respect for difference into praise for difference for its own sake, and finally into a culture of indifference.]

He continues:

> Seules les manifestations sporadiques d'*indignation*, face à des nuisances manifestes exercées contre les membres les plus fragiles de notre entourage, s'avèrent encore capables de réveiller nos sociétés de leur sommeil d'indifférence.

[Only sporadic manifestations of indignation in the face of harm meted out against the most vulnerable members of our species appear capable of awakening our societies from their slumber of indifference.][285]

Such indignation—the *saeva indignatio* of the moralist, itself only a stage in a process of adjustment to the otherness of others with the ultimate aim of absolute serenity—is seemingly at odds with the dispassionate analysis undertaken by the scholar, but I am not prepared to admit that intellectual pursuits should be divorced from ethical considerations. History shows us the danger of that split occurring: the ethical vacuum in which much Enlightenment science was conducted, lent authority, as the sociologist Dominique Schnapper has magisterially demonstrated, to subsequent racism: 'La pensée raciste du XIXe siècle est un enfant monstrueux des Lumières' [Nineteenth-century racist thinking is a monstrous product of the Enlightenment].[286] Other historians of racism confirm this position:

the history of European racism must be seen as originating in the eighteenth century, whatever antecedent elements might be discovered in earlier times. It was in the eighteenth century that the structure of racial thought was consolidated and determined for the next one and three-quarter centuries.[287]

George L. Mosse plausibly traces the sources of European racism in 'the new sciences of the Enlightenment and the Pietistic revival of Christianity' and in the reciprocal influence of science and aesthetics:

observations, measurements, and comparisons that were basic to the new eighteenth-century sciences were combined with value judgments following aesthetic criteria derived from ancient Greece. [...] Whatever the physical measurements or comparisons made, in the last resort the resemblance to ancient beauty and proportions determined the value of man. This continuous transition from science to aesthetics is a cardinal feature of modern racism.[288]

It is much to Lucie Cousturier's credit that her intuition should have led her to denounce such an association. She knew that socio-political considerations had to be balanced against moral ones. To recognise that the universalisation of western humanist values, however admirable, distorted and even destroyed other cultures is a key step in the process of relativisation.

Only by concentrating on individuals can we hope to escape from the debilitating trap of racism. As Kuoh-Moukoury writes:

> Ni les oppositions culturelles, ni les données historiques, ni les différences raciales n'empêchent les Noirs et les Blancs de tisser des liens d'amitié, d'affection et d'amour. Et les couples dominos réalisent une vie affective aussi solide, enrichissante, profonde, ou aussi banale et lamentable que les autres couples du monde.

> [Neither cultural oppositions, nor historical data, nor racial differences prevent Blacks and Whites from forging links of friendship, affection and love. And *couples dominos* enjoy an emotional life as solid, enriching and profound or as banal and lamentable as any other couples in the world.][289]

There is sufficient evidence from novels of recent years that, whatever the blandishments of black/white polarisation in the interest of providing a clear scaffolding for narrative, writers are more than ever alert to its dangers, to the point where skin-colour, even in a *Blanche/Noir* couple, becomes again, after more than a quarter of a millennium, supremely irrelevant. Such liberation from the chains of history by transcending it is of crucial importance.

Fanon asserts that ostracism, even castration, was traditionally meted out by Blacks to their fellows who slept with white women.[290] We have seen no instance of castration in the literature we have studied, but degrees of ostracism are clearly in evidence. The couple's cultural adventurousness—some would say adventurism—perceived as betrayal is criticised by society, black or white, bringing outside pressure to bear on the protagonists, while the inauthenticity to which it can give rise psychologically often undermines them from within. With ever easier travel and increased racial interaction, at least in urban centres, the persistent and perniciously stultifying mindset engendered on both sides by colonialism at long last shows signs of disappearing.

If we need a new symbol to help us to escape from polarisation and its parlous over-simplifications, there is one to hand which seems particularly apposite: the world-wide web. It is a metaphor that I have recommended elsewhere to supersede the binary entrapment and dis-honesty of the labels 'French' and 'Francophone' in relation to writing in French-language literatures from any source: 'la Francographie'.[291] It seems to me to have even more value as a guiding thread to lead us out of the labyrinth of hypocrisy and hatred in which western civilisation, self-seeking and exploitative, mesmerised by material gain, lost itself in respect of Blacks. No apologies on their part are necessary: on the contrary. There should be no centre to which they feel compelled to 'write back', as established postcolonial discourse has it, since each one is a centre, entire of itself. Yet as no man is an island, each weaves a web of relationships with those around him—and that increasingly means the whole world. The author reflects the patterns perceived; the reader brings more to bear. In the criss-crossing of such exchanges, we all have something to learn.

GENERAL NOTE TO THE READER

Where full bibliographical details are not given in the notes, they will be found in the select bibliography at the end of this volume. Page numbers are not given for creative writing (listed chronologically by date of publication—not composition—in section A of the bibliography) but they are for critical material (listed alphabetically by author in section B). It is my way of encouraging reading or re-reading of the creative works so as to replace the quoted extracts in their context.

In both text and notes, all translations are presented in square brackets immediately after the original; unless otherwise stated (in the cases of Fischer's 'William der Neger' and Duras's *Ourika* only), they are my own.

Introduction: Between Totem and Taboo

1   Henry Champly, *White Women, Coloured Men*, p. 261.
2   Albert Memmi, 1984 preface to *Agar* (first published 1955), p. 17.
3   Virginia Mason Vaughan, *Othello: a contextual history*, p. 51 (in chap. 3, 'Racial discourse: black and white', pp. 51–70, which is of general interest in the present context). A *locus classicus* for discussion of Otherness is Homi K. Bhabha, 'The Other Question', in *The Location of Culture*, pp. 66–84, and I would also point to the following essay, 'Of Mimicry and Man', pp. 85–92, as crucial to an understanding of our premises.
4   Sander L. Gilman, *Jewish Self-Hatred*, p. 11.
5   Leo Frobenius, *Histoire de la civilisation africaine*, tr. H. Back and D. Ermont, Paris: Gallimard, 1936 (the edition familiar to Senghor and Césaire) and Kenneth Clark, *Civilisation: a personal view*, London: BBC, John Murray, 1969.
6   John Locke, *Essay Concerning Human Understanding*, Oxford: Clarendon Press, 1975, p. 607. David Hume, footnote to 1753 reprint of his essay 'Of National Characters'. Both statements are quoted by Ronald Segal, *The Black Diaspora*, London: Faber, 1995, pp. 269–70.
7   Unattested in many recent dictionaries, the term *couple domino* seems to derive from the black and white of dominos, further overdetermined by the fact that they are joined together in the game (cf. *domino* 'connector' in an electrical circuit). My understanding of the slang term 'nutmegging' is that it applies exclusively to *Blanc/Noire* relations, but such dictionaries as record its use from the eighteenth century until today are unspecific on this point.
8   Ronald Hyam, *Empire and Sexuality*, p. 203.
9   This is the image used by Champly in *White Women, Coloured Men*, p. 300.

10 Freud's much-discussed term appears, in English in the original, in his 1926 essay 'The Question of Lay Analysis', in *The Standard Edition of the Complete Psychological Works of Sigmund Freud*, ed. James Strachey, London: The Hogarth Press, vol. XX, 1959, p. 212.

11 Gilman, *Difference and Pathology*, p. 120. Pius Ngandu Nkashama, *Vie et mœurs d'un primitif...* (1987), p. 107. Cf. Beth Day, *Sexual Life Between Blacks and Whites*, p. 5: 'Ironically the one area in which the black male can compete successfully with the white male is in bed.'

12 Gilman, 'Black Sexuality and Modern Consciousness', p. 50.

13 Dominique Schnapper, *La Relation à l'autre*, p. 59.

14 Aaron, in *Titus Andronicus*, being the unacceptable black other: both Othello and he are Moors having intimate relations with Europeans, but Othello is a Christian. It is interesting that Aaron, the 'coal-black Moor', 'chief architect and plotter of these woes', who stands in direct contrast to Othello in boasting: 'Aaron will have his soul black like his face', has never achieved the archetypal status of Othello. Rather surprisingly, in view of his importance in West Indian literature especially, Caliban proves not to be a relevant point of reference for present purposes.

15 My title and the first part of my sub-title refer indirectly to Sigmund Freud's *Totem and Taboo*, in *The Standard Edition...*, vol. XIII, 1955, pp. 1–162, and to Frantz Fanon's *Peau noire, masques blancs*, esp. chap. 3.

16 J.G. Frazer, *Totemism and Exogamy*, 4 vols, London: Macmillan, 1910.

17 Pierre-Antoine de La Place published his versions of both in 1745: see Margaret Gilman, *Othello in France*, p. 3.

18 The recent film, *White Man's Burden*, starring John Travolta, continues this race-reversal theme: see Adam Lively, *Masks*, p. 79, n. 1.

19 See the fascinating study by Jean-Claude Blachère, *Négritures*.

20 Jean-Paul Sartre, 'Orphée noir', in Léopold Sédar Senghor, ed., *Anthologie de la nouvelle poésie nègre et malgache de langue française*, Paris: Presses universitaires de France, 1948; 4ᵉ édition 1977, p. xiv.

21 I pursue this matter further in 'Fables of Melanocracy: "Race" Reversals in French Literature', *Forum for Modern Language Studies* (forthcoming).

22 See, e.g., at the titillating end of the spectrum, but still redolent of rape, the Black in colourful swimming trunks (the avowed object of the advertisement) carrying the supine and compliant white woman, fig. 271, p. 184 in Raymond Bachollet et al., *Négripub: l'image des Noirs dans la publicité*, Paris: Somogy, 1992; or, overtly and viciously racist, the gorilla raping the Aryan female from a 1920 issue of *Simplicissimus* reproduced in R. Grimm and J. Hermand, eds, *Blacks*

and German Culture, Madison: University of Wisconsin Press, 1986, p. 117. Lois Greenfield's stunning photograph of airborne black and white dancers used on the cover of the present volume is a fine exception, implicitly adding a moral dimension to the aesthetic one: see *The New Dance Photography of Lois Greenfield*, London: Thames and Hudson, 1998.

23 For examples of the former, see Abby L. Ferber, *White Man Falling*, esp. figs 3 and 4 between pp. 90 and 91; and of the latter, the *enquête* in the *Nouvel Observateur* of 14 February 1991 entitled 'Le Boom des mariages mixtes'.

24 Ferber, *White Man Falling*, p. 105.

25 See Thérèse Kuoh-Moukoury, *Les Couples dominos*. It is noteworthy that the cases of mixed-race children studied by Owen White in *Children of the French Empire* include none deriving from a *Blanche/Noir* union.

26 See in particular, apart from my own studies, the articles by Bauge-Gueye, Diefenthal and Schipper-De Leeuw, all dealing with the period 1950–80. For mixed-race relationships during the same period in English-language literatures, see Eliane Utudjian-Saint André, 'Unions mixtes et métissages dans quelques littératures noires d'Afrique anglophone' in *Unions mixtes et métissages*, ed. E. Hanquart-Turner, pp. 35–64.

I eschew the familiar phrase 'Francophone literature(s)' as an etymological absurdity. The case is argued in my paper '"La Francographie": a new model for "la Francophonie"', *African Literature Association Bulletin* [Philadelphia, PA], 25, 4 (Fall 1999), 28–36 and in *Littératures francophones: la problématique de l'altérité*, ed. C. O'Dowd-Smyth, Waterford: Waterford Institute of Technology (forthcoming).

27 Notable exceptions are the books by Fanoudh-Siefer, Hoffmann, Houssain, Martinkus-Zemp, Ruscio, Seeber and (specifically for the theatre) Chalaye. 'Doudouism' refers to the mawkish verse based on traditional French forms limply evoking the exotic flora and languorous Creole fauna of the tropics.

28 See Daouda Mar's 1996 thesis.

29 Mar, p. 731. In *Les Couples dominos*, Thérèse Kuoh-Moukoury confirms the pattern suggested here, but concentrates on the sociological, not the literary.

30 Schipper-De Leeuw, p. 166.

31 T.L. Richards with Stuart Gurr, *White Man, Brown Woman: The Life Story of a Trader in the South Seas*, London: Hutchinson, 1932, p. 267.

32 Eldridge Cleaver, *Soul on Ice*, p. 187.

33 Calixthe Beyala, *Amours sauvages*, Paris: Albin Michel, 1999, p. 119.

[34] Maryse Condé, *La Migration des cœurs*, Paris: Laffont, 1995; Pocket, 1997, p. 92.

[35] Munford, Jordan and Chalaye record several cases in their studies.

[36] Henri Lopes, *Le Chercheur d'Afriques*, Paris: Seuil, 1990, p. 257.

[37] The assertion by Iyay Kimoni, in *Destin de la littérature négro-africaine*, p. 69, that 'Il n'y a pas de continuité entre le thème nègre dans la littérature européenne, en particulier française, et le thème nègre inauguré par la littérature négro-africaine' [There is no continuity between the theme of the Negro in European, and especially French, literature and the theme of the Negro introduced in Black African literature] is immediately rendered suspect by his next sentence: 'La négrophilie, après avoir servi de mode littéraire, devient sous la plume des Noirs une force de changement' [Negrophilia, once a mere literary fashion, becomes, with Black pens, a force for change]. The power of each is best appreciated in relation to the other. It is furthermore inaccurate to suggest that anti-slavery fictions, in conjunction with various factual accounts, had no impact in generating support for the abolitionist movement: there is overwhelming evidence to the contrary.

[38] For 'hybridity as heresy', see Homi K. Bhabha, *The Location of Culture*, p. 225.

[39] L.-J.-B. Béranger-Féraud, *Les Peuplades de la Sénégambie*, Paris: Leroux, 1879, p. 379; Albert Gras, *La Zone torride: souvenirs du Sénégal*,Luxembourg: Imp. J. Beffort, 1885, p. 129, both cited by Mar, p. 709.

[40] Walvin, *Black and White*, p. 55, quoting Long's *Candid Reflections...*, London, 1772, p. 49. Walvin quotes extensively from Long's text, among other source documents on Blacks in Britain, in his valuable *Black Presence*. Guillaume Bosman had earlier registered his contempt for 'une certaine sorte de gens [...]; on les appelle *Tapoeyers* ou *Mulats*; ils sont nez d'un Européen & d'une Negre, ou bien d'un Blanc et d'une *Mulate*. Cette race bâtarde est portée à toute sorte de méchantez [*sic*] & de vices; ils n'aiment gueres les Negres plus que nous; [...] & tout ce que j'en peux dire, c'est qu'ils sont l'écume des Blancs & des Negres, & l'égout des vices des deux nations' [a certain type of people; they are called *Tapoeyers* or *Mulats*; they are the product of a European and a Negress or else of a White and a Mulatress. This bastard race is prone to all kinds of wickedness and vice; they like the Negroes scarcely any more than we do; and all I can say of them is that they are the scum of both Whites and Blacks, and the sewer for the vices of both nations], *Voyage de Guinée...*, Utrecht: Antoine Schouten, 1705 (9e lettre), pp. 145–46.

41 Alphonse Esquiros, 'Du mouvement des races humaines', p. 165. The eminent scientist Paul Broca would reiterate such ideas in 1864: see White, *Children of the French Empire*, p. 99.

42 Esquiros, p. 166.

43 Champly, p. 7. Italics in original. Cf. p. 6: '*The Coloured peoples have discovered the White woman*—as a marvel; as a wonder from the physical, the artistic, the social and even the religious points of view; as an idol worthy of being desired above all else.' And again, p. 276: 'during the bathing season the windows of our most up-to-date shops display feminine wax-dolls in swim-suits or beach-pyjamas, with their faces, their arms and their legs dyed a deep ochre. *This is the ideal of a fashion which is preparing the minds of White women to accept the idea of cross-breeding.*'

44 Yambo Ouologuem, *Lettre à la France nègre*, p. 40. Cf. Paul-Pierre Guebhard, *Mireille entre les négresses*, Paris: Éditions du monde moderne, 1925, p. 60 and Bernard Dadié, *Un Nègre à Paris*, Paris: Présence Africaine, 1959, p. 131.

45 Awa Thiam, *La Parole aux Négresses*, pp. 158–59.

46 A table of key dates for our theme in relation to France and her colonies is given at the beginning of this volume. For attitudes towards miscegenation in North America, see Winthrop D. Jordan, *White over Black*, esp. chap. IV.

47 See Victor Schœlcher, in a speech dating from 1880 among his writings collected under the title *Esclavage et colonisation*, Paris: Presses universitaires de France, 1948, p. 197. Cf. *abbé* Henri Grégoire, *Considérations sur le mariage et sur le divorce, adressées aux citoyens d'Haïti*, Paris: Baudouin, 1823; and *De la noblesse de la peau, ou du préjugé des blancs contre la couleur des Africains et celle de leurs descendans noirs et sang-mêlés*, Paris: Baudouin, 1826.

48 See esp. Henri Lopes, *Le Chercheur d'Afriques*, Paris: Seuil, 1990.

49 Albert Jacquard, preface to Barbara, *Les Couples mixtes*, p. 8.

50 Ferber, *White Man Falling*, p. 103.

Chapter 1: Eighteenth-century Enwhitenment

51 Nusayb the Younger (died 791), quoted in his own translation by Bernard Lewis, 'The Crows of the Arabs', in *'Race', Writing and Difference*, ed. Henry Louis Gates Jr., Chicago & London: Chicago University Press, 1986, p. 115.

52 *Le Pour et Contre*, XIV, 66 (1738), quoted by Régis Antoine, *Les Écrivains français et les Antilles*, p. 131.

53 See the case of *Jean Boucaux* vs *Verdelin* in Peabody, *'There are no slaves in France'*, esp. chaps 2–4.

54 *Le Code noir*, 1742, pp. 29–30, 493, 200–01 and 323–25 respectively.

55 See *Histoire de Louis Anniaba*, ed. R. Little, Exeter: University of Exeter Press, 2000.
56 Guillaume Bosman, *Voyage de Guinée...*, Utrecht: Antoine Schouten, 1705, letter 20, pp. 447–49. No reference is made here to Anniaba's marriage to a Frenchwoman.
57 Jean-Baptiste Labat, *Nouveau Voyage dans les isles de l'Amérique*, quoted by Hoffmann, *Le Nègre romantique*, p. 30.
58 Roger Mercier, *L'Afrique dans la littérature française*, p. 77.
59 Assini is now in Ghana, on the sea very near the Ivory Coast border.
60 These examples, noted in *The Irish Times* in 1992, could easily have been matched elsewhere.
61 See Aboubacry Moussa Lam, *De l'origine égyptienne des Peul*, Paris: Présence Africaine & Khépéra, 1994.
62 Hyam, p. 206.
63 See Yambo Ouologuem, *Le Devoir de violence*, Paris: Seuil, 1968, p. 43 and Christopher L. Miller, *Blank Darkness*, pp. 32–39.
64 See Chalaye, chap. II and esp. ref. to *Le Ballet du monde renversé*, pp. 56–57.
65 For other instances of such superficial transmogrification in literature and the *bande dessinée*, see my *Nègres blancs*, chap. 6, pp. 111–28.
66 See Mercier, p. 217, Little, *Nègres blancs*, pp. 119–21 and Chalaye, pp. 85–87.
67 This abolitionist 'sound-bite' featured widely, including on a ceramic medallion produced in 1787 by Josiah Wedgwood inspired by the British anti-slavery campaigners. For an illustration, see Hugh Honour, *The Image of the Black in Western Art*, IV: *From the American Revolution to World War I*, 1: *Slaves and Librators*, Cambridge, Mass. and London: Harvard University Press, 1989, p. 62, fig. 23.
68 Simone Weil, *L'Enracinement*, Paris: Gallimard, 1949, p. 146. The paradox was anticipated by abolitionist *philosophes* holding shares in slave-trading companies: see notably Louis Sala-Molins, *Les Misères des Lumières: sous la raison, l'outrage...*, Paris: Laffont, 1992. On the persistence of the paradox, see notably Jean-Loup Amselle, 'Black, Blanc, Beur, ou le fantasme du métissage', in Sylvie Kandé, ed., *Discours sur le métissage*, pp. 35–46.
69 See esp. Raynal's *Histoire philosophique et politique des ... Deux Indes* (1770), Condorcet's *Réflexions sur l'esclavage des Nègres* (Neuchâtel, Société Typographique, 1781) and, for modern overviews, Jean-Pierre Biondi & François Zuccarelli, *16 pluviôse an II: les colonies de la Révolution*, Yves Benot, *La Révolution française et la fin des colonies*, and Aimé Césaire, *Toussaint Louverture: la Révolution française et le problème colonial*.

70 Jean-François de Saint-Lambert, *Contes américains: L'Abenaki, Ziméo, Les Deux Amis*, ed. R. Little, Textes littéraires CIX, Exeter: University of Exeter Press, 1997.
71 'On Poetry', in *The Works of Dr. Jonathan Swift, Dean of St. Patrick's, Dublin*, London: C. Davis et al., 1754, vol. VII, p. 261.
72 See esp. William B. Cohen's valuable *The French Encounter with Africans*.
73 Maryse Condé, *La Civilisation du bossale: réflexions sur la littérature orale de la Guadeloupe et de la Martinique*, Paris: L'Harmattan, 1978, pp. 17–18.
74 Munford, *The Black Ordeal*, vol. III, p. 705.
75 E.g. Jean-Baptiste Radet's *Honorine, ou la femme difficile à vivre* (1795), see Carminella Biondi, p. 107 and Chalaye, pp. 117, 119, 122–26, 141–42: Zago loves Louise who, with regard to his different colour, remarks 'Je ne m'en aperçois guère' [I scarcely noticed].
76 Andréa de Nerciat, *Le Diable au corps* [1803], 10/18 edition, pp. 347–55.
77 In its original edition of 1818 it is also presented, but in error, as a *récit à dialogues* in the manner of *Le Diable au corps*.
78 Dubreuil's *Paulin et Virginie* (1794), in which Domingo (black) and Babet (white) fall in love, is based on *Paul et Virginie*. See Chalaye, pp. 115–16.
79 W.E.B. Du Bois, *The Souls of Black Folk* [1903], New York and Toronto: Knopf, Everyman Library, 1993, p. 16: 'The problem of the Twentieth Century is the problem of the color-line.'
80 Hoffmann, p. 144. My account of the novel is indebted to his analysis.
81 Hoffmann, pp. 145–46. A graphic image of the three races can be seen in the title-plate to Claude-Nicolas Le Cat's *Traité de la couleur de la peau humaine*, of 1765, reproduced as the frontispiece to my edition of Saint-Lambert's *Contes américains* [1759–60].

Chapter 2: From Taboo to Totem

82 William Blake, 'The Little Black Boy', in *Songs of Innocence*.
83 Chateaubriand, letter of October 1814, in *Correspondance générale*, II: *1808–1814*, ed. Pierre Riberette, Paris: Gallimard, 1979, pp. 218–21.
84 Hyam, p. 117.
85 Claire de Durfort, duchesse de Duras, *Ourika* [1823], ed. R. Little, Textes littéraires CV, Exeter: University of Exeter Press, 1998, p. 14. This and subsequent translations from *Ourika* are taken from the anonymous version, London: Longman, Hunt, Rees, Orme, Brown and Green, 1824, from which the last two words quoted are missing.
86 Echoing her visit to Guadeloupe from late 1801 to autumn 1802, Marceline Desbordes-Valmore published a poem in different versions

('Chanson créole', 1819; 'Le Réveil créole', 1820) in which the sex and colour of the speaker and addressee are unclear, but which could allude to a slave's desire for his mistress. See M. D.-V., *Œuvres poétiques*, ed. M. Bertrand, Grenoble: Presses Universitires de Grenoble, 1973, vol. II, pp. 585 (text), 772 (notes).

87 Quoted by Hoffmann, *Le Nègre romantique*, p. 159.

88 A further century on, Pierre Loti's first-hand experience would allow him, in *Le Roman d'un spahi* (1881), to continue this vein of escapism while eschewing its more extravagant noble sentiments in favour of Blacks.

89 'William der Neger', first printed in the *Zeitung für die elegante Welt* (1817), 97–101 and published in *Kleine Erzählungen und romantische Skizzen*, Posen and Leipzig, 1818, pp. 27–73; reprinted Hildesheim, Zürich, New York: Georg Olms, 1988. The English translation is quoted from 'William the Negro', in *Bitter Healing: German Women Writers from 1700 to 1830. An Anthology*, ed. Jeannine Blackwell and Suzanne Zantop, Lincoln and London: University of Nebraska Press, 1990, pp. 354–67. See also Judith Purver, 'Caroline Auguste Fischer, an introduction', in *Women Writers of the Age of Goethe*, Occasional Papers in German Studies 4, Lancaster: University, Department of Modern Languages, 1991, pp. 3–30; and, more sharply focused, 'Gender and the Representation of Cultural Difference in the Treatment of the Haitian Revolution in German Literature around 1800', an as yet unpublished paper by Nicholas Saul (to whom I am indebted for drawing this material to my attention) presented in July 1997 at the International Seminar at Trinity College, Dublin.

90 'Taking on Reality', *The Irish Times* (24 April 1999), Review section, p. 10.

91 In his 1826 preface to the first edition of *Bug-Jargal*, written in 1818 and printed in 1820 in that less fully developed version in the periodical *Le Conservateur littéraire*, Hugo noted: 'une ébauche de cet opuscule ayant été déjà imprimée [...] en 1820, à une époque où la politique du jour s'occupait fort peu d'Haïti, il est évident que si le sujet qu'il traite a pris depuis un nouveau degré d'intérêt, ce n'est pas la faute de l'auteur' [a sketch of this little piece having already been published in 1820, at a time when politicians took little interest in Haiti, it is scarcely the author's fault if the subject has subsequently acquired a new degree of interest]. Victor Hugo, *Romans*, I, Paris: Seuil, Coll. L'Intégrale, 1963, p. 149, col. 2.

92 Hoffmann, *Le Nègre romantique*, p. 202: 'Il n'est peut-être pas inutile de remarquer que outre Victor Hugo [dans *Bug-Jargal*], des quatre écrivains qui imaginent la possibilité d'un amour entre un Nègre et une Blanche, trois sont des femmes [Mmes Cashin, Doin et Ségalas]' [It is relevant to note that apart from Victor Hugo, of the four writers who

envisage the possibility of love between a Negro and a white woman, three are women].

Cf. Alain Ruscio, *Le Credo de l'homme blanc*, p. 221: 'Il y a, dans la littérature coloniale, des exemples, rares il est vrai, de couples de ce type unis par des réels sentiments d'amour. Est-ce par hasard que beaucoup de ces livres sont écrits par des femmes?' [There are, in colonial literature, some examples, albeit rare, of couples of this type joined by feelings of love. Is it mere chance that many of these books are written by women?].

93 Ruscio, p. 220.
94 Quoted in Ruscio, p. 221.
95 Chalaye, p. 167.
96 Hoffmann, 'Victor Hugo, les Noirs et l'esclavage', p. 65.
97 Ibid., p. 66.
98 *Bug-Jargal*, pp. 192–93. Hugo does not hesitate to emphasise the point heavily: 'Mais comment se fait-il qu'avec cela, reprit-elle, qu'il soit amoureux de moi? En es-tu sûr? / —Sûr maintenant, lui dis-je. [...] / — Vraiment, reprit Marie avec une naïve surprise, c'est ton rival!' [But how, she replied, can he possibly be in love with me? Are you sure? / Quite sure now, I said to her. [...] / Really, Marie continued with innocent surprise, he is your rival!], p. 193, col. 1.
99 In *Cornélie, nouvelle grecque, suivie de six nouvelles*, 1826, pp. 125–44.
100 Ibid., p. 173.
101 Saint-Leger Leger, 'Cohorte', in Saint-John Perse, *Œuvres complètes*, Paris: Gallimard, Bibliothèque de la Pléiade, 1972 (1978 printing), p. 683. As one would expect in a poet, the meaning is ambivalent: it is also 'social commerce'.
102 Othello embodies this tradition. Adam Lively is just the latest to set this notion in the broader context of the ancient debate as to why Blacks were black: see *Masks*, chap. 1, 'The Invention of Race'.
103 '[C]'est grâce aux connaissances de Zéphire, à la science qu'il possède des ressources offertes par la nature sauvage que le couple peut bâtir une maison, cultiver un jardin, se soigner contre les fièvres tropicales, arriver en somme à mener une vie idyllique' [It is thanks to Zéphire's skills and to his knowledge of the resources offered by nature in the raw that the couple can build a house, cultivate a garden, heal their tropical fevers, and in short manage to live an idyllic life]. Hoffmann, *Le Nègre romantique*, p. 145.
104 *Dictionnaire de biographie française*, ed. R. d'Amat and R. Limouzin-Lamothe, Paris: Letouzey et Ané, vol. XI, 1967, col. 433.
105 André Gide, *Journal 1939–1949*, Paris: Gallimard, Bibliothèque de la Pléiade, 1960, p. 52 (2 September 1940).
106 Ibid., p. 296 (24 February 1946).

Chapter 3: Traditions and Transitions

[107] Harriet Martineau, *Demerara: A Tale*, 1832, quoted by Lively, *Masks*, p. 55.

[108] Jean Price-Mars, *Ainsi parla l'oncle*, [1928], Ottawa: Leméac, 1983, p. 45.

[109] Alain Ruscio, *Le Credo de l'homme blanc*, p. 218.

[110] See esp. A. James Arnold, in 'The Gendering of *créolité*', who, *inter alios*, denounces Césaire and Fanon in this respect.

[111] Chalaye, *Du Noir au nègre*, pp. 189–90, 204–05, 210–13.

[112] M. l'abbé Dugoujon, *Lettres sur l'esclavage dans les colonies françaises*, Paris: Pagnerre, 1845, p. 76.

[113] See Hoffmann, *Le Nègre romantique*, p. 201 and Ruscio, p. 221.

[114] Chalaye, pp. 162–63, in an excellent section on 'Amours en noir et blanc: de la farce au drame', pp. 162–74.

[115] Chalaye, pp. 189–90, 202–03.

[116] Ibid., p. 225. On the remarkable real-life Saint-George (properly spelt thus), see the full and lively biography by Alain Guédé, *Monsieur de Saint-George, le Nègre des Lumières*, Arles: Actes Sud, 1999.

[117] Ibid., p. 213.

[118] I am indebted for this account to Chalaye, pp. 194–96.

[119] See Hoffmann, p. 201.

[120] Quoted in Hoffmann, p. 201.

[121] As Hyam records (p. 115), Tacitus quotes Caecina Severus in his *Annals*, III, 3: 'The rule which forbade women to be taken to provinces or foreign countries was salutary. A female entourage stimulates extravagance in peacetime and timidity in war. [...] Women are not only frail and easily tired. Relax control, and they become ferocious, ambitious schemers, circulating among the soldiers, ordering company-commanders about. [...] The wives attract every rascal in a province.'

[122] Mineke Schipper-De Leeuw, *Le Blanc vu d'Afrique*, p. 149. Along the same lines, Léon Fanoudh-Siefer notes, in *Le Mythe du Nègre*, p. 167: 'La bamboula, telle qu'elle est décrite dans la littérature coloniale, c'est tout simplement la licence, c'est la sensualité animale déchaînée et folle, c'est l'érotisme impudique, brutal et bestial, c'est la furie de la libido exaspérée collectivement par la magie du tam-tam' [The bamboula, as described in colonial literature, represents licentiousness, unbridled animal sensuality, immodest, brutal and bestial eroticism].

[123] Lt-Colonel [Albert-Ernest] Baratier, *À travers l'Afrique*, Paris: Fayard, n.d., p. 80, quoted by János Riesz, 'Les Métamorphoses d'un livre', p. 265.

124 Jean-Pierre Houssain, 'L'Afrique noire et les écrivains français', p. 218. His pages 371–75 are devoted to the image of the Black as a 'sexual beast' denounced by Fanon (*Peau noire, masques blancs*, chap. 6) in order to complete the picture presented by Fanoudh-Siefer and to qualify that of Ada Martinkus-Zemp in *Le Blanc et le Noir*.

125 Cf. Paul-Pierre Guebhard, *Mireille entre les négresses*, Paris: Éditions du monde moderne, 1925, pp. 17–18: 'Je me félicite au contraire de ce que, ne pouvant m'affranchir des soucis sexuels—auxquels le climat ici prédispose—j'aie pu faire leur part et mener paître la bête quand elle a faim, sans complications sentimentales et sans difficultés. J'ai l'amour avec la même facilité qu'en tournant le bouton électrique tu as la lumière, que tu bois quand tu as soif, que tu manges quand tu as faim. Si tu savais combien c'est commode et salutaire!' [I congratulate myself on the contrary that, unable to free myself from sexual concerns—to which the climate here predisposes one—I have been able to satisfy them and give the beast some food when it was hungry, without sentimental complications or any difficulties. I make love with the same ease that you turn a switch to light an electric lamp, drink when you are thirsty and feed when you are hungry. If only you knew how convenient and healthy it is!]; and Gaston Pichot, *La Brousse et ses dieux*, Paris: Éditions de la Revue mondiale, 1931, pp. 52–53, quoted by Houssain, p. 219: '... la femme noire: instrument de plaisir bref ou d'hygiène, mais certainement jamais élue d'amour et sœur en esprit' [the black woman: an instrument of brief pleasure or hygiene, but certainly never the chosen beloved or the spiritual sister]. Houssain, pp. 222–23, also quotes Louis Sonolet (*Le Parfum de la dame noire*, Paris: La Renaissance du livre, 1931 (first published in a shorter version in 1908), pp. 15, 172): 'Chez les Noirs, l'amour n'est pas un sentiment. Ce n'est qu'une fonction' [In Blacks, love is not a feeling. It is merely a function]. 'Pour l'Européen, l'épouse [noire] ne peut et ne doit être qu'un meuble' [For the European, the [black] wife can and must be a mere chattel].

126 Madeleine Poulaine, for example, who, from her lofty position of privilege, recounts her travels in French and Belgian Congo in *Une Blanche chez les Noirs: l'Afrique vivante*, Paris: Tallandier, 1931. (Her husband Robert Poulaine gives his version in *Étapes africaines: voyage autour du Congo*, Paris: Éditions de la Nouvelle Revue critique, 1930.) In Michelle Marty's *Moussa, le petit noir* (Paris: Crès, 1925), Moussa is almost totally absent, unworthy of notice after serving to attract certain readers by figuring in the title.

127 Rita Cruise O'Brien, *White Society in Black Africa*, p. 57. By 1928, Albert Londres would write (see *Terre d'ébène* [1929], Paris: Le Serpent à plumes, 1994, p. 17): 'La carrière s'est dangereusement embourgeoisée. Finis les enthousiasmes du début, la colonisation romantique, les

risques recherchés, la case dans la brousse, la conquête de l'âme nègre, la petite mousso! On s'embarque maintenant avec sa femme, ses enfants et sa belle-mère. C'est la colonie en bigoudis!' [Careers in the colonies have become dangerously middle-class. Gone are the early enthusiasms, the romance of colonisation, the risk-seeking, the hut in the bush, the conquest of the negro soul, the native girl! Nowadays, wife, children and mother-in-law go on board with you. It's the colony in curlers!]

[128] See e.g. Jean d'Esme, *Fièvres: roman de la forêt équatoriale*, Paris: Flammarion, 1935. Robert Randau writes in *Le Chef des porte-plume: roman de la vie coloniale*, Paris: Éditions du Monde nouveau, 1922, p. 57, n. 1: 'Au Sénégal, l'expression *Faire la Ligne* s'applique aux blanches demi-mondaines qui vont de gare en gare, sur les voies ferrées, et de poste en poste, sur le fleuve et au Soudan, se prostituer à tout venant' [In Senegal, the expression *faire la ligne* is used for demimondaines who go from station to station along the railway lines, and from trading-post to trading-post on the river or in the Soudan, selling themselves to all comers].

[129] Louis Le Barbier, *La Côte d'Ivoire*, Paris, 1916, pp. 206–07, quoted by White, *Children of the French Empire*, p. 24.

[130] See Pierre Mille, 'Marie-faite-en-Fer', in *Barnavaux et quelques femmes*, Paris: Calmann-Lévy, 1908; new edition, 1931.

[131] Roger Martin du Gard, *Les Thibault*, III: *La Belle Saison*, Paris: Gallimard, 1923; Bibliothèque de la Pléiade, 1969, pp. 1002–03: '... sans un mot, il laissait glisser son boubou le long de son petit corps. [...] Là-bas, l'amour, non, ça n'est pas du tout le même que le vôtre. Là-bas, c'est un acte silencieux, à la fois sacré et naturel. Profondément naturel. Il ne s'y mêle aucune pensée, d'aucune sorte, jamais' [without a word, he let his gown slip down his slight body. [...] Over there, it's a silent act, both sacred and natural. Profoundly natural. Thinking, of any sort, never comes into it].

[132] Quoted in Roland Lebel, *Les Établissements français d'outre-mer et leur reflet dans la littérature*, Paris: Larose, 1925, pp. 153–54.

[133] See Chalaye, pp. 361–62 and 314–18 respectively.

[134] Quoted by Ruscio, *Le Credo de l'homme blanc*, p. 220.

[135] Cf. the cartoon in *Rire* (23 janvier 1897), reproduced in Nederveen Pieterse, p. 220.

[136] See Claude Lévi-Strauss, *Tristes tropiques*, Paris: Plon, 1955; Coll. 10/18, 1966, chap. XXII.

[137] See e.g. pp. 121, 148 and, for their representation of flagrant racism in the army, pp. 153–54.

[138] An allusion to the movements led by Lamine Senghor and Blaise Diagne.

[139] *La Femme et l'homme nu*, p. 195. Demaison's qualities as an ethnological observer, widely acknowledged to be considerable, can be measured against Lucie Cousturier's even more perceptive ones by comparing this extract with the following remarks made in *Mes inconnus chez eux*, 2: *Mon ami Soumaré, laptot*, p. 81: 'Certes, pour préserver la famille, toutes les civilisations ont pris des mesures contre l'amour; mais il semble qu'aucune n'en ait pris d'aussi rigoureuses que la civilisation nègre. Elle est un chef d'œuvre de ce que certains appellent improprement la pudeur. On peut se promener indéfiniment dans des villages nègres sans apercevoir de commerce sentimental. La sensualité est réduite au minimum, le contact à l'essentiel' [It is true that, to preserve the family unit, every civilisation has taken measures against love, but none, it seems, so strict as those taken by Negro civilisation. It is a masterpiece of what is sometimes inaccurately termed modesty. You can walk endlessly in black villages without seeing any sign of an exchange of amorous feelings. Sensuality is reduced to a minimum, contact to basics.]

Chapter 4: Opposite Genders, Opposite Agendas

[140] Félicien Challaye, *Souvenirs sur la colonisation*, 1935, p. 4; 1998, p. 24.

[141] Jean Suret-Canale, *L'Afrique noire occidentale et centrale : l'ère coloniale (1900–1945)*, Paris: Éditions Sociales, 1964, p. 181, gives the figure of 164,000; others have suggested as many as 193,000: see Marc Michel, 'Le Recrutement des Tirailleurs en A.O.F. pendant la première guerre mondiale: essai de bilan statistique', *Revue française d'histoire d'outre-mer*, 221 (4e trimestre 1973), 644, and his *L'Appel à l'Afrique: contributions et réactions à l'effort de guerre en A.O.F.*, Paris: Publications de la Sorbonne, 1982. For deaths, see Marc Michel, 'Les Troupes noires, la Grande Guerre et l'armée française', in János Riesz and Joachim Schultz, eds, »*Tirailleurs sénégalais*«: *zur bildlichen un literarischen Darstellung afrikanischer Soldaten in Dienste Frankreichs — Présentations littéraires et figuratives de soldats africains au service de la France*, Frankfurt am Main, Bern, New York, Paris: Peter Lang, 1989, p. 19, n. 14. The figures for the second World War are some 180,000 recruits, with 63,000 coming to France, and 24,000 dead or disappeared.

[142] Martine Astier-Loutfi, *Littérature et colonialisme*, p. 139.

[143] Among the wounded rewarded with a medal is the eponymous hero of *La Randonnée de Samba Diouf*, Paris: Plon, 1922, by the Tharaud brothers, Jérôme and Jean (probably ghosting for André Demaison). They fall short of the satirical quality found in Ferdinand Oyono's *Le Vieux Nègre et la médaille*, Paris: Julliard, 1956; Union Générale d'Editions, Coll. 10/18, 1979.

[144] See Simone de Beauvoir, *Le Deuxième Sexe*, Paris: Gallimard, 1949, t. I, pp. 24–25.

[145] Houssain, pp. 229–30, quoting Marthe Bancel, *La Faya sur le Niger*, Paris: Éditions des Belles Lettres, 1923, p. 167.

[146] Diefenthal, p. 87. A somewhat arbitrarily restricted corpus (as is the case for Martinkus-Zemp) reduces the value of the analysis and findings of Diefenthal's thesis.

[147] Bauge-Gueye, 'La Femme blanche dans le roman africain', p. 101. We shall see that the narrator of Louise Faure-Favier's *Blanche et Noir* is not entirely free of this characteristic. Black feminist critics have cast doubt on western women's ideas about female sexuality: they are inevitably culture-bound: see notably Chandra Talpade Mohanty's now classic essay 'Under Western Eyes: Feminist Scholarship and Colonial Discourses' (pp. 259–68) and other essays grouped with it in the section 'Feminism and Post-colonialism' in Ashcroft, Griffiths and Tiffin, *The Post-colonial Studies Reader*, pp. 249–80.

[148] Fanon, *Peau noire, masques blancs*, p. 34.

[149] Bauge-Gueye, p. 101.

[150] Ibid., p. 102.

[151] Ouologuem, *Lettre à la France nègre*, p. 33.

[152] Schipper-De Leeuw, p. 166.

[153] Diefenthal, p. 88.

[154] In our area of study, Martinkus-Zemp, in *Le Blanc et le Noir*, tends to forget this.

[155] Schipper-De Leeuw, p. 166.

[156] See Houssain, pp. 127 and 143 n. 1. He adds (pp. 202–03): 'Lucie Cousturier est une voyageuse exceptionnelle non seulement à cause de sa sympathie pour les Noirs, mais aussi à cause des circonstances de son voyage. [Elle] visite—seule—le Sénégal, la Guinée et le Soudan, d'octobre 1921 à juin 1922. Elle bénéficie d'une mission officielle, mais préfère loger chez l'habitant...' [Lucie Cousturier is an exceptional traveller not simply because of her sympathy for Blacks, but also because of the circumstances of her journey. [She] visited—alone—Senegal, Guinea and the Soudan from October 1921 to June 1922. Although on an official mission, she preferred to sleep in native huts...].

[157] Houssain, p. 204. The errors stem from her lack of training as an ethnologist. Her innocent and sympathetic eye can nevertheless be enlightening.

[158] One example of irony among many, since it is closely related to our subject. In the first of two replies inserted at the head of the first volume of *Mes inconnus chez eux* (pp. 7–8), Cousturier, quoting the second volume, p. 198, addresses a sceptical reader: 'Louant un adminstrateur français, j'ai dit dans un fragment déjà publié de cet

ouvrage: "Ce capitaine agile et enjoué, ces Toma confiants, nouveau-nés à la domination française, cela me rappelle, observé ailleurs, un spectacle étrange et touchant d'innocence. C'était, en France, dans une ferme, au milieu d'un clapier, une pigeonne blanche qui couvait des lapereaux gris."

Ce petit trait d'histoire naturelle vous a paru invraisemblable en soi et intentionnellement injurieux envers la colonisation. Cependant, je n'ai jamais été plus que là véridique et exempte d'arrière-pensée. Je respecte et prise au plus haut degré l'enseignement donné par les bêtes. [...] Qu'est cela sinon le spectacle le plus beau qui se puisse voir d'une défaite des intérêts,—non pas seulement de classe et de race,—mais d'espèce même? Et qu'ai-je fait, sinon honorer, en l'y rattachant, la forme de colonisation que j'avais à peindre?'

[Praising a French administrator, I wrote in an extract of this book already published: 'This agile and cheerful captain, these confident Tomas new to French domination, remind me of a strange and innocent scene I observed elsewhere. It was in France, on a farm, in a hutch, where a white pigeon was sitting on some baby grey rabbits.'

This little reference to natural history seemed implausible to you and intentionally insulting to colonisation. Yet never have I been more accurate or innocent of any hidden agenda. I respect and value the lessons animals teach us. [...] What is it if not the finest spectacle you could see of self-interest being overcome—not simply of class and race—but even of species? What did I do other than to praise by association the form of colonisation I was trying to portray?]

This mocking biology lesson anticipates another suggested by Étiemble in his 'Esquisse d'une pédagogie antiraciste', *Présence afri-caine*, 26 (June–July 1959): 'Peut-être avez-vous lu ces jours-ci, dans la presse, la mésaventure du lapin noir qui, dans un livre américain à l'usage des petits enfants, se marie au clair de lune avec une lapine blanche. La vigilance des blancs de l'État d'Alabama réussit à accuser ces lapins d'intentions subversives et à les proscrire des librairies: ce qui est bon pour les lapins pourraient le devenir pour les hommes, écrivent là-bas les journaux racistes. S'il arrivait qu'un noir épousât une blanche, où irions-nous?'

[You have possibly read in the press recently the sad story of the black rabbit which, in an American children's book, married a white rabbit by moonlight. White vigilantes in the state of Alabama managed to accuse these rabbits of subversive activities and have them banned from the bookshops: what is good for rabbits might, the racist newspapers suggest, become good for people. If a black man married a white woman, what would we be coming to?] An illustrated account of the episode is presented by Werner Sollors, 'Can Rabbits

Have Interracial Sex?', in Sylvie Kandé, ed., *Discours sur le métissage*, pp. 163–89.

[159] Cousturier, *Mes inconnus chez eux*, 1: *Mon amie Fatou, citadine*, Rieder, 1925, p. 92. Houssain (p. 204) recalls the similar reaction of Isabelle Eberhardt in Algeria: 'Je voulais posséder ce pays, et ce pays m'a possédée' [I wanted to possess this country, and it has possessed me].

[160] See esp. chap. 2, 'Le Colonisateur qui se refuse'. The psychological mechanisms and peer-pressures articulated by Memmi parallel the scenario of many a 'liberal' short story or novel.

[161] Cousturier, *Mes inconnus chez eux*, 2: *Mon ami Soumaré, laptot*, p. 265.

[162] Houssain, p. 143, n. 1, quoting Serge Doubrovsky, *Pourquoi la nouvelle critique? Critique et objectivité*, Paris: Mercure de France, 1966, 1972, p. 95.

[163] Cousturier, *Des inconnus chez moi*, p. 135.

[164] Ibid., pp. 230–37.

[165] Ibid., p. 264. The comfort imagined by Cousturier recalls that of Isabelle Eberhardt as recorded in his *Notes et souvenirs* by Robert Randau (Paris: La Boîte à documents, 1989, 1997, pp. 114–15). Were it not for her husband's doughty opposition, she thought seriously of relieving the love-lorn Mbarek from his despair.

[166] Cousturier, *Mes inconnus chez eux*, 1: *Mon amie Fatou, citadine*, pp. 9, 11.

[167] Cousturier, *Des inconnus chez moi*, pp. 33, 40.

[168] Ibid., pp. 66–67.

[169] Ibid., p. 250.

[170] See Jean Laude, *La Peinture française et l'art nègre (1905–1914)*, Paris: Klincksieck, 1968. The aesthetic urge in writing by white men about Blacks sometimes masks a sexual one, as in certain homosexual responses recorded before it dared to speak its name. See e.g. Jean-Richard Bloch, *Première journée à Rufisque*, Paris: Sagittaire, 1926 (esp. chap. V, pp. 45–55) and Champly, *White Women, Coloured Men*, p. 23.

[171] Maurice Delafosse had begun before the war by publishing a novel (*Les États d'âme d'un colonial*, Paris: Comité de l'Afrique française, 1909; new edition under the title *Broussard ou les états d'âme d'un colonial, suivis de ses propos et opinions*, Paris: Larose, 1923) and a study (*Haut Sénégal–Niger*, Paris: Larose, 1912). He followed these with *Les Noirs de l'Afrique*, Paris: Payot, 1922; *L'Ame nègre* (an anthology comprising some thirty folktales, proverbs etc.), Paris: Payot, 1923; *Les Civilisations disparues: les civilisations africaines*, Paris: Stock, 1925; *Les Nègres*, Paris: Rieder, 1927.

[172] Houssain, p. 432, recalls the collections by *abbé* Grégoire, Baron Roger and Father Trilles in the nineteenth century, and by Auguste Dupuis,

known as Yacouba, and especially by François-Victor Équilbecq (who provided so many examples for Blaise Cendrars's *Anthologie nègre* of 1921) at the beginning of the twentieth century. In the 1920s, serious work was done by Louis Tauxier, Henri Labouret, Maurice Delafosse, Georges Hardy, Théodore Monod, Robert Delavignette et al.

173 Cousturier expresses a judgement on ethnography which will be found in sceptical minds only in the 1960s, after Negritude's period of approval: 'je n'aime pas l'ethnographie. Je l'aimerais si elle n'était qu'une science, même inexacte, comme les autres. Mais elle est un art de trahir les peuples pour les diviser, pire que l'histoire. Donner la vie de quelques individus pour la vie de tous, c'est la tromperie de l'histoire. Donner les formes collectives de la vie d'un peuple, pour ce peuple lui-même, c'est la trahison bien plus grave de l'ethnographie' [I do not like ethnography. I would like it if it were only a science, even an inexact one, like any other. But it is an art of betraying peoples by dividing them, worse than history. Presenting the life of some as everyone's life is the deceit of history. Presenting the collective forms of a people's life as their life itself is the more serious betrayal of ethnography]. *Mes inconnus chez eux*, 2: *Mon ami Soumaré, laptot*, p. 106.

174 Claude McKay, *Banjo* [1929], A Harvest Book, New York: Harcourt Brace Jovanovich Inc., [n.d.], pp. 205, 207. Ray continues: 'I can understand these ignorant black men marrying broken-down white women because they are under the delusion that there is some superiority in the white skin that has suppressed and bossed it over them all their lives. But I can't understand an intelligent race-conscious man doing it. Especially a man who is bellyaching about race rights. He is the one who should exercise a certain control and self-denial of his desires. Take Senghor and his comrades in propaganda for example. They are the bitterest and most humorless of propagandists and they are all married to white women. It is as if the experience has over-soured them. As if they thought it would bring them closer to the white race, only to realize too late that it couldn't' (p. 207). The reference to Senghor is not, of course, to Léopold Sédar of that ilk but to Lamine, the political activist of the interwar years: see Claude McKay's autobiography *A Long Way from Home* [1937], London: Pluto, 1985, chap. XXV: 'Marseilles Motley', esp. pp. 278–81.

175 Cited by Jordan, p. 239, n. 46.

176 For a near-contemporary anticipation of Fanon, where the black hero seduces a white friend's wife as revenge for the evils of colonisation, see Yvan Noë's play, *Marzouk*, of 1929. See Chalaye, p. 365.

177 Moray McGowan, 'Black and White?', p. 209.

178 Ibid., p. 211.

[179] Jean Genet, *Les Nègres*, Décines: L'Arbalète, 1958; Paris: Gallimard, Coll. Folio, 1980, p. 15.

[180] *Blanche et Noir*, pp. 168–69.

[181] Blaise N'Djehoya, 'Bwanaland', in Blaise N'Djehoya and Massaër Diallo, *Un regard noir*, Paris: Autrement, 1984, p. 20.

[182] Houssain, pp. 230–31.

[183] Ibid., p. 230.

[184] Ibid., pp. 188–94. The railway linking Dakar and Saint-Louis was opened in 1885 and encouraged a huge increase in the groundnut trade.

[185] On this myth, see Houssain, pp. 375–79.

[186] Fanon, *Peau noire, masques blancs*, p. 37, note.

[187] Ibid., pp. 211–12.

[188] Ibid., p. 212. Faure-Favier stops short of recalling Aristotle's observation that the sperm of Blacks was also white.

[189] Houssain, p. 217.

[190] Ruscio, p. 222. In fact, a Cousturier-like passage in the novel suggests that it was already being written in 1925: 'En 1925, la race blanche continue à mépriser la race noire, à la considérer comme inférieure. La traite des nègres est supprimée, l'esclavage est aboli, il n'est plus de négriers, plus de bateaux en partance pour l'Amérique, pleins de troupeaux noirs. C'est vers la France que les vaisseaux portèrent, en 1914, les combattants nègres au secours de la Patrie en péril... Les vaisseaux sont revenus singulièrement allégés. Et les survivants ont repris leur labeur pour la prospérité du territoire français.

Mais l'ostracisme dure toujours qui bannit le nègre de la société des blancs. Les Français de 1925 ont, vis-à-vis des noirs, le même dédain que les marins normands du quinzième siècle ou que les soldats conquérants du duc de Lauzun...'

[In 1925, the white race continues to despise the black race and consider it inferior. The slave-trade has been suppressed, slavery abolished, there are no more slave-traders or ships leaving for America full of human black cargo. Vessels brought to France, in 1914, black soldiers ready to fight for the Motherland in danger... The vessels returned noticeably lighter. And the survivors resumed their toil for France's prosperity.

But ostracism continues, banishing Blacks from white society. The French in 1925 have, *vis-à-vis* Blacks, exactly the same contempt as the Norman sailors in the fifteenth century or the Duke of Lauzun's conquering soldiers.] (*Blanche et Noir*, pp. 207–08).

[191] Paul Morand, *Paris-Tombouctou*, Paris: Flammarion, 1928, p. 266.

[192] See David Murphy, 'La Danse et la parole: l'exil et l'identité chez les Noirs de Marseille dans *Banjo* de Claude McKay et *Le Docker noir* d'Ousmane Sembène', forthcoming. The occasional writings in English

by Blacks before the 1920s—Olaudah Equiano, Frederick Douglass—are unequalled in French.

193 Houssain, p. 418.
194 Challaye, *Souvenirs sur la colonisation*, 1935, p. 201; 1984, p. 144.
195 Houssain, p. 247.
196 *Mes inconnus chez eux*, 2: *Mon ami Soumaré, laptot*, p. 263.
197 André Gide, *Voyage au Congo* [1927] *suivi de Le Retour du Tchad* [1928]: *carnets de route*, Gallimard, Coll. Folio, 1995, p. 27.

Chapter 5: The French Empire Writes Back

198 Victor Hugo, in the draft of an 1867 letter to the widow of Octave Giraud, the Guadeloupean abolitionist, quoted by Hoffmann in 'Victor Hugo, les Noirs et l'esclavage', p. 85.
199 Henri Crouzat, *Azizah de Niamkoko*, Paris: Presses de la Cité, 1959; Pocket, 1983, 1995, p. 137.
200 Nicolas Bancel and Pascal Blanchard observe (in 'Sauvage ou assimilé? Quelques réflexions sur les représentation[s] du corps des Tirailleurs sénégalais (1880–1918)', *Africultures*, 25 (Feb. 2000): *Tirailleurs en images*, p. 41) that relationships between *Tirailleurs* and their *marraines de guerre* gave rise to a wave of suspect iconography: 'Les images des soldats convalescents, entourés des attentions de jeunes infirmières ou au bras de jeunes femmes du monde, développent une vision paternaliste et stéréotypée. La suggestion d'une transgression—socialement impossible—des interdits relatifs aux relations sexuelles entre une femme blanche et un homme noir est clairement mise en scène. De ce phantasme apparaît celui—toujours suggérée—de la sexualité débridée des Noirs, toujours proches de la nature et donc incapables de dominer leurs propre corps et leur instinct.' [Images of soldiers convalescing, surrounded by attentive young nurses or arm in arm with young ladies, give rise to a stereotypical, paternalistic view. The hint of transgression—socially impossible—of taboos relating to sexual relations between a white woman and a black man is clearly presented. From this phantasm—always implicit—arises that of the unbridled sexuality of Blacks, ever close to nature and therefore incapable of mastering their own bodies and their instincts.]
201 See Ashcroft, Griffiths and Tiffin, *The Empire Writes Back*.
202 For this aspect of English-language material, see Eliane Utudjian-Saint André, 'Unions mixtes et métissages dans quelques littératures noires d'Afrique anglophone', in *Unions mixtes...*, ed. E. Hanquart-Turner, pp. 35–64.
203 Ousmane Socé, *Mirages de Paris*, p. 148.
204 The novel closes on a letter sent by Nelly Guérin from Guadeloupe: 'Je t'ai bien compris, et tu as raison: les qualificatifs de français, créoles

et mulâtres ne peuvent que paralyser inutilement l'élévation rapide et certaine de la population noire à la pleine conscience de sa dignité de race et de sa haute valeur humaine' [I have understood you perfectly, and you are right: the epithets French, Creole and Mulatto can only prevent the rapid and inexorable rise of the black population to full awareness of its racial dignity and high human value]. Also anticipatory of Césaire is the broadening of the concept of Negritude beyond Blacks: 'On peut être noir de couleur, on peut l'être par principe...'

[205] In his presentation of an *Anthologie de la nouvelle sénégalaise (1970–1977)*, Dakar, Abidjan: Nouvelles Éditions africaines, 1978, p. 10.

[206] See esp. Blachère, *Le Modèle nègre*.

[207] Paul Morand, *Magie noire*, Paris: Grasset, 1928, 1968, pp. 10, 206. In the same book (p. 260), Morand further indulges his taste for sweeping statement in declaring of the black Occide: 'Non, la vue d'une Blanche ne le rendait pas fou, comme prétendent les lyncheurs de Virginie; il prenait Paméla comme une autre, il avait pour les femmes, cet énorme et indifférent appétit du mâle noir, à qui la quantité seule importe' [No, the sight of a white woman did not make him mad, as the lynchers in Virginia claim; he took Pamela like any other woman; he had for women that enormous and indiscriminate appetite of the black male, for whom quantity alone counts].

[208] Houssain, p. 392. The public's appetite had also been whetted by stereotypes filling the popular theatre after the war. Referring to *Malikoko, roi nègre* (1919, revived in 1925 and 1930), by Mouëzy-Éon, Sylvie Chalaye asks (p. 310): 'Ce croque-mitaine moricaud, plus célèbre en son temps que Joséphine Baker, n'allait-il pas contribuer au décervelage de toute de génération?' [Did this dark-skinned bogey-man, more famous in his day than Josephine Baker, not contribute to a whole generation losing its senses?]

[209] 'Je déchirerai les rires *banania* sur tous les murs de France' [I shall tear down those *Banania* smiles from every wall in France]. Léopold Sédar Senghor, 'Poème liminaire', in *Hosties noires* [1948], in *Œuvre poétique*, Paris: Éditions du Seuil, Coll. Points, 1990, p. 55.

[210] See Raymond Bachollet et al., *Négripub: l'image des Noirs dans la publicité*, Paris: Somogy, 1992; and J. Nederveen Pieterse, *White on Black*.

[211] See Georges-Marie Haardt and Louis Audouin-Dubreuil, *La Première Traversée du Sahara en automobile: le raid Citroën de Touggourt à Tombouctou par l'Atlantide*, Paris: Plon, 1923 and *La Croisière noire: expédition Citroën Centre-Afrique*, Paris: Plon, 1927 (with a parallel film of the same title made by Léon Poirier).

212 See e.g. *La Révolution surréaliste*, n° 5 (nov. 1925), René Crevel, *Babylone*, Paris: Kra, 1927 and Philippe Soupault, *Le Nègre*, Paris: Kra, 1927.

213 Defence of the system is encapsulated in Victor Piquet's *Histoire des colonies françaises*, Paris: Payot, 1931.

214 Bernardin de Saint-Pierre, *Empsaël et Zoraïde*, ed. R. Little, p. 49.

215 Sander Gilman writes: 'For Hitler the linkage between the Jew and the black was a political one. It was the Jews who inspired the French to station black troops along the Rhine following the 1919 armistice, and it was therefore the intent of the Jews to loose those "barbarians belonging to a race inspired by Nature [...] with a tremendous sexual instinct into the heart of Europe."' *Jewish Self-Hatred*, p. 8.

216 See Chalaye, pp. 372–74.

217 *Peau noire, masques blancs*, p. 64.

218 In *Le Lys et le flamboyant* (Paris: Seuil, 1997, p. 195), Lopes has his narrator observe of the Europeans in the colony: 'C'était comme d'imaginer qu'un nègre séduisît une Blanche, ce qu'on n'avait jamais vu et que bien sûr, affimaient-ils, on ne verrait jamais, même quand les poules auraient des dents' [It was like imagining a Negro seducing a white woman, something that had never been seen or obviously, they asserted, that would ever be seen, even when pigs started flying].

Chapter 6: Struggles for Independence

219 Geneviève Billy, *Le Couple mixte*, p. 48.

220 As they are in Leïla Sebbar's *Le Chinois vert d'Afrique*, Paris: Stock, 1984: see Michel Laronde, 'Du métissage au décentrage: évolution du trope génétique dans la littérature post-coloniale en France', in Sylvie Kandé, ed., *Discours sur le métissage*, pp. 143–62.

221 Calixthe Beyala, *Le Petit Prince de Belleville*, Paris: Albin Michel, 1992; J'ai lu, 1993; *Maman a un amant*, Paris: Albin Michel, 1993; J'ai lu, 1995.

222 Schipper-De Leeuw, p. 161.

223 The Tunisian Albert Memmi's fine novel *Agar* dating from this time (Paris: Correa Buchet/Chastel, 1955; Gallimard, Coll. Folio, 1984) presents the self-destructive relationship of a Jewish Tunisian doctor and his Catholic French wife. The admirably lucid successive prefaces (1963, 1984) reprinted in the Folio edition affirm the link made between the psychology of the individual case and a view of society at large.

224 *Othello's Countrymen: the African in English Renaissance Drama*, London: Oxford University Press, 1965, p. 87.

[225] A student edition by Patrick Corcoran has been published: London: Methuen, 1986.

[226] Billy, *Le Couple mixte*, pp. 15–16.

[227] 1960 also saw the publication of William Conton's novel *The African* (London: Heinemann), dealing centrally with a *Blanche/Noir* relationship.

[228] 'La Fuite de la main habile', the first story in Henri Lopes's collection of short stories, *Tribaliques* (1971), continued the trend, which we shall investigate more closely in Daniel Biyaoula's *L'Impasse* (1996).

[229] Francis Fouet, 'Le Thème de l'amour...', p. 94. Cf. Billy, in *Le Couple mixte*, p. 43: 'D'ailleurs, l'amour est une notion qui échappe à l'homme africain, du moins selon le sens occidental du mot. Il peut y avoir estime, respect, désir, on peut s'apprécier mutuellement dans le couple africain sans toutefois montrer de sentiment. [...] Généralement il [l'Africain noir] ne s'attarde pas aux jeux de l'amour, romantisme et autres fadaises jugées indispensables par les Européens' {Moreover, love is a notion foreign to African men, at least in the western sense of the word. There may be esteem, respect, desire, mutual appreciation in the African couple, without feelings being shown. [...] In general, he spends no time on foreplay, Romanticism and other fooleries considered indispensible by Europeans].

[230] Kuoh-Moukoury, *Les Couples dominos*, p. 98.

[231] Which I exclude from detailed consideration here partly because it is so well known, partly because it deals with the relationship between a Frenchwoman and a North African rather than a Black, and partly because I can refer the interested reader to the study by Sarah Poole, *Etcherelli: Elise ou la vraie vie*, London: Grant & Cutler, Critical Guides to French Texts 104, 1994. For a survey of Maghrebi fact and fiction about mixed marriages, see Claude Liauzu, 'Guerres des Sabines et tabou de mariage. Discours sur les mariages mixtes, de l'Algérie coloniale à l'immigration en France', in Sylvie Kandé, ed., *Discours sur le métissage*, pp. 115–35.

[232] See Bertène Juminer, *La Revanche de Bozambo*, Paris: Présence Africaine, 1968, pp. 40–41.

Chapter 7: The Freedom to Choose

[233] Abdoul Doukouré, *Le Déboussolé*, Québec: Naaman, 1978, p. 79.

[234] See, e.g., *Mandingo*, London: Longman Green, 1959; Pan Books, 1961, and *Drum*, London: W.H. Allen, 1963; Pan Books 1965.

[235] See Barbara, *Les Couples mixtes*, pp. 34–35.

[236] For a fuller denunciation of Guy des Cars's plagiarism, see my articles 'Plagiarism as neocolonialism: *Sang d'Afrique*', *French Studies*

Bulletin, 70 (Spring 1999), 10–12, and 'More on plagiarism as neo-colonialism', *French Studies Bulletin*, 73 (Winter 1999), 19–20.

237 See A.-M. Vergiat, *Les Rites secrets des primitifs de l'Oubangui*, Paris: Payot, 1936. At least this debt is acknowledged in a prefatory note.

238 Such a racial switch, but in the other direction, is registered in the new title given by Senghor in 1961 to his 'Chants pour Naëtt': 'Chants pour Signare'. Echoing the colour of his successive wives, the sequence first published in 1949 is revised to take account of the change.

239 I confess, however, that there have been several items probably dating from the 1970s which purport to deal with *Blanche/Noir* couples but which, despite my best efforts, I have been unable to trace from inadequate references in secondary material. This is the case of Jean Michonet, *La Mémoire d'un fleuve* and Nadine Bari, *Noces d'absence et grain de sable*, Paris: Le Centurion.

240 While the film is presumably drawn from the novel by H.G. Wells (in James Whale's technically innovative version of 1933), it is not impossible that the author is surreptitiously alluding also to Ralph Ellison's powerful 1952 book of the same title (minus the article), in which the Black in the United States of America is so far beneath contempt that he is even beneath notice.

241 In a letter to the present writer dated 'Cotonou, le 30 Janvier 1997'.

242 See Dostoievsky's *Notes from Underground* and Césaire's *Cahier d'un retour au pays natal*, in both of which two plus two are said to make five.

243 Ogboni is a Yoruba word and the initiation society is found widely in Nigeria as well as in neighbouring Bénin.

Chapter 8: Liberty and Licence

244 Dany Laferrière, *Comment faire l'amour avec un nègre sans se fatiguer*, Montréal: VLB, 1985, p. 19.

245 For a fuller presentation of this link, see J.P. Little 'The Legacy of Medea: Mariama Bâ, *Un chant écarlate* and Marie Ndiaye, *La Femme changée en bûche*', *Modern Language Review*, 95, 2 (April 2000).

246 'Elle se souvint de la colère de son père:/— Tu connais «ça»?/Elle acquiesça:/— Ousmane était bien "ça"' [She remembered her father's anger. 'Do you know "that"?'/She acquiesced: 'Ousmane really was "that"']. Bâ, *Un chant écarlate*, p. 237; cf. p. 40. Again, 'id' is an undertone of 'that'.

247 Dominique Combe makes some interesting comments on the particular relationship between the *style indirect libre* and Francographic

writing in *Poétiques francophones*, Paris: Hachette, 1995, esp. pp. 143–45.

248 *'Lane-la?'* is glossed in a note as 'Qu'est-ce qu'il y a? Cri d'angoisse pour percer le contenu de l'événe-ment tragique' [What is it? Cry of anguish piercing the content of the tragic event].

249 Sembène Ousmane, *Le Dernier de l'Empire*, Paris: L'Harmattan, 1981, 1985, p. 242.

250 Abasse Ndione, *La Vie en spirale*, Dakar: Nouvelles Éditions africaines, 1984, p. 171.

251 Ashcroft, Griffiths and Tiffin, *The Empire Writes Back*, p. 85.

252 'Elle était smplement une femme forte. [...] Du coup, elle me fut tellement proche, tellement accessible, que je la regardai à nouveau, comme un mâle' [She was simply a big woman. [...] Immediately, she was so close to me, so accessible, that I looked at her with new eyes, as a male]. *Vie et mœurs d'un primitif...*

253 Maryse Condé, *Desirada*, Paris: Laffont, 1997; Pocket, 1999, p. 257.

254 Maryse Condé, *Traversée de la mangrove*, Paris: Mercure de France, 1989; Gallimard, Coll. Folio, 1993, p. 82. Condé has expressed her serious reservations over Negritude in several interviews.

Chapter 9: Full Circle

255 Denis Oussou-Essui, *La Souche calcinée*, Yaoundé: CLE, 1973, p. 198.

256 Geneviève Billy, *Le Couple mixte*, p. 48.

257 Cf. Marina Warner's fascinating novel *Indigo*, London: Chatto & Windus, 1992; Vintage, 1993, and Miranda's dream in it of 'the longed-for, missing Primitive' in her relationship with George Felix alias Shaka Ifetabe.

258 Sembene, 'Si j'étais une femme...', p. 88.

259 Sartre's Heideggerian phrase figures in 'Orphée noir', his seminal preface to Senghor's celebrated *Anthologie de la nouvelle poésie nègre...*, p. xxix.

260 Jacques Lacan, *Écrits I*, Paris: Seuil, Coll. Points, 1971, p. 91.

261 See the chapter on 'Nègres blanchis' in my *Nègres blancs*.

262 A further instance of verbal overdetermination occurs when Joseph is pleased to catch his reflection in windows as he walks along the street: 'Aussi, tout le long de ma route, le costume que je suis allé retirer chez le *blanchisseur* posé sur mon bras gauche, je ne cesse de guigner ici ou là' [So all the way home, the suit I'd collected from the *cleaner's*, draped over my left arm, I squinted at it from time to time]. Italics added. Here, as for the verb 'déteindre', the French has overtones lost in translation.

263 Cf. Ouologuem, *Lettre à la France nègre*, p. 30: 'ne voilà-t-il pas que tu t'es livré avec ta compagne blanche fraîchement épousée, à un acte

somme toute voisin d'un enlèvement des Sabines [...]?' [haven't you just indulged with your newly-wed white wife in an act very much like the rape of the Sabines [...]?]

264 In November 1996, on a visit to Dublin, Olympe Bhêly-Quenum kindly passed me a copy of a provisional and uncorrected typescript of *C'était à Tigony*. The author's wish that the novel should not be quoted verbatim prior to publication has been respected.

265 Letter of 14 February 1997 addressed from Cotonou to Roger and Patricia Little.

266 This, despite a plethora of free-floating mixed-race relationships in the novel, all of them involving, however, a white man and a black woman: apart from Gaëtan's, there are those between the journalist Greenough and both his housekeeper Séliki and the wealthy, high-flying politician Myriam.

267 In the definitive version of the novel, to be published by Présence Africaine and Nouvelles Éditions ivoiriennes in 2000, Gaëtan commits suicide, thereby obviating any intervention on his part.

268 Ouologuem, *Lettre à la France nègre*, pp. 32–33. Tadjo's novel closes precisely on images of the sun.

269 Bernard Dadié, *Un Nègre à Paris*, Paris: Présence Africaine, 1959, p. 183.

Conclusion: Beyond Difference and Indifference

270 A point I make in *Nègres blancs*, p. 12: see Tzvetan Todorov, *Nous et les autres*, Coll. Points, p. 439.

271 Jean-Luc Bonniol, 'Le métissage entre social et biologique. L'exemple des Antilles de colonisation française', in Sylvie Kandé, ed., *Discours sur le métissage*, p. 63.

272 Daniel Maximin, *L'Isolé soleil*, Paris: Seuil, 1981; Coll. Points, 1987, p. 98.

273 Ruth Morse, 'Not Beating But Joining: the traditions of mixed marriages in anglophone fiction', in *Unions mixtes...*, ed. E. Hanquart-Turner, p. 9.

274 Ibid., p. 17.

275 See Léopold Sédar Senghor, *Liberté 3: Négritude et civilisation de l'universel*, Paris: Seuil, 1977 and *Ce que je crois*, Paris: Grasset, 1988, chap. 5, pp. 201–34.

276 Lewis R. Gordon, *Her Majesty's Other Children*, p. 251.

277 Amin Maalouf, *Les Identités meurtrières*, p. 160.

278 Ouologuem, *Lettre à la France nègre*, pp. 30–31.

279 See my *Nègres blancs*.

280 The proposition is less fanciful than may at first appear: Alain Bosquet recalls that under Nazism, 'A Zloczew, le capitaine de S.S.

Detlew von Hebbelraue, se souvenant des chevaliers teutoniques, rassemblait sur la place du marché toute la population, soit sept cents hommes, et tonitruait: "La race blonde est supérieure aux races brunes et trapues; c'est pourquoi tous ceux qui n'ont pas les yeux bleus seront fusillés séance tenante"; il choisissait lui-même ses victimes, [...] se contentait d'un geste bref, écoutait le crépitement des balles, disait à ses subordonnés: "Le Führer trace les grandes lignes de sa politique; c'est à vous et à moi qu'incombent les détails"' [At Zloczew, S.S. captain Detlew von Hebbelraue, recalling the Teutonic knights, assembled the whole population of seven hundred men on the market-place, and bellowed: 'The fair-haired race is superior to the brown and stunted races; that is why anyone who does not have blue eyes will be shot forthwith'; he chose his victims himself, [...] made a brief gesture, listened to the crackle of gunfire, said to his subordi-nates: 'The Führer determines the outline policy; it is up to you and me to interpret the details']. *Ni guerre, ni paix*, Paris: Grasset & Fasquelle, 1983; Livre de poche, 1985, p. 235.

281 See my 'Fables of Melanocracy: "Race" Reversals in French Litera-ture', *Forum for Modern Language Studies* (forthcoming).

282 C.L.R. James, *The Black Jacobins: Toussaint l'Ouverture and the San Domingo Revolution* [1938], London: Allison & Busby, 1989, p. 370.

283 Henri Crouzat, *Azizah de Niamkoko*, Paris: Presses de la Cité, 1959; Pocket, 1983, 1995, p. 319.

284 Roland Barthes, *Fragments d'un discours amoureux*, Paris: Gallimard, 1977, p. 87.

285 Paul Ricœur, 'État actuel de la réflexion sur l'intolérance', in *L'Intolé-rance*, ed. F. Barret-Ducrocq, p. 22.

286 Dominique Schnapper, *La Relation à l'autre*, p. 45.

287 George L. Mosse, *Toward the Final Solution: A History of European Racism*, London: Dent, 1978, p. xvi.

288 Ibid., p. 2.

289 Kuoh-Moukoury *Les Couples dominos*, p. 173.

290 'Historiquement, nous savons que le nègre coupable d'avoir couché avec une Blanche est castré. Le nègre qui a possédé une Blanche est fait tabou par ses congénères' [Historically, we know that the Black guilty of sleeping with a white woman was castrated. The Black who had possessed a white woman is ostracised [literally: is made taboo] by his fellows], *Peau noire, masques blancs*, p. 58. Unfortunately, Fanon does not give his source for his affirmation about castration.

291 '"La Francographie": a new model for "la Francophonie"', *African Literature Association Bulletin* [Philadelphia, PA], 25, 4 (Fall 1999), 28–36 and in *Littératures francophones: la problématique de l'altérité*, ed. C. O'Dowd-Smyth, Waterford: Waterford Institute of Technology (forthcoming). I learned subsequently from my ever-

vigilant former postgraduate students Aedín Ní Loingsigh and David Murphy that I had not invented the word: it is applied, undeveloped, to a somewhat different concept in Blachère's *Négritures*. Assia Djebar further uses the term in its etymological sense in declaring: 'écrivain de langue française, je pratique sûrement une FRANCO-GRAPHIE' [as a writer in the French language, I surely engage in FRANCO-GRAPHY] ('Écrire, résister, transgresser', in *Francophone Voices*, ed. Kamal Salhi, Exeter: Elm Bank Publications, 1999, p. 67, the hyphen and capitals being editorial interpolations).

SELECT BIBLIOGRAPHY

A. Creative writing (in chronological order).
B. Critical works (in alphabetical order by author).

A. **Creative writing** and eye-witness accounts referring to *Blanche/Noir* couples (other items being excluded), in chronological order of the first edition or performance. The original date of publication or performance is indicated in square brackets when a later edition is quoted. To facilitate reference, the names or pseudonyms by which authors are known are highlighted in this section by capitalisation.

• signals major cases, while those other than in French are put in square brackets (details of modern cases in this latter category having been sacrificed to save space).

Where no bibliographical details are given for French items, performance dates are indicated, and further information may be found in Chalaye, *Du Noir au Nègre* (see B below).

[• SHAKESPEARE, *Titus Andronicus, c.*1589–90]

[• SHAKESPEARE, *Othello, c.*1604]

ANON., *Ballet du monde renversé,* 1625

[Thomas SOUTHERNE, *Oroonoko or the Royal Slave,* first performed 1695, published 1696; Imoinda is not black, as in Aphra Behn's novella of 1688, but white.]

VOLTAIRE, *Zaïre,* Paris: Les Comédiens ordinaires du Roi, 1732

ANON., *Histoire de Louis Anniaba, roi d'Essenie en Afrique sur la côte de Guinée,* Paris: Aux dépens de la Société, 1740; ed. R. Little, Exeter: University of Exeter Press, 2000

Claude-Prosper Jolyot de CRÉBILLON, *Le Sopha conte moral,* A Gaznah, De l'Imprimerie du Très-Pieux, Très-Clement et Très-Auguste Sultan des Indes. L'an de l'Hégire 1120 (=1742); ed. F. Juranville, Paris: GF Flammarion, 1995

VOLTAIRE, *Candide, ou l'Optimisme* [1759], in *Candide et autres contes,* ed. F. Deloffre, Paris: Gallimard, Coll. Folio, 1992

VOLTAIRE, *La Princesse de Babylone* [1768], in *Zadig et autres contes,* ed. F. Deloffre, Paris: Gallimard, Coll. Folio, 1992

Louis-Archambault DORVIGNY, *Le Nègre blanc,* Amiens: Veuve Godart, 1774

Nicolas-Edme RÉTIF de la Bretonne (pseud. of Nichols Donneraill, Timothée Joly, Jean-Pierre Linguet and Maribert de Courtnay), *La Paysanne pervertie ou les dangers de la ville,* Paris: Duchesne, 1784

265

Jean-Baptiste RADET and Pierre BARRÉ, *La Négresse ou le pouvoir de la reconnaissance,* 1787

* Andréa de NERCIAT, *Le Diable au corps* (prob. written 1789, publ. 1803), Paris: Union Générale d'Editions, Coll. 10/18, 1997

* BERNARDIN de Saint-Pierre, *Empsaël et Zoraïde, ou les Blancs esclaves des Noirs à Maroc* (completed c.1793, publ. 1818), ed. R. Little, Exeter: University of Exeter Press, 1995

Alphonse C. DUBREUIL, *Paulin et Virginie* (after Bernardin de Saint-Pierre), 1794

Jean-Baptiste RADET, *Honorine, ou la femme difficile à vivre* [1795], in *Suite du répertoire du théâtre français,* Paris: Veuve Dabo, 1823, 'Vaudevilles', t. IV, pp. 279–403

Charles-Antoine PIGAULT-LEBRUN, *Le Blanc et le noir, drame en quatre actes et en prose,* Paris: Mayeur & Barba, an IV (=1796)

Jacques GRASSET de Saint-Sauveur, *Hortense, ou la jolie courtisane. Sa vie libertine à Paris, et ses aventures tragiques avec le nègre Zéphire dans les déserts de l'Amérique,* Paris: Pigoreau, 1796

D.-A.-F. de SADE, *La Nouvelle Justine, ou les Malheurs de la vertu,* En Hollande, 1797

[Adrien-A.] de TEXIER, *Les Colons de toutes couleurs,* Berlin: Decker, 1798

Claude GODARD d'Aucourt de Saint-Just, *Le Nègre par amour,* 1809

Victor HUGO, *Bug-Jargal* (drafted 1818, printed 1820), Paris: U. Canel, 1826

Horace de St-Aubin (pseud. of Honoré de BALZAC), *Le Nègre,* 1822

Horace de St-Aubin (pseud. of Honoré de BALZAC), *Le Vicaire des Ardennes,* 1822

Claire de Durfort, duchessse de DURAS, *Ourika,* Paris: Imprimerie Royale, 1823; ed. R. Little, Exeter: University of Exeter Press, 1993, 1998

* Sophie DOIN, *Cornélie, nouvelle grecque suivie de six nouvelles,* Paris: Desauges et Leroy, 1826 (incl. 'Blanche et noir', pp. 123–44); repr. *Nouvelles blanches et noires,* Paris: Desauges, 1828

Eugène SUE, *Atar-Gull* [1831], in *Romans, nouvelles et histoires maritimes,* Paris: Gosselin, 1841

Victor ESCOUSSE, *Farruck, le Maure,* 1831

* Louis de MAYNARD DE QUEILHE, *Outre-mer,* Paris: Renduel, 1835

Alexis DE COMBEROUSSE and Benjamin ANTIER, *Le Marché Saint-Pierre,* 1839

* MÉLESVILLE (pseud. of Anne-Joseph Duveyrier) and Roger de BEAU-VOIR (pseud. of Roger de Bully), *Le Chevalier de Saint-Georges* [sic], comédie mêlée de chant en trois actes, Théâtre des Variétés, 15 févr. 1840, Paris: Mifliez & Tresse, Répertoire des auteurs contemporains, n° 50, 1840; ed. S. Chalaye, Paris: L'Harmattan, Coll. Autrement Mêmes, 2000

Charles LAFONT and Charles DESNOYER, *Le Tremblement de terre de la Martinique,* 1840

SELECT BIBLIOGRAPHY

- Alexandre DUMAS *père*, *Georges* [1843?] Paris: Michel Lévy, 1848; Paris: Gallimard, Coll. Folio, ed. L.-F. Hoffmann, 1974

Louis-T. HOUAT, *Les Marrons*, Paris: Ebrard, 1844

Anaïs SÉGALAS, 'Un Nègre à une Blanche', in *Poésies*, Paris: Desforges, 1844, p. 256

Anicet BOURGEOIS and Philippe DUMANOIR, *Le Docteur noir*, 1846

Madame A. CASHIN, *Amour et liberté*, Paris: Galignani, 1847

Anatole FRANCE, 'Balthasar' in *Balthasar*, Paris: Calmann-Lévy, 1889; repr. in *Œuvres*, ed. M.-Cl. Bancquart, Gallimard, Bibliothèque de la Pléiade, I, 1984, pp. 585–600

Oswald DURAND, *Rires et pleurs*, Corbeil: Impr. de E. Crété, 1896 (quoted in Roland Lebel, *Les Établissements français d'outre-mer et leur reflet dans la littérature*, Paris: Larose, 1925, pp. 153–54)

Alfred JARRY, *Ubu colonial* [1901] in *Tout Ubu*, Paris: Livre de Poche, 1962, pp. 420–31

Marius-Ary LEBLOND (pseud. of Georges Athénas and Aimé Merlo), *Le Zézère: amours de blancs et de noirs*, Paris: Fasquelle, 1903

Pierre MILLE, *Barnavaux et quelques femmes*, Paris: Calmann-Lévy, 1908, 1931

- Lucie COUSTURIER, *Des inconnus chez moi*, Paris: La Sirène, 1920; Paris: Les Belles Lectures, with intro. by René Maran, 1957; ed. R. Little, Paris: L'Harmattan, Coll. Autrement Mêmes, 2000

André SALMON, *La Négresse du Sacré-Cœur*, Paris: Gallimard, 1920, 1968

Georges RIBEMONT-DESSAIGNES, *Le Serin muet*, 1920, Paris: Au Sans Pareil, 1921

André-Paul ANTOINE, *Le Démon noir*, 1922

Gaston BATY, *Haya*, 1922

Jean-Victor PELLERIN, *L'Intimité*, 1922

Oruno LARA, *Question de couleurs (Blanches et Noirs): roman de mœurs*, Paris: Nouvelle Librairie Universelle, n.d. [1923]

Massyla DIOP, 'Le Chemin du salut', short story, 1923: see Pierre Klein, 'Présentation' in [Various], *Anthologie de la nouvelle sénégalaise (1970–1977)*, Dakar, Abidjan: Nouvelles Éditions africaines, 1978

- Pierre MILLE and André DEMAISON, *La Femme et l'homme nu*, Paris: Les Editions de France, 1924

Lucie COUSTURIER, *Mes inconnus chez eux*, 1: *Mon amie Fatou*; 2: *Mon ami Soumaré*, Paris: Rieder, 1925; Paris: Les Belles Lectures, with intro. by René Maran, 1956

Félicien CHAMPSAUR, *La Caravane en folie*, Paris: Fasquelle, 1926

Bakary DIALLO, *Force-bonté* [1926], Paris: Nouvelles Éditions africaines/ACCT, 1985

- Claire GOLL, *Le Nègre Jupiter enlève Europa*, Paris: Crès, 1928 (first published in German as *Der Neger Jupiter raubt Europa*, 1926; Munich, 1992)

Philippe SOUPAULT, *Le Nègre*, Paris: Kra, 1927; Paris: Gallimard, 1997

• Louise FAURE-FAVIER, *Blanche et Noir,* Paris: J. Ferenczi et fils, 1928

Yvan NOË, *Marzouk,* 1929

Madeleine POULAINE, *Une Blanche chez les Noirs: l'Afrique vivante,* Tallandier, 1931

Ombres roses, ballet as part of revue *1936* at Folies-Bergères, Paris, 1936 (see illustrations in Champly)

• Ousmane SOCÉ [DIOP], *Mirages de Paris* [1937]; Paris: Nouvelles Éditions Latines, 1964, 1977, 1986

• Jean-Paul SARTRE, *La P... respectueuse* [1946], Paris: Gallimard, 1947

• René MARAN, *Un homme pareil aux autres,* Paris: Arc-en-ciel, 1947

• André ROUSSIN, *La Petite Hutte* [1947], Paris: Du Rocher, 1966

Abdoulaye SADJI, *Nini, mulâtresse du Sénégal* [1947], Paris: Présence Africaine, 1953, 1988

• Maurice BEDEL, *Le Mariage des couleurs,* Paris: Gallimard, 1951

• Pierre BARILLET and Jean-Pierre GRÉDY, *La Reine blanche,* 1953

• Jean MALONGA, *Cœur d'Aryenne,* in *Présence Africaine,* 16 (n.d. [1953?]), pp. 159–285 (dated at end 'Brazzaville, le 14 juillet 1948')

• Robert SABATIER, *Alain et le Nègre,* Paris: Albin Michel, 1953, 1999

• Albert MEMMI, *Agar,* Paris: Correa Buchet/Chastel, 1955; Gallimard, Coll. Folio, 1984

Bernard B. DADIÉ, *Climbié* [1956], repr. in *Légendes et poèmes,* Paris: Seghers, 1966, pp. 95–223 (dated Abidjan 18 April 1953)

• SEMBÈNE Ousmane, *Le Docker noir,* Paris: Debresse, 1956; Paris: Présence Africaine, 1973, 1982

Ferdinand OYONO, *Une vie de boy,* Paris: Julliard, 1956

Benjamin MATIP, *Afrique, nous t'ignorons,* Paris: Lacoste, 1956

• SEMBÈNE Ousmane, *Ô pays, mon beau peuple!* Paris: Le Livre contemporain/Amiot-Dumont, 1957; Paris: Presses-Pocket, 1975; ed. Patrick Corcoran, London: Methuen, 1986.

• Christine GARNIER, *La Fête des sacrifices,* Paris: Grasset, 1959

• Ferdinand OYONO, *Chemin d'Europe,* Paris: Julliard, 1960; Paris: Union Générale d'Editions, Coll. 10/18, 1973, 1982

Ake LOBA, *Kocoumbo, l'étudiant noir,* Paris: Flammarion, 1960

• Léopold Sédar SENGHOR, *Nocturnes,* Paris: Editions du Seuil, 1961 (the first section, 'Chants pour Signare' is a revision of the 1949 collection *Chants pour Naëtt,* implicitly dedicated to his second (white) wife as opposed to his first (black) one)

• Bertène JUMINER, *Les Bâtards,* Paris: Présence Africaine, 1961

Charles NOKAN, *Le Soleil noir point,* Paris: Présence Africaine, 1962 (written 1959)

• Bertène JUMINER, *Au seuil d'un nouveau cri,* Paris: Présence Africaine, 1963

• Guy DES CARS, *Sang d'Afrique,* Paris: Flammarion, 1963; 2-vol. edition, I: *L'Africain,* II: *L'Amoureuse,* J'ai lu, 1971, 1974

• Cheik DIA, *Avant Liberté I,* Paris: Editions du Scorpion, 1964

Georges CONCHON, *L'État sauvage,* Paris: Albin Michel, 1964

SELECT BIBLIOGRAPHY

SEMBÈNE Ousmane, *Le Mandat*, Paris: Présence Africaine, 1966

CAMARA Laye, *Dramouss*, Paris: Plon, 1966; Presses Pocket, 1976

• Claire ETCHERELLI, *Élise ou la vraie vie*, Paris: Denoël, 1967

• Olympe BHÊLY-QUENUM, *Liaison d'un été*, Paris: SAGEREP, L'Afrique actuelle, 1968

Bertène JUMINER, *La Revanche de Bozambo*, Paris: Présence Africaine, 1968, 2000

• Marie CHAUVET, *Amour, colère et folie*, Paris: Gallimard, 1968

Henri LOPES, 'La fuite de la main habile' in *Tribaliques*, Yaoudé: CLE, 1971; Yaoundé and Paris: CLE and Presses Pocket, 1983

• Jean-Louis BAGHIO'O, *Le Flamboyant à fleurs bleues*, Paris: Calmann-Lévy, 1973; Paris: Éditions Caribéennes, 1981

Denis OUSSOU-ESSUI, *La Souche calcinée*, Yaoundé: CLE, 1973

Amadou Hampaté BÂ, *L'Etrange Destin de Wangrin*, Paris: Union Générale d'Editions, 1973, Coll. 10/18, 1979, 1996

• Abdou Anta KA, 'La Terrasse', in *Mal*, Dakar: Nouvelles Éditions africaines, 1975

Abdoul DOUKOURÉ, *Le Déboussolé*, Québec: Naaman, 1978

• Olympe BHÊLY-QUÉNUM, *L'Initié*, Paris: Présence Africaine, 1979

• Cheikh Aliou NDAO (pseud. of Sidi Ahmet Alioune Ndao), 'Le Nègre et la dame blanche', in *Le Marabout de la sécheresse*, Dakar: Nouvelles Éditions africaines du Sénégal, 1979, 1997

Michel TOURNIER, *Gaspard, Melchior & Balthazar*, Paris: Gallimard, 1980

• Mariama BÂ, *Un chant écarlate*, Dakar: Nouvelles Éditions africaines, 1981

René DEPESTRE, *Alléluia pour une femme-jardin*, Paris: Gallimard, 1981; Coll. Folio, 1986

• Geneviève BILLY, *La Piste de la soif*, 1: *Sahel*, 2: *Retour au Sahel*, Carcassonne: G. Billy, 1981–82

• MONGO BETI (pseud. of Alexandre Biyidi), *Les Deux Mères de Guillaume Ismaël Dzewatama, futur camionneur*, Paris: Buchet/Chastel, 1982

• MONGO BETI (pseud. of Alexandre Biyidi), *La Revanche de Guillaume Ismaël Dzewatama*, Paris: Buchet/Chastel, 1984

KEN BUGUL (pseud. of Mariétou Mbaye), *Le Baobab fou*, Dakar, Abidjan, Lomé: Nouvelles Éditions africanes, n.d. [1984], 1996

• Dany LAFERRIÈRE, *Comment faire l'amour avec un nègre sans se fatiguer*, Montréal: VLB, 1985 (edition quoted); modified edition, Paris: Belfond, 1989; Coll. J'ai lu, 1990

• Luc Blin NIAMKEY, *La Femme blanche de Monsieur Aka: comédie en quatre actes*, Abidjan: CEDA, 1985

• Michèle ASSAMOUA, *Le Défi*, Abidjan, Dakar, Lomé: Nouvelles Éditions africaines, 1987

Pius NGANDU NKASHAMA, *Vie et mœurs d'un primitif en Essonne quatre-vingt-onze*, Paris: L'Harmattan, 1987

Pius NGANDU NKASHAMA, *Les Étoiles écrasées*, Paris: Publisud, 1988

Henri LOPES, *Le Chercheur d'Afriques*, Paris: Seuil, 1990

René DEPESTRE, *Éros dans un train chinois: neuf histories d'amour et un conte de sorcier*, Paris: Gallimard, 1990; Coll. Folio, 1993

Aboubacry Moussa LAM, *La Fièvre de la terre*, Paris: L'Harmattan, 1990

• Diana MORDASINI, *Le Botillon perdu*, Dakar: Nouvelles Éditions africaines du Sénégal, 1990

• Chantal SPITZ, *L'Ile des rêves écrasés*, Papeete, Tahiti: Éditions de la Plage, 1991

Pius NGANDU NKASHAMA, *Un jour de grand soleil*, Paris: L'Harmattan, 1991

KEN BUGUL (pseud. of Mariétou Mbaye), *Cendres et braises*, Paris: L'Harmattan, 1994

Maguy KABAMBA, *La Dette coloniale*, Montréal: Humanitas, 1995

• Daniel BIYAOULA, *L'Impasse*, Paris: Présence Africaine, 1996

Olympe BHÊLY-QUENUM, *La Naissance d'Abikou*, Cotonou (Benin): Phoenix Afrique, 1998

Daniel BIYAOULA, *Agonies*, Paris: Présence Africaine, 1998

• Véronique TADJO, *Champs de bataille et d'amour*, Abidjan: Nouvelles Éditions ivoiriennes and Paris: Présence Africaine, 1999

• Laurence GAVRON, *Marabouts d'ficelle*, Paris: Baleine–Le Seuil, 2000

• Olympe BHÊLY-QUENUM, *C'était à Tigony*, Paris: Présence Africaine and Abidjan: Nouvelles Editions ivoiriennes, forthcoming (read in typescript)

B. Critical works with a direct and significant bearing on the *Blanche/ Noir* theme as treated above. Bibliographical details of other items are given on the first occurrence in the notes and may be found by reference to the index.

Adams, Michael Vannoy, *The Multicultural Imagination: 'Race', Colour and the Imaginary*, London: Routledge, 1995

Alibhai-Brown, Yasmin & Anne Montague, *The Colour of Love: Mixed Race Relationships*, London: Virago, 1992

Allport, Gordon W., *The Nature of Prejudice*, New York, 1958

Antoine, Régis, *Les Écrivains français et les Antilles: des premiers Pères blancs aux surréalistes noirs*, Paris: Maisonneuve et Larose, 1978

Arnold, A. James, 'The gendering of *créolité*: the erotics of colonialism', in M. Condé and M. Cottenet-Hage, eds, *Penser la créolité*, Paris: Karthala, 1995, pp. 21–40

Ashcroft, Bill, Gareth Griffiths and Helen Tiffin, *The Empire Writes Back: Theory and Practice in Post-colonial Literatures*, London and New York: Routledge, 1989

—, —, — and — —, eds, *The Post-colonial Studies Reader*, London and New York: Routledge, 1995

SELECT BIBLIOGRAPHY

Astier-Loutfi, Martine, *Littérature et colonialisme: l'expansion coloniale vue dans la littérature romanesque française, 1871–1914*, Paris-La Haye: Mouton, 1971

Bancel, Nicolas, Pascal Blanchard & Laurent Gervereau, *Images et colonies: iconographie et propagande coloniale sur l'Afrique française de 1880 à 1962*, Paris: BDIC/ACHAC, 1993

Barbara, Augustin, *Les Couples mixtes*, Paris: Bayard Éditions, 1993, preface by Albert Jacquard, new edition of *Mariages sans frontières*, Paris: Éditions du Centurion, 1985; tr. David E. Kennard, *Marriage Across Frontiers*, Clevedon, Avon; Philadelphia, PA: Multilingual Matters, 1989

Barret-Ducrocq, Françoise, ed., *L'Intolérance*, Paris: Grasset & Fasquelle, 1998

Bauge-Gueye, Martine, 'La Femme blanche dans le roman africain', *Notre Librairie*, 50 (nov.–déc. 79), 95–103

Ben Jalloun, Tahar, *La Plus Haute des solitudes*, Paris: Seuil, Coll. Points actuels, 1977

Benot, Yves, *La Révolution française et la fin des colonies*, Paris: La Découverte, 1989

Bhabha, Homi K., *The Location of Culture*, London: Routledge, 1994

Billy, Geneviève, *Le Couple mixte*, La Chapelle St Mesmins: La Piste de la soif, 1986

Biondi, Carminella, 'Le Héros noir dans le théâtre révolutionnaire', in Daniel Droixhe and Klaus H. Kiefer, eds, *Images de l'Africain de l'antiquité au XXe siècle*, Frankfurt, Bern, New York, Paris: Peter Lang, Bayreuther Beiträge zur Literaturwissenschaft 10, 1987, pp. 103–11

Biondi, Jean-Pierre and François Zuccarelli, *16 pluviôse an II: les colonies de la Révolution*, Paris: Denoël, Coll. Destins croisés: L'Aventure coloniale de la France, 1989

Blachère, Jean-Claude, *Le Modèle nègre: aspects littéraires du mythe primitiviste au XXe siècle chez Apollinaire, Cendrars, Tzara*, Dakar, Abidjan: Nouvelles Éditions africaines, 1981

—, —, *Négritures: les écrivains d'Afrique noire et la langue française*, Paris: L'Harmattan, 1993

Bonniol, Jean-Luc, *La Couleur comme maléfice*, Paris: Albin Michel, 1992

Cazenave, Odile Marie, 'White Othello: White Women and Interracial Relationships in the West African Novel of French Expression', Ph.D., Pennsylvania State University, 1988. (See *Dissertation Abstracts*, XLIX (1988/1989), 2654A–2655A.)

Césaire, Aimé, *Toussaint Louverture: la Révolution française et le problème colonial*, Paris: Club français du livre, 1960; Paris: Présence Africaine, 1981

Chalaye, Sylvie, *Du Noir au Nègre: l'image du Noir au théâtre de Marguerite de Navarre à Jean Genet (1550–1960)*, Paris: L'Harmattan, 1998

271

Challaye, Félicien, *Souvenirs sur la colonisation*, Paris: Picart, 1935; reprinted with complementary material under title *Un livre noir du colonialisme: Souvenirs sur la colonisation*, Paris: Les Nuits rouges, 1998

Champly, Henry, *Femmes blanches, hommes de couleur*, Paris: Tallandier, 1935; *White Women, Coloured Men*, tr. Warre Bradley Wells, London: Long, 1936

Charles, Jean-Claude, *Le Corps noir*, Paris: Hachette, 1980

Chevalier, Jean-Louis, Mariella Colin and Ann Thomson, eds, *Barbares et sauvages: images et reflets dans la culture occidentale. Actes du colloque de Caen, 26–27 février 1993*, Caen: Presses universitaires de Caen, 1994

Childs, Peter and R.J. Patrick Williams, *An Introduction to Post-Colonial Theory*, London, New York etc.: Prentice Hall/Harvester Wheatsheaf, 1997

Chinard, Gilbert, *L'Amérique et le rêve exotique dans la littérature française au XVIIe et au XVIIIe siècles*, Paris: Hachette, 1913; Paris: E. Droz, 1934

Cleaver, Eldridge, *Soul on Ice*, New York: McGraw-Hill, 1967; London: Cape, 1969 (esp. 'On Becoming' and 'The Allegory of the Black Eunuchs')

Le Code noir, ou Recueil des réglemens rendus jusqu'à présent concernant le Gouvernement, l'Administration de la Justice, la Police, la Discipline et le Commerce des Negres dans les Colonies Françoises, et les Conseils et Compagnies établis à ce sujet, Paris: Prault, 1742

Cohen, William B., *The French Encounter with Africans: White Responses to Blacks*, Bloomington: Indiana University Press, 1980

Coquery-Vidrovitch, Catherine, *L'Afrique occidentale au temps des Français: colonisation et colonisés 1860–1960*, Paris: La Découverte, 1992

—, — and Charles-Robert Ageron, *Histoire de la France coloniale*, III: *Le Déclin*, Paris: Armand Colin, 1991 (see also under Meyer, Thobie)

Cruise O'Brien, Rita, *White Society in Black Africa*, London: Faber, 1972

Daniels, Jessie, *White Lies: Race, Class, Gender and Sexuality in White Supremacist Discourse*, New York: Routledge, 1997

Day, Beth, *Sexual Life between Blacks and Whites: The Roots of Racism*, New York: World Publications, 1972; London: Collins, 1974

Debrunner, Hans Werner, *Presence and Prestige: Africans in Europe: A History of Africans in Europe before 1918*, Basel: Basler Afrika Bibliographien, 1979

Diefenthal, Anna Maria, 'La Perception de l'Européen dans le roman sénégalais', thèse de 3e cycle, UCAD, 1997 (esp. pp. 86–128 on *couple domino*)

Duchet, Michèle, *Anthropologie et histoire au siècle des Lumières*, Paris: Maspéro, 1971; Paris: Flammarion, 1977

Egbujor, Eronini Emma C., 'Le Couple dans le roman négro-africain de langue française des années 1950 aux années 1980', Ph.D., University of Sherbrooke, 1988

Esquiros, Henri-Alphonse, 'Du mouvement des races humaines', *Revue des Deux Mondes* (avril–juin 1845), 152–86

Eterstein, Claude, *Le Bon Sauvage*, Paris: Gallimard, 1993

Fall, Mar, *Des tirailleurs sénégalais aux... Blacks: des Africains noirs en France*, Paris: L'Harmattan, 1986 (N.B. cover reverses order of title and subtitle)

Fanon, Frantz, *Peau noire, masques blancs*, Paris: Seuil, 1952; Coll. Points, 1971

Fanoudh-Siefer, Léon, *Le Mythe du nègre et de l'Afrique noire dans la littérature française (de 1800 à la 2ᵉ guerre mondiale)*, Paris: Klincksieck, 1968; Dakar, Abidjan, Lomé: Nouvelles Éditions africaines, 1980

Ferber, Abby L., *White Man Falling: Race, Gender, and White Supremacy*, Lanham, Boulder, New York, Oxford: Rowman & Littlefield, 1998

Fouet, [Francis], 'Le Thème de l'amour chez les romanciers négro-africains d'expression française', Colloque sur les écrivains africains d'expression française, Université de Dakar, 26–29 mars 1963, typescript of papers bound in one volume, B.U., UCAD, Dakar (shelf-mark L7895), pp. 94–108

Frederickson, George M., *The Black Image in the White Mind: The Debate on Afro-American Character and Destiny, 1817–1914*, New York: Harper & Row, 1971

Freud, Sigmund, *Totem and Taboo*, in *The Standard Edition of the Complete Psychological Works of Sigmund Freud*, ed. and tr. James Strachey, vol. XIII, London: Hogarth Press and Institute of Psycho-Analysis, 1955

Fryer, Peter, *Staying Power: The History of Black People in Britain*, London: Pluto Press, 1984

Gates, Henry Louis, Jr., ed., *'Race', Writing and Difference*, Chicago & London: Chicago U.P., 1986

Gilman, Margaret, *Othello en France*, Paris: Édouard Champion, 1925

Gilman, Sander L., *Difference and Pathology: Stereotypes of Sexuality*, Ithaca, New York and London: Cornell University Press, 1985

—, —, *Jewish Self-Hatred: Anti-Semitism and the Hidden Language of the Jews*, Baltimore and London: Johns Hopkins University Press, 1986

—, —, 'Black Bodies, White Bodies: Toward an Iconography of Female Sexuality', *Critical Enquiry*, 12, 1 (Autumn 1985), 204–42

—, —, 'Black Sexuality and Modern Consciousness', in R. Grimm and J. Hermand, eds, *Blacks and German Culture*, Madison: University of Wisconsin Press, 1986, pp. 35–53

Gobineau, Joseph-Arthur, comte de, *Essai sur l'inégalité des races humaines*, 4 vols, Paris: Firmin Didot, 1853–55

Gordon, Lewis R., *Her Majesty's Other Children: Sketches of Racism from a Neocolonial Age*, London, Boulder, New York, Oxford: Rowman & Littlefield, 1997 (esp. chap. 4, 'Sex, Race, and Matrices of Desire in an Antiblack World', pp. 73–88)

—, —, T. Denean Sharpley-Whiting and Renée T. White, eds, *Fanon: A Critical Reader*, Oxford: Blackwell, 1996

Göröög-Karady, Veronika, *Noirs et Blancs: leur image dans la littérature orale africaine*, Paris: SELAF, 1976

Grégoire, Henri, *abbé*, *Considérations sur le mariage et sur le divorce, adressées aux citoyens d'Haïti*, Paris: Baudouin, 1823

—, —, *De la noblesse de la peau, ou du préjugé des blancs contre la couleur des Africains et celle de leurs descendans noirs et sang-mêlés*, Paris: Baudouin, 1826

—, —, *Lettre aux citoyens de couleur et nègres libres de Saint-Domingue et des autres îles françoises de l'Amérique*, Paris: Le Patriote françois, 1791 (dated 8 juin 1791 at end, i.e. before insurrection)

Hanquart-Turner, E., ed., *Unions mixtes et métissages dans le monde anglophone*, Paris: Éditions A3, 1998

Heath, Stephen, *The Sexual Fix*, London: Macmillan, 1982

Henriques, Louis Fernando M., *Children of Caliban: Miscegenation*, London: Secker & Warburg, 1974

Hoffmann, Léon-François, *Le Nègre romantique: personnage littéraire et obsession collective*, Paris: Payot, 1973

—, —, 'Victor Hugo, les Noirs et l'esclavage', *Francofonia: studi e ricerche sulle letterature di lingua francese* [Florence], XVI, 31 (aut. 1996), 47–90

Houssain, Jean-Pierre, 'L'Afrique noire et les écrivains français entre les deux guerres', Doct. d'état, Université de Paris-Sorbonne, 1981 (esp. chap. VIII, 'L'Amour exotique', pp. 217–32, within which: 'Blanche et Noir', pp. 229–32)

Hufton, Olwen, *The Poor of Eighteenth-Century France*, Oxford: Clarendon Press, 1974

Hyam, Ronald, *Empire and Sexuality: The British Experience*, Manchester: Manchester Univrsity Press, 1990

Ignatiev, Noel and John Garvey, eds, *Race Traitor*, New York: Routledge, 1996

Jordan, Winthrop D., *White over Black: American Attitudes toward the Negro, 1550–1812*, Chapel Hill, N.C.: University of North Carolina Press, 1968; New York: Norton, 1977

Jourda, Pierre, *L'Exotisme dans la littérature française depuis Chateaubriand*, Paris: Presses universitaires de France, 1956

Kandé, Sylvie, ed., *Discours sur le métissage, identités métisses: en quête d'Ariel*, Paris: L'Harmattan, Montréal: L'Harmattan Inc., 1999

Kesteloot, Lilyan, review of Thérèse Kuoh-Moukoury, *Les Couples dominos* (see below) in *Éthiopiques* [Dakar], n.s. II, 1 (1er trim. 1984), 97–99

Kimoni, Iyay, *Destin de la littérature négro-africaine ou problématique d'une culture*, Kinshasa: Presses universitaires du Zaïre and Sherbrooke, Québec: Naaman, 1975

Kristeva, Julia, *Étrangers à nous-mêmes*, Paris: Fayard, 1988; Paris: Gallimard, Coll. Folio essais, 1991

Kuoh-Moukoury, Thérèse, *Les Couples dominos: aimer dans la différence*, Paris: Julliard, 1973; Paris: L'Harmattan, 1983

Laplantine, François and Alexis Nouss, *Le Métissage*, Paris: Dominos/Flammarion, 1997

Lebeau, André, *De la condition des gens de couleur libres sous l'ancien régime*, Paris: Guillaumin, 1903

Lebel, Roland, *L'Afrique occidentale dans la littérature française (depuis 1870)*, Paris: Larose, 1925

—, —, *Etudes de littérature coloniale*, Paris: Peyronnet, 1928

—, —, *Histoire de la littérature coloniale en France*, Paris: Larose, 1931

Leblond, Marius-Ary, *Après l'exotisme de Loti, le roman colonial*, Paris: Vald-Rasmussen, 1926

Liauzu, Claude, *Race et civilisation: l'autre dans la culture occidentale*, Paris: Syros/Alternatives, 1992

Lips, Julius E., *The Savage Hits Back: The White Man Through Native Eyes*, with an Introduction by Bronislaw Malinowski, tr. Vincent Benson, New Haven: Yale University Press; London: Lovat Dickinson, 1937 (esp. chap. X, pp. 215–28)

Little, Roger, *Nègres blancs: représentations de l'autre autre*, Paris: L'Harmattan, 1995

—, —, 'Escaping Othello's Shadow: *Un homme pareil aux autres*, *Ô pays mon beau peuple!* and *Un chant écarlate*', *ASCALF Yearbook 1*, Bristol: Association for the Study of Caribbean and African Literature in French, 1996, pp. 95–112

—, —, 'The "Couple Domino" in the Writings of Olympe Bhêly-Quenum', *Research in African Literatures*, 29, 1 (Spring 1998), 66–86

—, —, 'Keeping up Appearances: Biyaoula's *L'Impasse*', *Présence Africaine*, 157 (1er semestre 1998), 141–56

—, —, 'From Taboo to Totem: Black Man, White Woman in Caroline Auguste Fischer and Sophie Doin', *Modern Language Review*, 93, 4 (October 1998), 948–60

—, —, '*Blanche et Noir*: Louise Faure-Favier and the Liberated Woman', *Australian Journal of French Studies*, XXXVI, 2 (May–August 1999), 214–28

—, —, 'Blanche et Noir aux années vingt', in *Regards sur les littératures coloniales*, II: *Afrique francophone: Approfondissements*, ed. J.-Fr. Durand, Paris: L'Harmattan, 1999, pp. 7–50

Lively, Adam, *Masks: Blackness, Race and the Imagination*, London: Chatto & Windus, 1998; Vintage, 1999

Maalouf, Amin, *Les Identités meurtrières*, Paris: Grasset, 1998

Mar, Daouda, 'La Vision du Sénégal dans les comptes rendus de mission (1620–1920) et ses prolongements dans la littérature sénégalaise', Doctorat d'État, Université Cheikh Anta Diop, Dakar, 1996

Martinkus-Zemp, Ada, *Le Blanc et le Noir: essai d'une description de la vision du Noir par le Blanc dans la littérature française de l'entre-deux-guerres*, Paris: Nizet, 1975

Mathorez, J[ules], *Les Étrangers en France sous l'ancien régime: histoire d e la formation de la population française*, 2 vols., Paris: É. Champion, 1919 (see esp. 'Les Nègres', vol. I, pp. 387–404)

McCloy, Shelby T., *The Negro in France*, Lexington: University of Kentucky Press, 1961

McGowan, Moray, 'Black and White?: Claire Goll's *Der Neger Jupiter raubt Europa*', in E. Robinson and R. Vilain, eds, *Claire Goll — Yvan Goll: Texts and Contexts*, Amsterdam: Rodopi, Internationale Forschungen zur allgemeinen und vergleichenden Literaturwissenschaft 23, 1997, pp. 205–18

Meek, Ronald L., *Social Science and the Ignoble Savage*, Cambridge: Cambridge University Press, 1976

Memmi, Albert, *Portrait du colonisé, précédé du Portrait du colonisateur et d'une préface de Jean-Paul Sartre*, Paris: J.-J. Pauvert, 1966; Paris: Payot, 1973.

Mercier, Roger, *L'Afrique noire dans la littérature française: les premières images (XVIIe–XVIIIe siècles)*, Dakar: Université de Dakar, Faculté des Lettres et Sciences humaines, Publications de la section langues et littératures n° 11, 1962

Meunier, Claude, *Ring noir: quand Apollinaire, Cendrars, Picabia découvraient les boxeurs nègres*, Paris: Plon, 1992

Meyer, Jean, *Les Européens et les autres de Cortès à Washington*, Paris: Armand Colin, 1975

—, —, Jean Tarrade and Annie Rey-Goldzeiguer, *Histoire de la France coloniale*, I: *La Conquête*, Paris: Armand Colin, 1991 (see also under Coquery-Vidrovitch, Thobie)

Michel, Marc, *L'Appel à l'Afrique: contributions et réactions à l'effort de guerre en A.O.F.*, Paris: Publications de la Sorbonne, 1982

Miller, Christopher L., *Blank Darkness: Africanist Discourse in French*, Chicago: University of Chicago Press, 1985

—, —, *Theories of Africans*, Chicago & London: University of Chicago Press, 1990

Moreau de Saint-Méry, Médéric-Louis-Élie, *Description topographique, physique, civile, politique et historique de la partie française de l'isle Saint-Domingue* [1797–98], 3 vols, Paris: Société d'histoire des colonies françaises et Librairie Larose, 1984

Munford, Clarence J., *The Black Ordeal of Slavery and Slave Trading in the French West Indies 1625–1715*, 3 vols., Lewiston, Queenston, Lampeter: Mellen, 1991

Musgrave, Marian E., 'Literary Justifications of Slavery', in R. Grimm and J. Hermand, eds, *Blacks and German Culture*, Madison: University of Wisconsin Press, 1986, pp. 3–21

N'Diaye, Jean-Pierre, *Élites africaines et culture occidentale: assimilation ou résistance?*, Paris: Présence Africaine, 1969

N'Djehoya, Blaise and Massaër Diallo, *Un regard noir*, Paris: Autrement, 1984

Notre Librairie, 90 and 91: *Images du Noir dans la littérature occidentale*, 1: *Du Moyen-âge à la conquête coloniale* (oct.–déc, 1987) and 2: *De la conquête coloniale à nos jours* (janv.–févr. 1988)

Oliver, Caroline, *Western Women in Colonial Africa*, Westport, Conn.: Greenwood, 1982

Ouologuem, Yambo, *Lettre à la France nègre*, Paris: Nalis, 1968 (esp. 'Lettre aux couples mixtes', pp. 29–35)

Pakenham, Thomas, *The Scramble for Africa*, London: Weidenfeld & Nicolson, 1991

Peabody, Sue, '*There are no slaves in France*': *The Political Culture of Race and Slavery in the Ancien Régime*, New York, Oxford: Oxford University Press, 1996

Philippe, Claudine, Gabrielle Varro and Gérard Neyrand, eds, *Liberté, égalité, mixité... conjugales*, Paris: Anthropos, Coll. Exploration interculturelle et sciences sociales, 1998

Pieterse, J. Nederveen, *White on Black: Images of Africa and Blacks in Western Popular Culture*, New Haven and London: Yale University Press, 1992

Pluchon, Pierre, *Nègres et Juifs au XVIIIᵉ siècle: le racisme au siècle des Lumières*, Paris: Tallandier, 1984

Prévost, *abbé* Antoine-François, 'Si l'on peut supposer une femme blanche amoureuse d'un noir', *Le Pour et Contre*, XIV (1738), 66–67

Raynal, *abbé* Guillaume, *Histoire philosophique et politique et des établissements des Européens dans les deux Indes* [1772], selection ed. Y. Benot under title *Histoire philosophique et politique des deux Indes*, Paris: Maspéro, 1981

Riesz, János, 'Les Métamorphoses d'un livre: textes et images dans la littérature coloniale française (1900–1945)', in *L'Historien et l'image: de l'illustration à la preuve. Actes du colloque tenu à l'université de Metz 11–12 mars 1994*, ed. H. D'Almeida-Topor and M. Sève, Metz: Centre de recherche histoire et civilisation de l'université de Metz, 1998, pp. 255–69

— , — and Joachim Schultz, eds, *Tirailleurs sénéglais: présentations littéraires et figuratives de soldats africains au service de la France*, Frankfurt am Main, Bern, New York, Paris: Peter Lang, 1989

Romano, Dugan, *Intercultural Marriage: Promises and Pitfalls*, Yarmouth, Maine: Intercultural Press, 1997

Rousseau, Jean-Jacques, *Discours sur l'origine et les fondements de l'inégalité parmi les hommes*, Amsterdam: Marc Michel Rey, 1755; ed. J. Roger, Paris: Garnier-Flammarion, Coll. GF, 1971 (with *Discours sur les sciences et les arts*)

Roussel, Louis, *Le Mariage dans la société française*, Paris: Presses universitaires de France, 1975

Ruscio, Alain, *Le Credo de l'homme blanc*, Brussels: Complexe, 1995

Said, Edward, *Culture and Imperialism*, London: Chatto & Windus, 1993; Vintage Books, 1994

Sala-Molins, Louis, *Les Misères des Lumières: sous la raison l'outrage*, Paris: Laffont, 1992

Schipper-De Leeuw, Mineke, *Le Blanc vu d'Afrique: le Blanc et l'Occident au miroir du roman négro-africain de langue française, des origines au Festival de Dakar, 1920–1966*, Yaoundé: Clé, 1973 (esp. chap. VII: 'La Femme blanche', pp. 135–67)

Schnapper, Dominique, *La Relation à l'autre: au cœur de la pensée socio-logique*, Paris: Gallimard, 1998

Seeber, Edward Derbyshire, *Anti-Slavery Opinion in France during the Second Half of the Eighteenth Century*, Baltimore, MD: Johns Hopkins University Press, London: Humphrey Milford, Oxford University Press, Paris: Les Belles Lettres, 1937; New York: Greenwood Press, 1969

—, —, 'Oroonoko in France in the XVIIIth Century', *Publications of the Modern Language Association of America*, LI (1936), 935–59

Segalen, Victor, *Essai sur l'exotisme: une esthétique du divers*, Montpellier: Fata morgana, 1978; Paris: Librairie générale française, Livre de poche, 1986

Sembene, Ousmane, 'Si j'étais une femme, je n'épouserais jamais un Africain', *Peuples noirs/peuples africains*, 14e année, 8 (mars-avril 1991), 88

Singh, Jyotsna, 'Othello's identity, postcolonial theory, and contemporary African rewritings of *Othello*', in *Women, 'Race', and Writing in the Early Modern Period*, ed. M. Hendricks and P. Parker, London and New York: Routledge, 1994

Stein, Robert L., *The French Slave Trade in the Eighteenth Century: An Old Régime Business*, Madison: University of Wisconsin Press, 1979

Stember, Charles Herbert, *Sexual Racism: The Emotional Barrier to an Integrated Society*, New York: Elsevier, 1976

Sypher, Wylie, *Guinea's Captive Kings: British Anti-Slavery Literature of the XVIIIth Century*, Chapel Hill: University of North Carolina Press, 1942; New York: Octagon Books, 1989

Thiam, Awa, *La Parole aux Négresses*, Paris: Denoël, 1978

—, —, *Continents noirs*, Paris: Tierce, 1987

Thobie, Jacques and Gilbert Meynier, *Histoire de la France coloniale*, II: *L'Apogée*, Paris: Armand Colin, 1991 (see also under Coquery-Vidrovitch, Meyer)

Thomas, Hugh, *The Slave Trade: The History of the Atlantic Slave Trade, 1440–1870*, London: Picador, 1997

Todorov, Tzvetan, *Nous et les autres: la réflexion française sur la diversité humaine*, Paris: Seuil, 1989; Coll. Points, 1992

Turbet-Delof, Guy, *L'Afrique barbaresque dans la littérature française aux XVIᵉ et XVIIᵉ siècles*, Geneva: Droz, 1973

Vaughan, Virginia Mason, *Othello: A Contextual History*, Cambridge: Cambridge University Press, 1994 (esp. chap. 3, 'Racial discourse: black and white', pp. 51–70)

Vinsonneau, Geneviève, 'Les Repésentations familiales du noir africain séjournant en milieu intellectuel français', in Pierre Tap, ed., *Identité collective et changements sociaux*, Privat, 1980, pp. 213–17.

Walvin, James, *The Black Presence: A Documentary History of the Negro in England, 1555–1860*, London: Orbach & Chambers, 1971

—, —, *Black and White: the Negro and English Society, 1555–1945*, London: Allen Lane, The Penguin Press, 1973

—, —, ed., *Slavery and British Society 1776–1846*, London: Macmillan, 1982

White, Owen, *Children of the French Empire: Miscegenation and Colonial Society in French West Africa 1895–1960*, Oxford: Clarendon Press, 1999

Wilkinson, Doris Y., ed., *Black Male/White Female: Perspectives on Interracial Marriage and Courtship*, Cambridge, Mass.: Schenkman, 1975

Young, Robert J.C., *Colonial Desire: Hybridity in Theory, Culture and Race*, London and New York: Routledge, 1995

INDEX

INDEX